P9-CDT-184

Tom Clancy's
RAINBOW SIX™
ROGUE SPEAR™

Tom Clancy's
RAINBOW SIX™
ROGUE SPEAR™
MISSION PACK: URBAN OPERATIONS

PRIMA'S OFFICIAL STRATEGY GUIDE

Michael Knight

Prima Games
A Division of Prima Communications, Inc.

3000 Lava Ridge Court
Roseville, CA 95661
(916) 787-7000
www.primagames.com

ROGUE SPEAR

Project Editors David Mathews, Patrick Cunningham
Product Manager: Renee Middleton

ISBN: 0-7615-2871-7
Library of Congress Catalog Card Number: 00-10174
Printed in the United States of America

00 01 02 03 BB 10 9 8 7 6 5 4 3 2 1

TABLE OF CONTENTS

ROGUE SPEAR

Noronha, Alejandro 31
Novikov, Arkadi 32
Pak Suo-Won 33
Petersen, Einar 34
Price, Eddie 35
Rakuzanka, Kazimiera 36
Raymond, Renee 37
Sweeney, Kevin 38
Walther, Jorg 39
Weber, Dieter 40
Woo, Tracy 41
Yacoby, Ayana 42

CHAPTER THREE:
Tools of the Trade 43

Firearms 43
Primary Weapons 43
HK MP5A4 43
HK MP5SD5 44
HK MP5/10A2 44
HK MP5/10SD 44
HK UMP45 45
HK UMP45SD 45
HK MP5K-PDW 45
M4 Carbine 45
HK G3A3 46
G36K 46
Enfield L85A1 46
Steyr Aug 46
M16-A2 47
M-14 47
Barrett Model 82A1 47
PSG-1 48
Walther WA2000 48
Benelli M1 48
SPAS-12 49
Secondary Weapons 49
Beretta 92FS 9mm 49
Beretta 92FS 9mm-SD 50
HK .40 USP 50

iv — Tom Clancy's RAINBOW SIX · Rogue Spear · PRIMA'S OFFICIAL STRATEGY GUIDE

ROGUE SPEAR

CHAPTER SIX:
The Campaign 80

Part II
Mission Pack:Urban Operations
CHAPTER 8:
New Features in Urban Operations 227

CHAPTER 9:

ACKNOWLEDGEMENTS

I would like to thank Charles Holtzclaw, Gary Stelmack, and the rest of the Red Storm Entertainment team for all of their assistance and support during this project. Once again, they have created a great game that I enjoyed being a part of. Thanks also go out to David Mathews, Renee Middleton, and Jon Goetzman at Prima Games for their help in getting this book to print.

Most of all I would like to thank my family. The deadlines required to get a book to print on time can put strain on a family. However, my wife, Trisa, was a great support. My daughters, Beth and Sarah, also were great, though the additions to the text made by Sarah when I was away from the computer had to be deleted. My newborn son, Connor, also helped Daddy keep his sanity under the pressure of deadlines. Hugs and kisses all to all four of you.

FOREWORD

The year is 2002. The world is a very dangerous place. As the fragments of the former Soviet Union slide deeper and deeper into chaos, the forces of crime and terror expand to fill the vacuum. There is war in the Balkans, war in the Middle East—war in a dozen hot spots around the world. Outnumbered and under siege, the western democracies desperately struggle to keep the growing disorder from spilling across their borders. On the front lines of this strange war is the counter-terrorism taskforce code-named RAINBOW. Operating out of bases on both sides of the Atlantic, RAINBOW operatives are poised to strike at a moment's notice anywhere on the globe. Although their existence is secret, their combined courage and vigilance have saved the lives of millions.

Yet even now a new enemy looms in the east, an enemy greater than any RAINBOW has faced, an enemy able to strike when and where he pleases—bound only by his own hatred and ambition, an enemy armed with the most fearsome weapon known to man....

INTRODUCTION

RAINBOW Is Needed Again

A little over a year ago, I had the opportunity to play and write a strategy guide for a new type of game. *Rainbow Six* was a first-person shooter with more strategy, tactics, and planning than anyone thought could be put into that type of game. *Rainbow Six* was made to be realistic, with a lot of study and research done to make it so. As a result, the game was very popular and—more than a year after its release—is still one of the top 10–selling games. The Eagle Watch mission pack expanded the game even further.

As with any successful game, a sequel was in order. However, instead of just adding a few new weapons and operatives and providing different missions, the team at Red Storm Entertainment created a completely new game. Although it still has the same feel and may at first glance seem the same as the original, *Rogue Spear* contains a new gaming engine and adds several new features such as snipers, more control over AI Operatives, and better AI for the tangos. If you like *RAINBOW Six*, you'll love *Rogue Spear*. However, if you never played the predecessor, you can still hop aboard now with the sequel.

Rogue Spear: The Strategy Guide

This guide will help you become an efficient soldier in the war against terrorism. In *Rogue Spear*, you must combine strategy, tactics, and eye-hand coordination to make your way to the game's climactic finale. Because you're probably not an expert in the techniques of anti-terrorism and hostage rescue, this book takes you step by step, giving you the information you need to lead RAINBOW to another victory.

The first chapter covers the skills you need to progress through the game. It includes tutorials where you can practice what you learn. Chapter 2 provides dossiers on each RAINBOW Operative, as well as important information on how to use them. RAINBOW provides an arsenal of weapons and equipment for battling terrorists; Chapter 3 goes over all the items you can carry and how best to use them. Chapter 4 discusses tactics for completing your missions. It includes more tutorials to help you reach the operational level necessary to tackle the campaign.

You can't just run through a mission, single-handedly blowing everyone away. You must organize various Operatives into teams. To order each team what to do during the mission, you must plan the mission in detail. Chapter 5 gives you the plan on planning. Next, Chapter 6 provides strategies, tactics, and maps for each of the campaign's 18 missions.

Finally, Chapter 7 covers the additional games included in *Rogue Spear*, other than the campaign game. This includes tips and tactics for multiplayer games, as well as for the Lone Wolf and Terrorist Hunt missions.

The Urban Operations Mission Pack

The *Urban Operations* mission pack adds a lot of new features to an already great game. The latter part of this guide covers the mission pack. Chapter 8 discusses the many types of missions available through the new Custom Mission Builder. Here you can create several different types of missions on all the maps included in *Rogue Spear* and the *Urban Operations* mission pack. Also covered are the new types of weapons. Chapter 9 contains walkthroughs for each of the five new missions in the Urban Operations Campaign. Chapter 10 has the walkthroughs for the Classic Campaign, five missions from the original *Rainbow Six* brought into the new engine. Finally, Chapter 11 contains maps and strategies for each of the eight new multiplayer maps.

Dedication

This book is dedicated to my new son, Connor. He is a bundle of joy and likes watching me play games and write strategy guides from his little bouncy chair. In a few years, maybe he'll become my partner in writing about computer games.

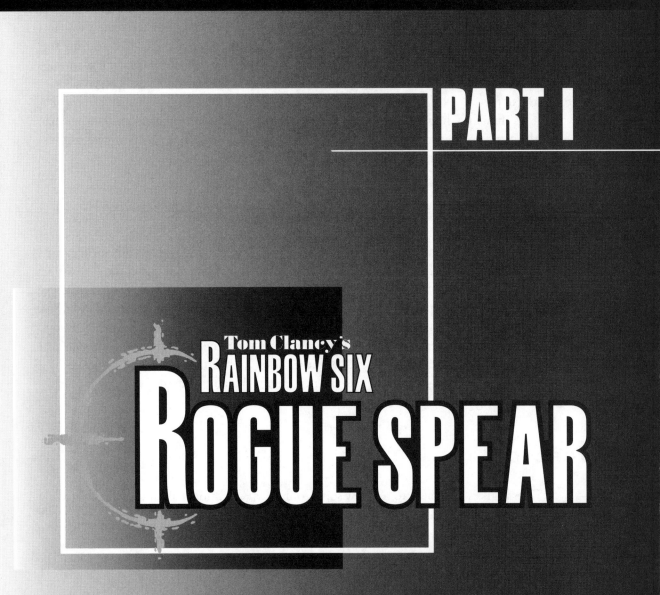

PART I

Tom Clancy's
RAINBOW SIX
ROGUE SPEAR

Controlling the Characters

During any mission, you control one team member directly. The others rely on orders you issue during the planning phase.

In combat, you must handle both movement and weapons smoothly and simultaneously. To achieve this, first master them individually and then put them together.

Movement

In *Rogue Spear,* you can control your team members with a joystick or other game controller, but I suggest using the keyboard and mouse combination for greater control and finer targeting.

Use W, S, A, and D to move forward and backward and strafe left and right. The mouse controls the direction your character faces, as well as the elevation of his or her line of sight. Move the mouse forward to look down and back to look up. Left and right motions turn your character in the corresponding direction. Press the right mouse button to run as you move forward. You also have the ability to look around corners by pressing Q (lean left), and E (lean right).

To crouch, press C. Press SPACEBAR to manipulate your environment: open doors, climb ladders, surmount obstacles, and the like. You may have noticed that "jump" is missing. This is intentional. Jumping is an uncontrolled movement. Once you're in the air, you can't stop or change direction until your feet hit the ground again. Teams such as RAINBOW avoid uncontrolled movement. Their missions are difficult and deadly enough without further variables. Besides, none of the training exercises or missions require jumping.

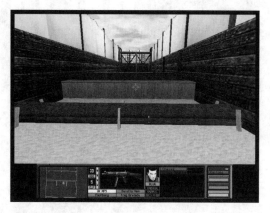

The Obstacle Course tests your ability to control a character.

The Obstacle Course

To practice what you've learned about movement, select Training from the main menu. Under Fire and Movement, highlight Obstacle Course, then click Start Tutorial. You'll get control of Rainbow team member Antonio Maldini, and begin at one end of the course. Press [F1] to toggle between first- and third-person views. For this exercise, use third person.

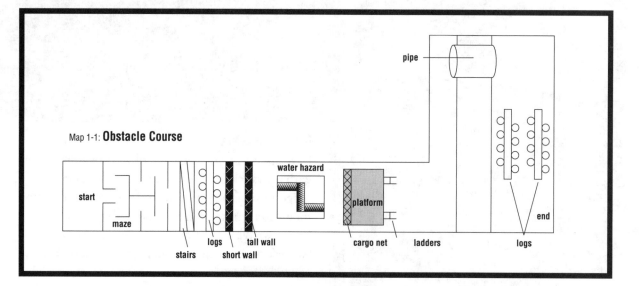

Map 1-1: **Obstacle Course**

The maze lies straight ahead. The lower-right corner of the screen displays a minimap of your surroundings. Press [[] or []] to zoom in and out, and [T] for a full-screen view of the map. Press [T] again to return to action view. Using the mouse to "steer," press the arrow keys to move through the maze to the end.

When you exit the maze, you come to a short flight of stairs. Climb up and walk off the end to fall back to the ground. The next obstacle is a pair of logs: hold down the right mouse button and run forward to clear the logs easily. Next, you face a pair of walls, the first short and the other of medium height. Move close to the first and press [SPACEBAR]. Maldini will climb to the top. Walk off the other edge and repeat at the next wall.

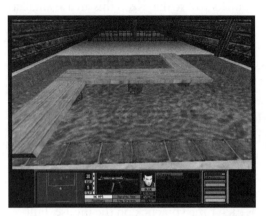

The water hazard requires careful footwork.

Now, carefully cross the wood planks over the water hazard. This is good practice for negotiating ledges and other narrow paths. Try this looking down and straight ahead, in both first- and third-person views. If you fall off, move to the water's edge and press (SPACEBAR) to climb out.

Your next obstacle is the climbing platform. Move close to the cargo net and press (SPACEBAR) to climb. Press the arrow key as if you were moving forward to continue to the top. Hold down the right mouse button to climb more quickly. At the top, move across the platform to a ladder. Press (SPACEBAR) again to climb down.

The final part of the course involves crouching. You must move down a depression. Once in the depression, crouch down by pressing (C). Then waddle through the pipe and on to the logs. You can stand up by pressing (C) again. Notice how your operative can hide behind the logs while crouched, then stand up to fire over them. Crouching is a good way to avoid detection during a mission and also makes it harder for the enemy to hit you.

Congratulations! You've completed the Obstacle Course and are ready for weapons training.

At the climbing platform you must climb up a cargo net and down a ladder.

Firearms

Moving can be fun, but this game is about combat. The weapons in *Rogue Spear* are realistically modeled after weapons counterterrorist groups actually use. (Chapter 3 covers weapons in greater detail.)

During the Obstacle Course exercise, a targeting reticle (a circle with four lines extending in the four compass directions) is always in the center of your view. The reticle shows you where your rounds probably will hit. Although the circle remains the same, as accuracy changes, the four short lines move out from the circle, reflecting the area where your bullets will strike. Keep this area as small as possible.

Factors that affect accuracy include fatigue, health, distractions, movement, and taking hits. As your character becomes tired or wounded, his or her accuracy decreases permanently for the rest of the mission. Distractions such as flashbangs, seeing a teammate or hostage go down, or hearing an alarm go off decrease accuracy temporarily.

To fire a gun, click the left mouse button. You may select a rate of fire—that is, the number of rounds fired each time you click the mouse—for any gun. Each gun has a safety and single-shot setting. When the safety is on, the weapon won't fire. The single-shot setting fires one round each time you pull the trigger (click on the mouse). Most submachine guns and assault rifles have two additional settings—three-round burst and full-automatic. The first fires three rounds each time you click on the mouse. Full-automatic continues firing as long as you hold the fire button down, until the clip is empty. To change a weapon's rate of fire, press B.

Tip *The three-round burst is the best rate of fire during missions. It's nearly as accurate as single-shot, yet packs a punch that will knock the target down. Use full-automatic only when you want to hose down an area with lead and you have ammunition to spare.*

Each firearm affords its own level of accuracy. A pistol is less accurate than a rifle, largely because of its shorter barrel. Rate of fire affects accuracy, as well. For example, firing at full-automatic, the first few rounds probably will hit the target, but the remaining rounds will scatter. This is the main reason for the three-round burst setting: studies show accuracy decreases dramatically after firing three rounds. When a gun fires once, its recoil alters the aim just a bit. The effects of multiple recoils in a short amount of time during full-automatic firing can change the aim significantly. When a three-round burst is used, all the rounds should hit the target. Then the shooter can correct his or her aim and fire again. Full-automatic is suited only for spraying a lot of bullets into an area when accuracy and ammunition aren't concerns. Remember, a round that misses its target will hit *something*. Take care that hostages and other team members aren't on the receiving end of your stray bullets.

A shooter's motion also affects accuracy. When a person is walking, it's harder to keep a firearm trained on a target. Running increases the difficulty. When you move, the gun tends to move up and down and side to side along with your body. You'll notice how forward and backward motion affect accuracy, but it's turning that really decreases it. If possible, avoid turning and sidestep instead when you fire.

Shooting Range

You can practice using all firearms in the *Rogue Spear* arsenal from all ranges at the Shooting Range. Select Shooting Range I from the training menu to go there. Your character will be armed with an HK MP5A4, the best weapon available and an extremely accurate one.

Three team members improve their firearms skills at the Shooting Range—not a welcome sight for a terrorist.

Walk toward the short range and up to the counter. To change the weapon's rate of fire, press B. Choose full-automatic, take aim at a target, and empty the clip. Most rounds should strike the target, but you can see how they spread. Press Z to load a second clip. Changing a magazine in *Rogue Spear* takes time, just as it does in real life. Select single-shot and fire six rounds at another target. Notice that they're close together, with little spread. Finally, fire the remainder of the clip at the third target using three-round bursts. You'll notice the groupings are very close together—much better than on full-automatic.

Map 1-2: **Shooting Range**

walk-up range
short range
medium range
long range
start
snipper range
counter

Practice moving fire at the walk-up exercise area.

Reload and move to the walk-up range. Here you shoot at the black target as you walk along the short gravel path, both to practice shooting on the move and to see how such movement affects your accuracy. Press 2 on the regular keyboard to pull out your pistol and repeat the walk-up shooting exercise. You'll find the pistol isn't as accurate. Try it out at the short range, too.

Next, move on to the medium range and try both weapons. For a better view of your targets and where your rounds hit, press ← SHIFT to activate Sniper mode. This zooms in the view. You should discover that your accuracy decreases as range increases, especially when you fire at full-automatic. Do the same at the long range. For this training session, you also have a pair of binoculars. After firing at targets on the longer ranges, use the binoculars to see where you hit the targets. Pressing ← SHIFT changes the magnification level of the binoculars.

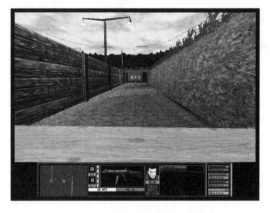

You may need to use the Sniper view when firing at the long range, both to see where your shots hit and for targeting.

After experimenting with the HK MP5A4, exit the shooting range and load the Shooting Range II tutorial. It's the same range, but now your character uses a PSG-1 sniper rifle. This is one of the best weapons for shooting at long range. Try it on the sniper range. Press ← SHIFT once or twice to zoom in at two different magnification levels. Sniper rifles can only fire single shots. However, they are extremely accurate and in the hands of a trained sniper, a single shot is all that's needed.

You can return to the shooting range under Open Training at the Training menu, as well. With this, you can choose any team member and practice with them using different weapons. Try out each of the weapons in the RAINBOW arsenal so you are comfortable with each and learn which is best for different conditions.

Breaching

Most of *Rogue Spear's* missions involve combat in urban environments, and nearly all require your teams to enter buildings. In this section, you'll learn how to enter buildings using breaching devices and explosives. Your mother may have taught you to knock, but antiterrorist tactics require you to open the doors for yourself.

When you confront a closed door, you must choose how you want to open it. To open a door normally, walk over to it and press (SPACEBAR). Normally it takes a few seconds to open. If it takes a lot longer, it's locked. If silence is key to a mission, let your character pick the lock. You do this the same way you open the door; it just takes a lot longer. A lockpick kit, either your character's or another team member's, will shorten the time it takes to pick a lock.

A few shotgun blasts will blow in most locked doors.

When stealth isn't a factor, you have more choices. Blasting a door's lock with a shotgun will open it easily. Or try a door charge. This involves placing small amounts of explosives around a door, and then detonating them to blow it in—removing the door from your path and stunning the room's occupants for a moment. To use a door charge, select it as your active item. Move to a door and click the mouse. It takes time to place the charge. Step back a bit and click the mouse again to detonate it. Quickly switch back to holding a gun before running into the room.

Door Breaching

Select Door Breaching from the Training menu to go to the Demolitions Range. Your character will be armed with a shotgun and some breaching charges. Walk to the Breaching Room and stand next to the door on the right. Press (SPACEBAR). The door is locked, so hold down the key until it opens. It would have taken less time if you'd had a lockpick kit.

Sidestep to the center door and aim the shotgun at the lock. Fire until it blows open. You've just performed a shotgun breach. Now position your character in front of the last locked door. Press keyboard [3] to select the breaching charge, and hold down the left mouse button to place it. Now back away from the door and click the mouse again. This detonates the charge, blasting the door out of your way. The breaching charge also acts as a flashbang to those on the other side of the door.

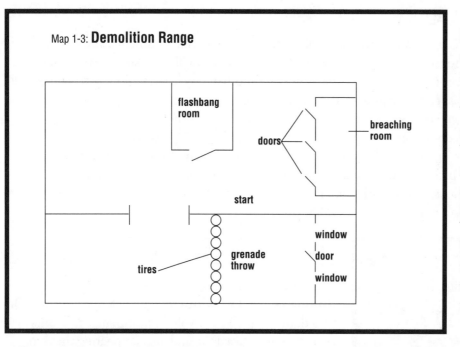

Map 1-3: **Demolition Range**

flashbang room

breaching room

doors

start

grenade throw

tires

window

door

window

Place the other breaching charge on the door to the flashbang room. Then switch back to the shotgun or pistol. You needn't detonate the charge right away. When you're ready, make the charge your active item and click the mouse to detonate it. You can practice more breaching, including using the lockpick, at the Demolitions Range under Open Training.

The breaching charge is ready to detonate. The explosion blasts the door in and stuns the room's occupants.

Grenades

Grenades can help significantly when it comes to entering a room or building safely. Rainbow operatives have two types at their disposal—flashbangs and fragmentation grenades. Flashbangs explode with a loud noise and a bright flash of light. They're also called stun grenades, because the detonation briefly stuns persons nearby. The effect lasts only a few seconds, but this can be long enough for your team to enter a room and kill all the terrorists within.

Fragmentation grenades are used by the military. When they explode, they send shards of shrapnel flying in all directions, killing those close by and wounding others farther away. Take care when using fragmentation grenades. Their blast radius may be greater than the distance your character can throw them. Make sure you have some cover to hide behind after you throw one.

Grenade Practice

Throw the flashbang through the doorway. Don't stand too close, or you'll end up stunning yourself.

This exercise takes place on the Demolition Range. First, walk to the flashbang room and open the door any way you choose. Press keyboard 3 to make flashbangs your current item. Aim the reticle at the door and press the left mouse button. Release it to throw. The longer you hold down the button, the farther you'll throw the grenade. If you're too close to the flashbang when it goes off, the screen will go black briefly: you've stunned yourself. Back away from the door or sidestep after throwing to avoid the blast. After a few tries, try running into the room after the grenade goes off without being stunned.

Throw the fragmentation grenades over the tires, or you'll kill your character. Practice throwing grenades through the doorway and windows.

Now walk to the grenade-throwing area, near the stacked tires. Many first-time grenade users stand right next to the tires. Often the grenade will hit the tires, fall next to your character, and kill him or her. Instead, back away from the tires a bit. Throw a flashbang or two over the tires before trying a fragmentation grenade. Move the reticle up and down to adjust your throwing angle. Throw a fragmentation grenade through the door of the mock building. If you're really good, try throwing a grenade though each window. For more practice using grenades, go to the Demolitions Range under Open Training.

Additional Practice

You've practiced shooting at stationary targets as you lean on a counter. It's time to advance to the next level. The next training sessions deal with room clearing and hostage rescue. They are discussed in Chapter 4 because they are used to teach tactics.

From the training menu, you can choose Open Training and return to the Shooting Range or Demolitions Course. In Open Training, you can select your operatives as well as the weapons and equipment they use for training. This allows you to experiment with everything in the RAINBOW arsenal.

CHAPTER TWO
THE RAINBOW OPERATIVES

Rouge Spear puts you in command of a team of operatives from around the world. Each has unique strengths and weaknesses, and it's up to you to assign them roles that maximize their skills. This chapter covers each Rainbow operative, providing background, personal information, attributes, and suggestions for how best to use him or her during operational missions.

Attributes

Attributes fall into two categories: profile and skill. The first four stats are considered profiles. These are inherent or learned attributes that demonstrate psychological make-up and physical endurance. Skills, on the other hand, are learned attributes that relate to using equipment, or to movement.

- **Aggression:** An operative's basic nature. It comes into play only when an operative "snaps," or loses self-control. An aggressive operative may use extreme force when he or she snaps, endangering hostages and teammates alike. In similar circumstances, a passive operative may freeze, or panic and run away.

- **Leadership:** Teamwork and self-control attributes. A leader with a low leadership rating reduces the values of those under his or her command. The higher the value, the better the bonus. Leadership applies whether the team leader is player or computer controlled.

- **Self-control:** Likelihood that a nonplayer operative will snap during combat. Once a operative snaps, his or her aggression level determines the outcome.

- **Stamina:** How many wounds it takes to incapacitate a operative. This attribute also affects fatigue levels at the end of a mission.

- **Assault:** Operative's base accuracy with pistols, shotguns, submachine guns and rifles, and how actions such as movement and firing affect it.

- **Demolitions:** How long it takes a operative to place a demo charge or disarm a bomb, and how many shots it takes to breach a locked door with a shotgun. High demolition value means quicker time and fewer shotgun blasts.

- **Electronics:** Time it takes an operative to place bugs, pick locks, bypass security systems, and splice video.

- **Grenades:** Operative's fragmentation grenade and flashbang accuracy and throwing time.

- **Sniper:** Operative's base accuracy when using a sniper rifle or a rifle while in Sniper view or mode.

- **Stealth:** How much noise an operative makes as he or she moves. The higher the value, the quieter the operative. Those with low stealth values can be heard even walking slowly on normally quiet surfaces.

Specialties

Each operative has a specialty—an area of expertise reflecting additional training and experience—and shows values for related attributes.

- **Assault:** Operatives with the assault specialty have good firearms values. Use them for taking out terrorists and other combat actions.

- **Demolitions:** Operatives with this specialty are great for breaching doors and creating access for teammates. Use them for defusing bombs and other explosives, as well. They have high demolitions and grenade values.

- **Electronics:** Electronics specialists are trained to plant bugs, deactivate security systems, and the like. Keep them out of firefights whenever possible—only two operatives have this specialty.

- **Recon:** Use recon operatives for surveillance and scouting. Their job is to locate the enemy without being detected, so their stealth values are high. They usually have high firearms values, as well, but keep them out of the fray when you can.

- **Sniper:** These operatives are especially skilled at sniping and also have high stealth values. Use them only for sniping tasks and always give them a good sniper rifle for the job.

Arnavisca, Santiago

Personal Information

Identification Number: RCT0031-A1044
Nationality: Spanish
Specialty: Assault
Date of Birth: 01 January 1968
Height: 186 cm
Weight: 81 kg
Hair: Brown
Eyes: Blue
Gender: Male

Background

Born in Málaga, Spain, the second in a family of eight. Although the family's holdings shrank considerably under Franco's rule, the Arnaviscas still control large tracts of farmland around Córdoba and the Guadalquivir River valley. His elder brother is a deputy in the Adalucian parliament. Attended University of Seville, 1983–88. Joined the *Guardia Civil* after graduation. Brigade commander 1994–96 in the Western European Union (WEU) administration of Mostar in Bosnia, where he was instrumental in rebuilding the local police force. *Guardia Civil's* counterterrorism unit, the *Unidad Especial de Intervención* (UEI) recruited him in 1997 as part of its focus on the growing threat of terrorism within the European Union by former citizens of Yugoslavia.

Arnavisca is an expert marksman, having participated in shooting competitions since childhood. In addition to his native Spanish, he speaks English, German, and Italian fluently and can make himself understood in most other European languages. Despite his aristocratic bearing, he is more comfortable acting as lieutenant and advisor than team lead. Tenacious in combat, he remains calmly detached in the tensest situations.

Attributes

Aggression: 72
Leadership: 81
Self-control: 94
Stamina: 83
Assault: 100
Demolitions: 24
Electronics: 34
Grenades: 65
Sniper: 49
Stealth: 82

Notes

Arnavisca is a superb marksman and one of the two best operatives with firearms. You can use him as team leader in a pinch, but he serves far better in a supporting role. He stays cool during the hottest firefights. Arnavisca is perfect to include in the team that's under player control.

Beckenbauer, Lars

Personal Information
Identification Number: RCT0031-A1044
Nationality: German
Specialty: Demolitions
Date of Birth: 21 August 1953
Height: 176 cm
Weight: 87 kg
Hair: Blond
Eyes: Blue
Gender: Male

Attributes

Aggression: 55
Leadership: 78
Self-control: 77
Stamina: 81
Assault: 76
Demolitions: 100
Electronics: 91
Grenades: 80
Sniper: 31
Stealth: 72

Background

Born on a farm near Chemnitz on the Czechoslovakian border in what was then the German Democratic Republic (East Germany). Drafted into the East Germany Army, 1970. Specialized in bomb disposal and demolitions. Assigned to East German Border Patrol, 1971–76. Arrested by the GDR State Security Service (Stasi) in 1976 under suspicion of involvement in high-profile defections. Released for lack of evidence and discharged from the army in 1977. Movements and activities 1977–84 unknown. The current German government will neither confirm nor deny rumors that he was a member of the *Libellen,* an underground group responsible for bombings of East German governmental offices in and around Berlin in the summer of 1981. Resurfaced in 1985 and granted asylum by West Germany after a risky crossing of the Baltic Sea in a small sailboat. Opened Pyrotechno GmbH, a security consulting firm, in 1989. Since then, he has acquired a reputation as Germany's leading expert on explosives and demolitions. Married, 1995. Two children.

Beckenbauer has an encyclopedic knowledge of explosive devices. His years of working with bombs make him extremely meticulous. He overlooks no detail and leaves nothing to chance. Because he focuses completely on the job at hand and considers personal interactions dangerous distractions, the rest of the team may perceive him as cold and distant.

Notes

Beckenbauer is Rainbow Six's demolitions expert and is proficient in electronics, as well. His other attributes are normal or lower. He is no leader and prefers to work alone. Put him in a team that has a strong leader and will engage in minimal combat.

Bogart, Daniel

Personal Information

Identification Number: RCT0047-A1109
Nationality: American
Specialty: Assault
Date of Birth: 12 October 1954
Height: 188 cm
Weight: 82 kg
Hair: Black
Eyes: Blue
Gender: Male

Background

Born in Keokuk, Iowa, USA. Father is a local deputy sheriff, mother a homemaker. Two brothers. Attended University of Iowa on a track and field scholarship, 1972–76. Graduated with honors with a degree in law enforcement. Patrolman with Keokuk Police Department for three years. Hired in 1980 by the Federal Bureau of Investigation. Member, FBI Hostage Rescue Team, 1987–97. Married, 1979. Wife and two teenage children live in Maine, USA.

Bogart makes an excellent team leader. He has exceptional tactical skills and situational awareness from his years with HRT. Cool under fire, he is a crack shot and won marksmanship awards during his tenure at the FBI. His low-key demeanor and laconic sense of humor make him well-liked among RAINBOW team members.

Notes

Bogart is a good choice for team leader. He is highly proficient with firearms, as well. Use him for your main assault teams.

Attributes

Aggression: 89
Leadership: 96
Self-control: 93
Stamina: 97
Assault: 98
Demolitions: 20
Electronics: 20
Grenades: 50
Sniper 51
Stealth: 73

Burke, Andrew

Personal Information

Identification Number: RCT0049-A2267
Nationality: British
Specialty: Assault
Date of Birth: 12 January 1968
Height: 176 cm
Weight: 72 kg
Hair: Red
Eyes: Blue
Gender: Male

Attributes

Aggression: 91
Leadership: 85
Self-control: 75
Stamina: 94
Assault: 93
Demolitions: 75
Electronics: 53
Grenades: 67
Sniper 36
Stealth: 78

Background

Born in Manchester, England. Whereabouts of father unknown. Mother is a secretary at a plastics processing plant in Leeds. Three siblings—two brothers and a sister. Joined Royal Marines, 1986. Two tours with British Special Air Service (SAS), 1989–91 and 1996–99. Received Military Cross, 1998. Has taken part in SAS actions in 22 countries on four continents. Further service record details are sealed. Unmarried.

Burke is a seasoned veteran of numerous covert operations. Although not reckless, he has a strong can-do attitude and confidence in his abilities. As a leader, he is decisive and demanding. He has a quick sense of humor and often uses jokes to relax his team before a mission. He maintains contact with his immediate family, but he considers the service to be his home.

Notes

Burke is a well-rounded operative. He has experience in most areas, but excels in none. A poor choice for team leader, he serves well in a support role for assault or other teams needing his firearms skills.

Chavez, Ding

Personal Information

Identification Number: RCT0047-X0566
Nationality: American
Specialty: Assault
Date of Birth: 12 January 1968
Height: 176 cm
Weight: 72 kg
Hair: Black
Eyes: Brown
Gender: Male

Background

Born in Los Angeles, California, USA. Joined U.S. Army, 1983. Served with the 7th Infantry Division (Light), 1984–87. Achieved rank of staff sergeant before the American Central Intelligence Agency (CIA) recruited him in 1987 for narcotics interdiction operations in South America. Discharged, 1988; became a full-time CIA employee under John Clark the same year. Service records for years 1989–99 are sealed. Earned B.S. degree in political science, George Mason University, 1995. M.A., international relations, from the same institution, 1999. Married.

Chavez is an excellent light infantry soldier with an exceptional grasp of small-unit tactics and close-quarters battle. Although small in stature, he is powerfully built and agile, a formidable opponent with a wide range of weapons and in hand-to-hand combat.

Notes

Chavez is operational leader of Rainbow Six. Put him in command of the team with the most important objectives. He is expert at firearms and stealth, with good experience in several other areas. His high leadership value boosts other team members with lower self-control and teamwork attributes. Put less-experienced operatives in his team. You will probably want to control Chavez, but, because he will follow your orders better than anyone else, you should leave him under AI control.

Attributes

Aggression: 95
Leadership: 100
Self-control: 92
Stamina: 97
Assault: 100
Demolitions: 71
Electronics: 67
Grenades: 74
Sniper: 63
Stealth: 100

DuBarry, Alain

Personal Information

Identification Number: RCT0013-A5436
Nationality: French
Specialty: Electronics
Date of Birth: 27 September 1967
Height: 174 cm
Weight: 66 kg
Hair: Black
Eyes: Brown
Gender: Male

Attributes

Aggression: 72
Leadership: 81
Self-control: 76
Stamina: 91
Assault: 84
Demolitions: 76
Electronics: 100
Grenades: 81
Sniper: 66
Stealth: 73

Background

Born in Chantilly, France. Father is manuscript curator at a local museum, mother a journalist. Four sisters, two brothers. Second-oldest sister is a prominent professor of mathematics at the University of Paris. Attended *l'École Supérieure d'Ingénieurs en Electrotechnique et Electronique* (ESIEE) in Paris, 1984–89. Graduated with degrees in electronics engineering and computer science. Joined the *Gendarmerie Nationale* in 1990 as an officer in their computer crime division. Instrumental in thwarting a 1994 attempt by Algerian nationals to bring down the French Minitel computer network using a virus spread by telephone switching software. *Groupe d'Intervention Gendarmerie Nationale* (GIGN), France's elite counterterrorist unit, recruited him in 1996 as a specialist in telephony and electronic surveillance. Unmarried.

DuBarry is expert in computers and computer nets, and in more conventional forms of surveillance. Although his role in CT actions is usually intelligence-gathering and communications, as a veteran of GIGN's extensive combat training, he is fully qualified to participate in armed operations. Introverted, thoughtful, and an excellent tactician, he often makes connections other team members miss. Off duty, he is an avid amateur scuba diver and an officer in the *Confédération Mondiale des Activités Subaquatiques* (CMAS).

Notes

DuBarry is Rainbow Six's electronics expert. He's proficient in the use of firearms and grenades, as well. He'll do well in a team with a good leader. Keep him out of combat when you can, because he is one of only two electronics specialists available to you. His death can seriously hamper future missions.

Filatov, Genedy

Personal Information
Identification Number: RCT0069-A1772
Nationality: Russian
Specialty: Assault
Date of Birth: 12 February 1964
Height: 183 cm
Weight: 84 kg
Hair: Blond
Eyes: Hazel
Gender: Male

Background
Born in Pskov, Pskovskaya Oblast in the former Soviet Union. No information on family. Served in army of former Soviet Union, 1981–85, including one tour in Afghanistan. Recruited by *Alfa* counterterrorist group, 1987. Operated in all major territories of the former Soviet Union and eastern Europe. Resigned from *Alfa* in 1991 in response to that organization's ambiguous response to the failed Soviet coup. Director of operations for private security firm, 1991–96. Returned to *Alfa* during its 1997 restructuring under the Russian Federal Security Service. Married, no children.

Filatov is a solid counterterrorism operative. His training and background are unorthodox by Western standards, but he has a wealth of real-world experience from his years in the security forces of the former Soviet Union and numerous contacts across eastern Europe and Asia. His steady nerves and methodical approach to threats make him particularly valuable in combat situations. Do not let his world-weary manner mislead you; he is no pessimist, but, rather, a realist, and he prides himself on being the voice of reason and conservatism in any debate.

Attributes
Aggression: 82
Leadership: 82
Self-control: 87
Stamina: 83
Assault: 91
Demolitions: 62
Electronics: 36
Grenades: 85
Sniper: 59
Stealth: 70

Notes
Filatov is an average operative with good values in all attributes except electronics. Although he is not a leader, he does well in a support role.

Galanos, Kure

Personal Information
Identification Number: RCT0031-A1044
Nationality: Greek
Specialty: Sniper
Date of Birth: 25 July 1975
Height: 167 cm
Weight: 58 kg
Hair: Black
Eyes: Brown
Gender: Female

Attributes

Aggression: 100
Leadership: 88
Self-control: 90
Stamina: 90
Assault: 50
Demolitions: 45
Electronics: 22
Grenades: 83
Sniper: 96
Stealth: 99

Background

Born in Nicosia, Cyprus. Galanos was thrust into the ethnic tensions on Cyprus from an early age, when her family lost their homes during widespread clashes between Turkish and Greek rioters. The Galanos family, while never physically harmed by the tensions, continued to suffer difficult times for many years due to the unrest. Eventually they fled the city, and Galanos' father, an ex-ELDYK sniper, taught her his trade in extended hunting trips through the center of the island. Galanos attempted to join the Greek MYK force, but was denied due to her gender. Instead, she joined the civilian police force and quickly rose to prominence as a sniper with a reputation for precise shooting in less-than-optimal conditions.

Galanos is, at times, a sheer force of nature. What she cannot achieve by skill alone, she often completes by force of will. Teammates often claim her piercing gaze does more damage than her bullets. She displays no antipathy towards Turks, or indeed any other nationality or criminal. She treats assignments as problems to be solved, and she solves them with a single, clean trigger pull.

Notes

Galanos is one of your better snipers. In addition, she can stay cool no matter what. This attribute is extremely important to snipers, because excitement ruins their accuracy.

Haider, Karl

Personal Information

Identification Number: RCT0007-A3709
Nationality: Austrian
Specialty: Assault
Date of Birth: 10 September 1975
Height: 196 cm
Weight: 117 kg
Hair: Black
Eyes: Blue
Gender: Male

Background

Born in Graz, Austria. Father is a petroleum distributor, mother a homemaker. Two siblings, a brother and a sister, both still in school. Joined the regular Austrian army in 1992. Transferred to *Gendarmerieeinsatzkommando Cobra* (GEK Cobra) in 1996. Trained with Germany's GSG-9 and Israel's *Sayeret Mat'Kal*. Participated in GEK Cobra raid on Deissenmayr GmbH headquarters in Vienna in 1998, single-handedly saving the lives of seven hostages. Married, 1999. No children.

In combat situations, Karl is unstoppable. He is extremely aggressive and will not hesitate to use any methods necessary to complete his mission. He is fanatical about protecting hostages and innocent bystanders, to the point of jeopardizing his own life. Off the job, he is soft-spoken and private, but he has an iron determination.

Notes

Haider is one tough soldier, but he needs a strong leader. He provides good support for Chavez's team.

Attributes

Aggression: 100
Leadership: 75
Self-control: 71
Stamina: 96
Assault: 89
Demolitions: 42
Electronics: 55
Grenades: 71
Sniper: 61
Stealth: 74

Hanley, Timothy

Personal Information
Identification Number: RCT0005-A1299
Nationality: Australian
Specialty: Assault
Date of Birth: 14 April 1965
Height: 187 cm
Weight: 85 kg
Hair: Blond
Eyes: Brown
Gender: Male

Attributes

Aggression: 93
Leadership: 86
Self-control: 84
Stamina: 100
Assault: 91
Demolitions: 75
Electronics: 65
Grenades: 84
Sniper: 43
Stealth: 85

Background

Born in Margaret River, Australia. Father is a winery foreman; mother is a homemaker. Two siblings, a brother and a sister. Attended Australian Defense Forces Academy in Canberra, 1983–87. Upon graduation, the Special Air Service Regiment (SASR) recruited him into its newly formed 1st squadron; he remained with this unit when it was reorganized into the Australian Tactical Assault Group (TAG) shortly thereafter. He has served his entire career with TAG, except one tour with the Australian Intelligence Corps (AustInt), 1993–96. Has led counterterrorist teams on three continents and cross-trained with both U.S. Delta Force and British Special Air Service. Unmarried.

Hanley is a career CT officer. He is a veteran of dozens of assaults and approaches even the most dangerous missions with easygoing good humor. Off duty, he is an experienced backpacker and mountaineer who has taken part in amateur expeditions to many of the world's major peaks. He is in superb physical condition and has demonstrated an ability to endure even the most extreme physical hardship.

Notes

Hanley is another good support operative with good values across the board. In a pinch, you can even use him for demolitions work.

Johnston, Homer

Personal Information

Identification Number: RCT0047-B0381
Nationality: American
Specialty: Assault
Date of Birth: 23 August 1972
Height: 183 cm
Weight: 73 kg
Hair: Blond
Eyes: Brown
Gender: Male

Background

Born in Boise, Idaho, USA. Father logger, mother secretary at lumber mill. Brought up in true mountain-man fashion. Shot his first deer at age 10. Former Green Beret and Delta Force member. Part of 101st AirMobile, Fort Campbell, Kentucky. Found his way into Black Ops by 1989. Definitive distance runner. Relies on stealth and speed to set up his sniper locations. Expert with all rifle types. Spends free time hunting with Weber and visiting his parents. Unmarried.

Notes

Johnston is one of the snipers assigned to the RAINBOW team. As such, he has great firearms and stealth skill levels. With the PSG-1 rifle, he's deadly at long range. Assign Johnston to a team that must pick off tangos from a distance. He'll give you a new understanding of the sniper motto, "One shot, one kill."

Attributes

Aggression: 89
Leadership: 83
Self-control: 87
Stamina: 98
Assault: 42
Demolitions: 55
Electronics: 50
Grenades: 70
Sniper: 100
Stealth: 100

Lofquist, Annika

Personal Information

Identification Number: RCT0030-A3224
Nationality: Swedish
Specialty: Electronics
Date of Birth: 02 November 1966
Height: 179 cm
Weight: 68 kg
Hair: Blonde
Eyes: Blue
Gender: Female

Attributes

Aggression: 80
Leadership: 92
Self-control: 77
Stamina: 82
Assault: 85
Demolitions: 61
Electronics: 97
Grenades: 69
Sniper: 58
Stealth: 69

Background

Born in Göteborg, Sweden. Father was a retired admiral in the Swedish Navy, now deceased. Mother is professor of Romance languages at Göteborg University and is active in *Miljöpartiet de Gröna*, the Swedish Green Party. Three brothers. The entire family sails avidly. Attended Stockholm University, 1984–87; earned a B.S. in physics. After a stint as engineer with the Swedish semiconductor giant Microelektronik AB (1988-92), Lofquist joined the Stockholm police force as an expert on electronic surveillance. *Ordningspolisens Nationella Insatsstyrka* (ONI), the national rescue unit of the Stockholm police force, recruited her in 1994. From 1997 to 1999, she led ONI intelligence and surveillance teams in more than a dozen counterterrorist actions, including the high-profile 1998 Red Cell occupation of the trading floor of the Stockholm futures exchange. Unmarried.

Lofquist is an electronics genius. Her name is on 14 patents held by Microelektronik, her old employer, and she continues to consult with their engineers while serving as a member of the RAINBOW team. Most of her innovations are in the area of electronic eavesdropping. She is confident and courageous, but at times her lack of military training can lead her to overestimate her ability to handle a situation. Off duty, she keeps to herself, and lives alone on a sailboat in Saltsjobaden, outside Stockholm.

Notes

Lofquist is proficient in electronics and makes a good team leader. As with DuBarry, keep her safe. However, in a firefight, she is good with a gun.

Loiselle, Louis

Personal Information

Identification Number: RCT0013-B5928
Nationality: French
Specialty: Assault
Date of Birth: 06 June 1968
Height: 178 cm
Weight: 68 kg
Hair: Black
Eyes: Brown
Gender: Male

Background

Born in Paris, France. Married to Elaine, three years. Father former commercial pilot, mother a clerk at local department store in Avagion. Former member, French Parachute Division. Detailed to DGSE. Part of action group Service 7. Involved in tactical espionage and counterespionage throughout Europe. Began training DGSE recruits in 1985. On assignments, he's a utility player and doesn't disturb easily. He's a marksman with pistols and rifles, but he's experienced in all forms of counterterrorism. He spends most free time reading and with his wife.

Notes

Loiselle is a good choice for an assault team in the support role. He'll do a great job covering your back during a mission, and he'll stay calm, even when stuff begins hitting the fan. Place him in a team's second slot.

Attributes

Aggression: 90
Leadership: 85
Self-control: 100
Stamina: 85
Assault: 94
Demolitions: 49
Electronics: 70
Grenades: 70
Sniper: 50
Stealth: 78

Maldini, Antonio

Personal Information
Identification Number: RCT0023-A2009
Nationality: Italian
Specialty: Recon
Date of Birth: 14 October 1966
Height: 179 cm
Weight: 68 kg
Hair: Blond
Eyes: Blue
Gender: Male

Attributes

Aggression: 50
Leadership: 60
Self-control: 80
Stamina: 95
Assault: 90
Demolitions: 65
Electronics: 65
Grenades: 50
Sniper: 38
Stealth: 100

Background

Born in Milano, Italy. Father manages a textile factory; mother is a homemaker. Five siblings. Attended *Universiti degli Studi di Ferrara,* 1984–88. Degree in chemistry. Joined *l'Arma dei Caribinieri* in 1989. On completion of training, he was assigned to the *Comando Caribinieri Antidroga,* the Caribinieri's antinarcotics agency. Transferred in 1995 to the *Gruppo Intervento Speciale* (GIS), Italy's elite counterterrorism team. Married since 1990. Three children.

Maldini's specialty is stealth. At GIS, his ability to occupy positions undetected by the enemy earned him the nickname "Invisible Man." He is in excellent physical condition and is quick on his feet. His demeanor is calm and somewhat aloof. Although a solid team member, he is too introspective to be a truly effective commander. Off duty, he is an amateur marathoner and has competed in races throughout Europe. Extremely intelligent and well-spoken.

Notes

Maldini is extremely stealthy and can sneak up on enemies undetected. Use him for quiet strikes or to gain intelligence on enemy locations. He is no leader but is useful in either a support role or alone.

McAllen, Roger

Personal Information

Identification Number: RCT0011-A1932
Nationality: Canadian
Specialty: Demolitions
Date of Birth: 06 June 1964
Height: 185 cm
Weight: 95 kg
Hair: Brown
Eyes: Hazel
Gender: Male

Background

Born in Toronto, Ontario, Canada. Father is a senior officer with the Royal Bank of Canada. Mother deceased. He has one sister, who resides in Toronto. Joined Canadian Army as field engineer, 1981. One tour, 1981–85. Received advanced training in combat diving and explosive ordnance disposal. Upon discharge, joined the Royal Canadian Mounted Police (RCMP) and, in 1988, became a member of the Special Emergency Response Team (SERT), the RCMP's elite counterterrorism unit. When SERT was disbanded in 1993, he helped coordinate the transition of counterterrorist responsibilities to the Canadian Armed Forces' newly formed Joint Task Force Two (JTF-2). McAllen reenlisted in 1994 and became a full member of JTF-2 the same year. He has participated in counterterrorist actions on three continents, including JTF-2 extended operations against war criminals in Bosnia, 1996–97. Married, 1984; divorced, 1992. One child, a daughter, born 1986, lives with her mother in London, Ontario, Canada.

McAllen specializes in several areas. He is an excellent shot and is aggressive in combat situations, and so makes a good assault team member, but he also has extensive experience with bomb disposal and demolitions. He is an amateur power-lifter and his strength and stamina make him a formidable opponent. Team leads should be warned that he performs better as a subordinate than in a command position. He has a hearty, good-natured manner and spends his off-duty time socializing with a wide circle of friends, most military or ex-military men.

Attributes

Aggression: 70
Leadership: 70
Self-control: 70
Stamina: 98
Assault: 96
Demolitions: 97
Electronics: 71
Grenades: 100
Sniper: 65
Stealth: 70

Notes

McAllen is proficient in demolitions and firearms and expert with grenades. Although he is not a leader, he is helpful as support when breaching doors and for additional firepower.

Morris, Gerald

Personal Information

Identification Number: RCT0047-A0781
Nationality: American
Specialty: Demolitions
Date of Birth: 24 December 1965
Height: 186 cm
Weight: 96 kg
Hair: Black
Eyes: Brown
Gender: Male

Attributes

Aggression: 40
Leadership: 72
Self-control: 80
Stamina: 79
Assault: 80
Demolitions: 99
Electronics: 54
Grenades: 97
Sniper: 63
Stealth: 71

Background

Born in Birmingham, Alabama, USA. Father is a retired furniture salesman; mother is a homemaker. Two younger sisters, both still living in Birmingham. High school valedictorian; National Merit Scholar, 1982. Attended Rice University in Houston, Texas, 1983–87; earned a B.S. in material science and a B.A. in Russian literature. Joined the American Bureau of Alcohol, Tobacco, and Firearms (BATF) in 1988 as an agent in their explosives division. Earned an M.S. degree in inorganic chemistry from the University of New Orleans during leave of absence from BATF, 1992–94. His thesis, "Applications of Micro-stress Analysis in Accelerant Identification," is considered a landmark in the forensic analysis of bomb debris. Upon his return in 1995 to active duty in the BATF, he was assigned to their International Response Team (IRT). Since 1998, Morris has been on extended assignment in South Korea with the Korean counterterrorism task force, the National Police 868 Unit, training them in bomb detection, bomb disposal, and postbombing investigation techniques. His wife and two daughters currently live in Seoul, South Korea.

Morris is a team player who likes his operations run strictly by the book. His primary specialty is forensics, but he is also expert at setting and disarming of all types of explosive devices. Although he is experienced in conducting counterterrorist assaults from his years working with the 868 Unit, he prefers to take an indirect approach in hostage situations. Morris likes to spend his off-duty hours with his family. In his spare time he collects antique blues recordings and memorabilia.

Notes

Morris is very good with demolitions and grenades. Use him for support, much as you would McAllen.

Murad, Jamal

Personal Information
Identification Number: RCT0031-A1044
Nationality: Egyptian
Specialty: Assault
Date of Birth: 03 April 1971
Height: 170 cm
Weight: 74 kg
Hair: Black
Eyes: Black
Gender: Male

Background
Born in Bani Suwayf, Egypt. Murad is the son of an influential moderate Muslim cleric, and grew up learning a great deal about both the religious and secular worlds. To the dismay of his pacifistic parents, Murad joined the Egyptian armed forces rather than continue his scholarship. Privately upset by the reputation of Egypt's Unit 777, Murad set out to change the organization from within. His contacts with U.S., British, and German training units convinced him there was a better way, but that Egypt would not be taking that path soon enough for him. His exceptional skills, both linguistic and military, landed him a frequent cross-training position with the SAS, where he came to the attention of RAINBOW.

    In combat, Murad is a swift and lethal presence. Once he has committed a plan to memory, nothing stands in his way to accomplish that plan. Prior to the mission, Murad questions every detail of every plan, often infuriating the planning officers but ensuring that every possible consequence and complication have been well thought out. His insistence that there is a "Right Way" has won him many admirers, if few friends.

Attributes
Aggression: 99
Leadership: 86
Self-control: 99
Stamina: 65
Assault: 87
Demolitions: 16
Electronics: 50
Grenades: 78
Sniper: 42
Stealth: 88

Notes
Murad is great for an assault team as one of the team. However, his leadership skill levels are not as high as others, so put him in second or third in a team.

Narino, Emilio

Personal Information

Identification Number: RCT0031-A1044
Nationality: Colombian
Specialty: Sniper
Date of Birth: 12 January 1967
Height: 164 cm
Weight: 82 kg
Hair: Black
Eyes: Brown
Gender: Male

Attributes

Aggression: 95
Leadership: 80
Self-control: 54
Stamina: 84
Assault: 39
Demolitions: 60
Electronics: 56
Grenades: 67
Sniper: 97
Stealth: 90

Background

Born in Cartagena, Colombia. Narino's early activities are shrouded in mystery, a situation he enhances with conflicting stories regarding his training and upbringing. At various times, Narino has claimed to be the nephew of a Colombian drug lord, a failed university professor, an ex-police officer, and a freedom fighter. Most team members believe that he learned his trade as a CIA assassin, a belief that Narino alternately encourages with outrageous stories or flatly denies with cold stares. Regardless, everyone agrees that Narino is a cool and composed marksman with a disquieting ability to sneak into exposed positions without being seen.

Narino is a study in unpredictable mood swings. One minute he's joking and talkative, the next tight-lipped and silent. This never interferes with his professionalism on the job, but it has kept Narino at arm's length from the easy camaraderie pervading most of the team. This distance is especially noticeable during planning sessions, where he doesn't contribute unless it is to point out an unorthodox sniping position.

Notes

Narino is a good and capable sniper. Use him if the other snipers need to rest because they are fatigued by the last mission.

Noronha, Alejandro

Personal Information

Identification Number: RCT0009-A1538
Nationality: Brazilian
Specialty: Assault
Date of Birth: 08 June 1959
Height: 175 cm
Weight: 70 kg
Hair: Brown
Eyes: Brown
Gender: Male

Background

Born in Belo Horizonte, Brazil. His late father ran an import business. His mother is a homemaker. One older brother, two younger sisters. Attended college at the Brazilian military academy, *Colègio Militar do Rio de Janeiro* (CMRJ), 1977–81. Served two terms of duty with the regular Brazilian army before recruitment into the CounterTerrorist Detachment (CTD) of the 1st Special Forces Battalion in 1987. Since 1995 he has commanded one of CTD's three squadrons. He has cross-trained with the U.S. Delta Force, Chile's *Unidad Anti-Terroristes* (UAT), Argentina's *Brigada Especial Operativa Halcon,* and Colombia's *Agrupacion De Fuerzas Especiales Urbanas* (AFEU). In 1997, he was one of a group of senior Brazilian CTD operators who assisted the Peruvian armed forces in ending the occupation of the Japanese embassy by the Tupac Amaru Revolutionary Movement (MRTA). Married, 1985. His wife and two daughters live in Rio de Janeiro.

Noronha has spent most of his military career as a CT operator. He is well-known in the CT community, particularly in North and South America and has a reputation as a stern taskmaster. Although he has conducted actions in a variety of terrain and circumstances, he is particularly proficient in jungle operations and long-range intelligence-gathering. In combat situations, he is extremely aggressive and expects the same from any team that serves under him. He has no sense of humor and considers it unprofessional in others. His only passion (aside from work and family) is classical music and opera.

Attributes

Aggression: 91
Leadership: 91
Self-control: 91
Stamina: 82
Assault: 94
Demolitions: 50
Electronics: 32
Grenades: 75
Sniper: 56
Stealth: 73

Notes

Noronha makes a good team leader. Although he is an assault specialist, you can assign his teams to other objectives, such as electronics or demolitions actions. He provides good leadership and protection to other types of specialists.

Novikov, Arkadi

Personal Information
Identification Number: RCT0031-A1044
Nationality: Russian
Specialty: Assault
Date of Birth: 24 May 1966
Height: 201 cm
Weight: 125 kg
Hair: Black
Eyes: Brown
Gender: Male

Attributes

Aggression: 74
Leadership: 99
Self-control: 80
Stamina: 83
Assault: 94
Demolitions: 32
Electronics: 85
Grenades: 60
Sniper: 75
Stealth: 70

Background

Born in Minsk, in what is now Belarus. Novikov is the son of a career army officer; his family is politically very well connected and has made the transition from the USSR to the CIS very well indeed. Novikov enjoyed the finest education and living standard available, including an engineering degree from the University of Moscow. He spurned the regular army to take a prized field position in the enforcement arm of the KGB, only to find it disintegrating beneath him. When his co-workers joined the forming Russian Mafias, Novikov returned to Minsk where the newly independent Belarus army offered him a chance to lead a CT team of his own creation. A series of low-profile but well-planned and -executed missions brought him to the attention of RAINBOW, which Novikov gladly joined.

Novikov combines the broad build of the Russian athlete with an incisive mind and stern leadership. He is capable of working much higher in the organization, but prefers field duty, even if it means taking more orders than he gives. Other team members feel comfortable with Novikov in charge, as his personal bravery combines with sharp planning to virtually guarantee success.

Notes

Novikov makes for an excellent leader, nearly on par with Chavez. Use him to lead one of your assault teams.

Pak Suo-Won

Personal Information
Identification Number: RCT0031-A1044
Nationality: South Korean
Specialty: Recon
Date of Birth: 12 December 1973
Height: 159 cm
Weight: 45 kg
Hair: Black
Eyes: Brown
Gender: Male

Background
Born in Kangnung, South Korea. Pak is a member of a large family of fishermen; he has four brothers and three sisters. He entered the South Korean army at the youngest age he could, so long as he wouldn't have to serve on a boat, ever again. Despite (or perhaps because of) his slight build, Pak developed a reputation for physical prowess, particularly endurance. He was accepted into the 707th Special Mission Battalion, making battalion history by being the only inductee to exceed every one of the punishing physical tests exacted upon the battalion during training. He further built up his reputation by succeeding at lengthy solo infiltration missions behind North Korean lines, often in disguise for extended periods of time.

Pak is cheerful and optimistic at all times. While Recon operatives are not used in all missions, Pak manages to be in the center of the planning and discussion stages all the same.

Notes
Pak is a stealthy recon specialist who gets the job done even when wounded due to his high pain tolerance.

Attributes
Aggression: 60
Leadership: 70
Self-control: 88
Stamina: 100
Assault: 89
Demolitions: 25
Electronics: 67
Grenades: 65
Sniper: 51
Stealth: 99

PETERSEN

Petersen, Einar

Personal Information

Identification Number: RCT0031-A1044
Nationality: Norwegian
Specialty: Sniper
Date of Birth: 14 September 1970
Height: 189 cm
Weight: 73 kg
Hair: Brown
Eyes: Brown
Gender: Male

Attributes

Aggression: 88
Leadership: 75
Self-control: 100
Stamina: 98
Assault: 36
Demolitions: 24
Electronics: 49
Grenades: 75
Sniper: 99
Stealth: 89

Background

Born in Hamar, Norway. Parents owned and operated a ski resort high in central Norway. Began skiing at an early age; soon added hunting and shooting, to become an accomplished biathlete. Attempted and failed to win entry to Norway's Olympic Biathlon Team in 1988 and 1992, missing by fractions of a point each time. Joined Beredskapstroppen in 1990, after his sister was wounded in a terrorist attack while traveling in the Middle East.

Petersen is a nearly unstoppable sniper if allowed the proper setup time. He projects an air of icy calm at all times, prompting teammates to devise various pranks and embarrassing situations to disturb that calm. All attempts so far have failed. While he is aloof, his unerring accuracy has endeared him to the rest of the team. When not on duty, Petersen often embarks on lengthy solo cross-country skiing trips, disappearing into dense terrain for days at a time.

Notes

Petersen is an excellent sniper. He is extremely accurate as well as patient, waiting for hours for the perfect shot.

Price, Eddie

Personal Information
Identification Number: RCT0049-B4197
Nationality: British
Specialty: Assault
Date of Birth: 21 September 1958
Height: 186 cm
Weight: 84 kg
Hair: Brown
Eyes: Green
Gender: Male

Background
Born in London, England. Father deceased, mother living in Cambridge, retired nurse. Price is a former color sergeant, serving in the 22nd SAS at Hereford. Spot-promoted to sergeant major. Spent time in Northern Ireland for the 14th Intelligence Company. Highly trained in techniques including CQB, IR photography, and covert surveillance, "the Company" performs in Northern Ireland, monitoring known IRA terrorists and preemptively striking terrorist targets. Involved in hostage rescue, Colombia, 1984. Extremely physically fit and an expert marksman. Enjoys reading, smoking his pipe, and working out with Weber. Unmarried.

Notes
Price is the first sergeant of Chavez's team in the novel. With more experience than any of the other operatives, Price makes a great team leader. Not only does he have great leadership skills, but he's also very proficient with firearms.

Attributes
Aggression: 80
Leadership: 95
Self-control: 90
Stamina: 87
Assault: 96
Demolitions: 71
Electronics: 63
Grenades: 77
Sniper: 52
Stealth: 89

Rakuzanka, Kazimiera

Personal Information

Identification Number: RCT0027-A2057
Nationality: Polish
Specialty: Assault
Date of Birth: 29 February 1964
Height: 165 cm
Weight: 61 kg
Hair: Blonde
Eyes: Brown
Gender: Female

Attributes

Aggression: 85
Leadership: 85
Self-control: 60
Stamina: 96
Assault: 96
Demolitions: 50
Electronics: 52
Grenades: 70
Sniper: 73
Stealth: 80

Background

Born Kazimiera Koziol in Gdansk, Poland. Her father and brothers worked in the shipyards and she was active from an early age in the movement later known as *Solidarnosc.* In 1981, when she was 17, she was beaten seriously enough by police to require hospitalization; in 1982 she was arrested during a street demonstration and spent the following year in jail. Upon her release in 1983, she resumed activity in the Solidarity underground while working odd jobs in and around Gdansk. Married in 1986 to fellow activist Andrzej Rakuzanka. With the shifting of political winds in 1989 and the founding of the Republic of Poland, she was able once again to make public her affiliation with Solidarity. In 1990, she joined the reconstructed Gdansk police force and quickly moved into undercover work to battle the growing organized crime problem in the newly liberated country. In 1993, she joined the Grupa *Reagowania Operacyjno Mobilnego* (GROM), Poland's newly formed counterterrorist unit. Initially she was involved purely in intelligence-gathering activities, but in 1994, when her unit took part in Operation Restore Democracy—the American-led invasion of Haiti—she was promoted to full-fledged CT operator. She led her first assault team in 1998 and has since crosstrained with the U.S. Delta Force, Norway's *Beredskapstroppen,* and Finland's *Osasto Karhu.* Her husband and two daughters reside in Gdansk.

Rakuzanka is a survivor. Despite her unassuming appearance, she has an iron constitution and can endure extreme hardship. She is a strong team player and an excellent shot. She can be sarcastic but reserves her sharpest barbs for the rich and powerful. Friends and family call her "Kazi," colleagues, "Kamikazi" (but never to her face).

Notes

Rakuzanka is a good assault specialist in a support role. She is best at firearms, average in other areas.

Raymond, Renee

Personal Information

Identification Number: RCT0047-A1342
Nationality: American
Specialty: Assault
Date of Birth: 30 March 1968
Height: 172 cm
Weight: 64 kg
Hair: Black
Eyes: Brown
Gender: Female

Background

Born in Kansas City, Missouri, USA. Father is a retired U.S. Army colonel; mother is a homemaker. Two older brothers. Attended University of Oklahoma, 1986–89, under Reserve Officers Training Corps (ROTC) program, majoring in political science. Entered regular U.S. Army upon graduation. Served in Kuwait, 1991. Recruited into U.S. Special Operations Psychological Operations (PSYOPS), 1992. Served in Bosnia, 1996–97. In 1998, participated in U.S. Army trial introduction of women into special operations ground combat forces. Trained with 1st Special Forces Operational Detachment–Delta (1st SFOD-D, "Delta Force"). Married, 1993. Husband is a lieutenant in U.S. Army, stationed in Frankfurt, Germany. One child, a daughter, born 1995.

Raymond is self-reliant and resourceful. An excellent combat soldier, she is also well-versed in psychological warfare and understands how both soldiers and civilians react under the stress of combat. Although she is an experienced officer, she is too much of a loner to be at her best as team lead. Use her to maximum advantage in a support role. She doesn't speak much, and weighs her words carefully when she does.

Attributes

Aggression: 75
Leadership: 79
Self-control: 90
Stamina: 91
Assault: 97
Demolitions: 30
Electronics: 23
Grenades: 85
Sniper: 68
Stealth: 96

Notes

Raymond is not only excellent in combat, with great firearms and grenades attributes, but her great ability to move about quietly renders her useful for reconnaissance. Keep her in the support role; other team members are better leaders.

Sweeney, Kevin

Personal Information
Identification Number: RCT0049-A3964
Nationality: British
Specialty: Recon
Date of Birth: 30 March 1968
Height: 177 cm
Weight: 83 kg
Hair: Black
Eyes: Brown
Gender: Male

Attributes
Aggression: 45
Leadership: 65
Self-control: 95
Stamina: 85
Assault: 90
Demolitions: 30
Electronics: 96
Grenades: 50
Sniper: 59
Stealth: 99

Background

Born in Birmingham, England. Father was a waiter, mother a cleaning woman. Two brothers, one younger, one older. Joined Birmingham Police Force as patrol officer, 1987. Promoted to detective, 1991. Spent the next five years working a variety of undercover operations in the Special Branch. In the fall of 1996, in collaboration with the British Security Service (MI5), coordinated a series of raids that broke the back of the "Field of Gold" terrorist underground in the British Isles. MI5 recruited him as an agent in 1997, and he left his position with the Birmingham force. Assigned to their counterterrorism branch (T Branch), and working out of London, Sweeney has planned and executed over two dozen covert actions in Great Britain and British territories. Unmarried.

Despite his youthful appearance, Sweeney is a master of covert operations. His knack for blending into the background served him well during his years working under-cover on the streets of Birmingham. He is an excellent burglar and, despite his large build, can move quickly and quietly when he must. He is a good actor and maintains his composure in even the most stressful situations. Professionally, he is soft-spoken and earnest. He prefers consensus to confrontation.

Notes

Sweeney is not only stealthy and good with firearms, he also has a knack for electronics. He makes a good choice for sneaking into an area and disabling security systems and such. If he is not operating alone, use him in the support role.

Walther, Jorg

Personal Information

Identification Number: RCT0017-A1615
Nationality: German
Specialty: Assault
Date of Birth: 17 May 1974
Height: 190 cm
Weight: 105 kg
Hair: Brown
Eyes: Blue
Gender: Male

Background

Born in Saarbrücken, Germany. Father is a safety engineer with Lufthansa German Airlines; mother is a homemaker. Three younger siblings—two sisters and a brother. Amateur archer, competing in Germany junior national championships, 1990. Entered the German Federal Border Police Force (*Bundesgrenzschutz*) in 1994, at the top of his cadet class. Stationed at Saarbrücken, 1994–98. Recruited into Germany's elite counterterrorist force, *Grenzschutzgruppe 9* (GSG-9) in 1998. Completed GSG-9 training in record time, again at the top of his class. Temporarily attached to GSG-9/1, the group's primary CT strike unit, before reassignment to RAINBOW. Married, 1996. No children.

Walther is the youngest member of the current RAINBOW team. His extraordinary drive and determination compensate for his inexperience in the field. He learns quickly and makes an exceptional team member who follows every order without hesitation or question. Although trained primarily in assault, he is well-versed in wiretapping and electronic surveillance. *Bundesgrenzschutz* command clearly is grooming him for advancement; his assignment to RAINBOW reflects the German government's long-term commitment to international CT collaboration.

Attributes

Aggression: 76
Leadership: 97
Self-control: 90
Stamina: 96
Assault: 96
Demolitions: 71
Electronics: 89
Grenades: 83
Sniper: 71
Stealth: 97

Notes

Walther makes a great team leader. Not only is he good with firearms, but he is useful for electronics work, as well.

Weber, Dieter

Personal Information

Identification Number: RCT0017-B7682
Nationality: German
Specialty: Assault
Date of Birth: 09 July 1971
Height: 191 cm
Weight: 98 kg
Hair: Blond
Eyes: Brown
Gender: Male

Attributes

Aggression: 93
Leadership: 73
Self-control: 84
Stamina: 100
Assault: 45
Demolitions: 53
Electronics: 61
Grenades: 72
Sniper: 95
Stealth: 96

Background

Born in Munich, Germany. Father ironworker, mother deceased. Graduate of German Army's *Berger Fuhrer* (Mountain Leader) schools, one of the world's toughest, physically. Came from GSG-9 team, part of the former Border Guards, the Federal Republic's counterterrorism team. He's fluent in English and German, and his marksmanship is matched by only a few team members. Spends free time hunting, working out with Price, and practicing tae kwon do. Unmarried.

Notes

Weber is another one of RAINBOW's snipers. While he has great firearms and stealth skill levels, he's not the best leader. You may want to control him, however, so either put him in charge of a small team or keep him alone at a distance from the action to supply fire support.

Woo, Tracy

Personal Information

Identification Number: RCT0047-A2715
Nationality: American
Specialty: Recon
Date of Birth: 14 July 1971
Height: 155 cm
Weight: 44 kg
Hair: Black
Eyes: Brown
Gender: Female

Background

Born in Los Angeles, California, USA. Father is a doctor, mother a lawyer. No siblings. Amateur gymnast, competed in West Coast regional championships 1987–88. Attended UCLA 1989–92; graduated with a B.A. in psychology. Joined Los Angeles Police Department in 1992; transferred to Metro Division Special Weapons and Tactics (SWAT) team in 1994, specializing in surveillance and negotiation. Commended for bravery for her role in ending the New Millennium occupation of Los Angeles City Hall in 1999. Unmarried.

Woo is expert in reconnaissance and surveillance. She moves quickly and quietly through terrorist-controlled areas and is skilled in the installation and removal of a variety of electronic intelligence-gathering devices. She handles command well but has an independent nature and has been known to argue with superiors. Her combat skills are average. Outspoken and self-reliant.

Attributes

Aggression: 50
Leadership: 75
Self-control: 85
Stamina: 96
Assault: 80
Demolitions: 30
Electronics: 85
Grenades: 50
Sniper: 61
Stealth: 98

Notes

Woo is a good support operative in recon missions.
Although she is very stealthy, her combat and other skills are below average, (except for electronics, in which she is fairly proficient).

YACOBY

Attributes

Aggression: 95
Leadership: 65
Self-control: 70
Stamina: 95
Assault: 97
Demolitions: 30
Electronics: 86
Grenades: 60
Sniper: 54
Stealth: 97

Yacoby, Ayana

Personal Information

Identification Number: RCT0022-A4242
Nationality: Israeli
Specialty: Recon
Date of Birth: 03 March 1973
Height: 163 cm
Weight: 57 kg
Hair: Brown
Eyes: Brown
Gender: Female

Background

Born in Tel Aviv, Israel. Father is a greengrocer; mother died when Yacoby was three. One younger brother, professional soccer player, *Beitar Jerusalem.* Joined regular Israeli army, 1992. Transferred to *Sayeret Mat'Kal* in 1995, where she served in the general staff reconnaissance unit. Mossad recruited her in 1997. Specializes in infiltration and intelligence gathering. In addition to her native Hebrew, speaks fluent English and Arabic. Unmarried.

Yacoby is master of the silent kill. Her training enables her to move stealthily into hostile territory and neutralize any threats. She is extremely intelligent with little tolerance for fools. The quintessential professional, she has complained about the "cowboy mentality" of some other team members. Ruthless in combat, in nonmilitary situations she may err on the side of excessive force.

Notes

As with most recon specialists, Yacoby is no leader. However, she is expert when it comes to firearms and stealth. Her lower self-control value means you should use her in support of good leaders.

CHAPTER THREE
TOOLS OF THE TRADE

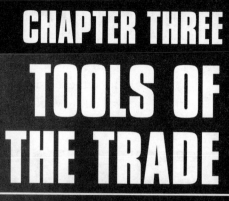

The Rainbow team must use a number of items to complete its missions. Firearms first come to mind, but making an antiterrorist operative's job (and rescued hostages) safer requires other equipment. The diverse circumstances confronting team members involve using a variety of uniforms, as well. The following sections detail the many tools Rainbow uses to complete its missions.

Firearms

The firearms in the RAINBOW arsenal are selected based on accuracy, firepower, and reliability. Each team member carries a primary weapon—a submachine gun, assault rifle, sniper rifle, or shotgun—and a pistol. The needs of the mission determine which weapon is assigned. Sometimes stealth and silence are vital; other circumstances demand firepower at long range. Give your team members the best weapons for the tasks they must accomplish.

Primary Weapons

HK MP5A4

The preferred submachine gun of counterterrorist operatives around the world, Heckler & Koch's MP5 is known for its reliability and accuracy, even when firing on full-automatic. RAINBOW uses the 9mm MP5A4 fitted with single, triple, and full-auto trigger group.

Notes

This is the standard RAINBOW firearm, and it's one of the most accurate firearms available to your operatives. Unless you need long-range fire or stealth, this is the weapon to use.

HK MP5SD5

Terrorists throughout the world fear Heckler & Koch's MP5SD. Its integral silencer is so effective that the report of the bullet is minuscule compared to the click of the bolt operating. RAINBOW uses the 9mm MP5SD5 whenever both accuracy and stealth are essential.

Notes

The MP5SD5 is essentially an MP5 with a silencer built on. Use this weapon when you must take out enemy units while maintaining stealth and secrecy. It's the only primary weapon with a silencer. Assign it to your recon teams.

HK MP5/10A2

The HK MP5/10A2 is a product-improved variant of the venerable HK MP5 chambered for a 10mm round. The increased stopping power of the heavier round is offset by increased recoil. It is equipped with a single and full-auto trigger group.

Notes

This is a good weapon if you want the ease of use of the MP5A4, but prefer a little more punch. If you expect the terrorists to be wearing light body armor, this is a good choice.

HK MP5/10SD

An HK MP5/10A2 equipped with a sound suppresser gives a nice mix between power and silence. Because the suppression is not integral (like the MP5SD), the suppression is not quite as complete.

Notes

If possible, it's always better to use silenced weapons. This one gives you more take-down power than the MP5SD, but does make a bit more noise.

HK UMP45

The HK UMP45 is the newest submachine gun from veteran gun manufacturer HK. The stopping power of its .45 caliber round comes at the price of an increased recoil and lower rate of fire.

Notes

This weapon fills the gap between submachine gun and assault rifle. Its size makes it a bit more difficult to handle in close quarters, but still much better than a rifle. This is a good choice when the enemy is wearing medium body armor.

HK UMP45SD

This weapon is an HK UMP45 equipped with a sound suppresser. While the suppression is not as complete as the integral suppresser of the MP5SD, the HK UMP45SD is a good choice when a balance between power and silence is required.

Notes

This weapon is the largest caliber primary weapon equipped with a silencer. If you still need stealth, but with as much take down as possible, use the HK UMP45SD.

HK MP5K-PDW

Heckler & Koch's 9mm MP5K-PDW is a compact version of the classic MP5. Its folding stock and light weight make it an ideal choice when a full rifle or submachine gun is unmanageable and a handgun is a poor compromise. It is equipped with the single and full-auto trigger group.

Notes

The PDW is RAINBOW's close-quarters submachine gun. Although not as accurate at the MP5A2, it's good for clearing rooms with full-automatic bursts.

M4 Carbine

A compact version of the M-16, the M4 Carbine is commonly used when the firepower of an assault rifle is needed, but the weight and size is not. It is commonly used by U.S. and Israeli special forces. It comes standard with a single and full-auto trigger group.

Notes

Issue the M4 to firepower support teams. It's best used outside, but its compact size allows it to be used effectively inside buildings, as well.

HK G3A3

The G3A3 is Heckler & Koch's standard assault rifle. It fires the powerful 7.62mm NATO round. This is the most accurate assault rifle in RAINBOW's arsenal.

Notes

This is your best weapon choice for long-range, non-sniper shooting. Give it to your teams providing cover from a distance when you need more firepower than is available from a sniper rifle.

G36K

The Heckler & Koch G36K is their latest assault rifle entry. Its compact design makes it useful in close quarters, while its 5.56mm round will penetrate most body armor.

Notes

Firing the same round as the M-16, the G36K gives added punch to assault teams working at short range with little room to maneuver. Use this against tangos wearing body armor when you must advance through narrow corridors or other such areas.

Enfield L85A1

The Enfield L85A1 (also known as the Enfield Individual Weapon or SA80) is the standard infantry weapon of the British Army. Its bullpup design trades accuracy for maneuverability.

Notes

With the magazine built into the stock, the L85A1 provides a longer barrel in shorter gun. Similar to an M-16 in firepower, it is much easier to use in close quarters where accuracy is less important.

Steyr Aug

The standard weapon of the Austrian Army, the Steyr Aug is a futuristic-looking assault rifle with a compact bullpup design. It is well suited for missions requiring the maneuverability of a submachine gun combined with the punch of an assault rifle.

Notes

This weapon also bridges the gap between submachine guns and rifles. A bit more accurate than the L85A1, the Steyr is a good choice for indoor missions as well as outdoor ones.

M16-A2

When extra range or firepower is needed, RAINBOW turns to Colt's M16A2. Tried and true, its 5.56 caliber easily pierces Level II body armor, and it has the longest range of any of RAINBOW's standard weapons. It comes standard with a single and three round trigger group.

Notes

The M-16A2 is RAINBOW's heavy firepower. It's the standard infantry weapon of the U.S. military, but it's quite large by RAINBOW standards. This weapon is best for support-fire teams and is best used outside, where range is a factor. It's difficult to use in room-to-room combat because of its size.

M-14

The direct descendant of the classic M1 Garand, the M-14 fires a 7.62 round with extreme accuracy. It has been used by the U.S. Army since 1957.

Notes

The M-14 fills the gap between assault rifle and sniper rifle in both accuracy and firepower. This is definitely an outdoor weapon. It fires a larger round than any of the assault rifles at a longer range. However, its rate of fire is less.

Barrett Model 82A1

The Barrett "Light Fifty" M82A1 was the first .50 caliber sniper rifle to achieve widespread use. Its massive length (1.55 m) and weight (13.4 kg) make it the most accurate sniper rifle in RAINBOW's arsenal. Extreme care should be used in employing this weapon, as its high-powered .50 Browning round can tear through multiple targets just as easily as it can through an engine block.

Notes

This sniper rifle is definitely an outdoor weapon. Its very long barrel makes it hard to use indoors. Because it has a range of over a mile, you can position your snipers away from terrorists' fire.

PSG-1

Arguably the most accurate off-the-shelf sniper rifle available and a favorite of police forces around the world, the PSG-1 comes standard with a 6x sight and fires the NATO 7.62 round.

Notes

This will be your standard sniper rifle for most missions. It fits between the other two sniper rifles in terms of range and maneuverability.

Walther WA2000

The shortest sniper rifle used by the RAINBOW team, the Walther WA2000's bullpup design and light weight make it a favorite of snipers needing to move stealthily into difficult positions. Its powerful .300 Winchester round has more punch than the more common 7.62 NATO round.

Notes

This sniper rifle is a good choice for indoor missions. Its length and weight allow it to be carried in close quarters though it should still be used for long-range shooting.

Benelli M1

Whether used for door breaching or highly lethal close-quarters combat, a good tactical shotgun is an essential part of all antiterrorist teams. RAINBOW uses the Benelli M1 Tactical 12-Gauge, largely because its superb recoil characteristics enable a skilled operator to fire five rounds accurately in less than one second.

> **Tip** *When reloading a shotgun, you reload a single shell at a time. In the weapons display, the bottom number lists the number of shells the operative is carrying rather than the number of magazines. Whenever you get a chance, be sure to top off a shotgun so it will have a full load when you need it.*

Notes

The shotgun is best suited to breaching doors. It's useful against terrorists, as well, but if they have any body armor at all, a single blast rarely will take them down. Breaching teams should include at least one shotgun-armed member. Don't assign it to a team leader because he or she usually will be the first through a door and will need a high rate of fire with deadlier ammunition.

SPAS-12

The SPAS-12 is a fully automatic combat shotgun capable of emptying its clip in 1.75 seconds. This makes it ideal for quickly clearing a room of all hostiles.

Notes

This is an excellent weapon for close-quarters combat against terrorists who aren't wearing any body armor. If stealth and range are not a factor in a mission, give this shotgun a try. You'll be impressed.

Secondary Weapons

Your team members will use their pistols rarely, usually if a primary weapon jams or runs out of ammo. Pistols are inaccurate at medium or long range. If you must use one, fire several times at your target: they allow only for single shots and it may take more than one to drop a terrorist, especially one in body armor.

Beretta 92FS 9mm

The Beretta Model 92FS is RAINBOW's 9mm pistol of choice. Its primary advantage is low recoil and a large magazine compared to the bulkier .45.

Notes

The Beretta fires a smaller caliber round than the Mark 23, so its magazine can hold more ammunition. If you're going to use a pistol a lot during a mission, then this is a good choice. This is the standard sidearm of the U.S. military.

Beretta 92FS 9mm-SD

The specially designed sound and flash suppresser on this Beretta Model 92FS minimizes weight and length to maintain accuracy while boasting an impressive 32dB of sound reduction. It is the favorite pistol of RAINBOW's recon specialists.

Notes

This is a great pistol for recon teams or any team that needs a silenced sidearm to supplement a nonsilenced submachine gun or assault rifle. Some missions may demand stealth at first and tremendous firepower later on. Use this pistol for the early kills.

HK .40 USP

Heckler & Koch's .40 caliber USP is a favorite among those desiring a balance between size and firepower.

Notes

This pistol is similar to the MK23, but it fires small-caliber ammunition, and so it's a little lighter. It's usually a better idea to take an MK23 because of its greater punch.

HK .40 USP-SD

This Knight Armament Corp. silencer provides excellent sound suppression to the HK .40 USP.

Notes

Again, if you need a silenced pistol, the MK23-SD is a better choice.

HK .45 Mark 23

The extreme ruggedness, reliability, and match-grade accuracy of Heckler & Koch's .45 Caliber Mark 23 ACP have made it the handgun of choice for all U.S. Special Forces.

Notes

The Mark 23 is one of the best pistols available to RAINBOW operatives. The weapon is accurate and the .45 round has the necessary stopping power.

HK .45 Mark 23-SD

The specially designed sound and flash suppresser on this HK MK23 virtually eliminates muzzle flash and provides more than 35dB of sound reduction. It's an essential part of any RAINBOW mission requiring both firepower and discretion.

Notes

The Mark 23-SD is nearly as accurate as the standard MK23, and its silencer allows your team to kill without alerting others to your presence.

.50 Desert Eagle

The IMI .50 Desert Eagle is a very powerful handgun. It's capable of punching through body armor, but it has a limited seven-round magazine.

Notes

Although the Desert Eagle has only a seven-round magazine, given the limited use a secondary firearm gets, this shouldn't be a problem. Besides, with a .50-caliber round, it takes only a single shot to drop your target, even if you don't hit the tango in the head. Unless you must stay quiet, take one of these pistols along. If you must resort to your secondary weapon, this is one you can count on.

.357 Desert Eagle

The smaller cousin of the Desert Eagle .50, the IMI Desert Eagle's .357 Magnum round packs a punch capable of piercing body armor at close range. It carries a limited eight-round magazine.

Notes

This pistol is a bit smaller and easier to handle than the Desert Eagle .50. It also carries an additional round in the magazine.

Ammunition

Rogue Spear allows you to select the type of ammunition your operatives will use in their firearms during a mission. All firearms, except shotguns, can fire either full metal jacket or jacketed hollow point rounds. Shotguns can fire buckshot, slugs, or rubber batons. Let's take a look at each of these types of ammunition.

Full Metal Jacket (FMJ)

This is the common military round. The soft lead projectile is covered or "jacketed" by a harder metal. This prevents the round from breaking up when it hits something, allowing the full impact to strike at a small point. As a result, the penetrative power is increased.

Full metal jacket ammunition has a longer range than jacketed hollow point and is better for use against body armor. It is the default selection for all weapons.

Jacketed Hollow Point (JHP)

This round is often used by law enforcement. Similar to the full metal jacket round, the jacketed hollow point surrounds a lead center with a harder metal jacket. However, instead of the round coming to a pointed tip, it instead drilled out to form a cone-shaped opening. When this round strikes a target, it flattens—creating a larger surface and causing a lot more damage. As the round flattens, it also decreases its ability to penetrate body armor since the force is spread across a larger area.

Because of the shape and ballistics of the round, jacketed hollow point have a short range. So do not use them for long-range firing. However, they're very effective for short- to medium-range firing and best used against terrorists not wearing body armor.

.00 Buckshot

This is the standard load for RAINBOW's shotguns. The shell contains a number of small round projectiles that separate and spread out after leaving the barrel. While not effective for penetrating body armor or for medium- and long-range fire, buckshot is great for unarmored targets in close-quarters combat. The spread increases the chance of hitting the target. Buckshot is also effective for shooting out a lock and breaching doors.

Slugs

Rather than being filled with buckshot, a shotgun shell can contain a single, large projectile. Though it does not have the penetrative power of a standard bullet, a slug has a lot of mass and will knock down whatever it hits. Slugs are not effective against body armor, but will still knock the target off his/her feet. While buckshot is often a better choice, slugs are great when you must avoid hitting nearby hostages with the spread of buckshot.

Rubber Batons

This round allows a shotgun to be used with nonlethal force. The shell contains a rubber slug-like projectile. As such, it will not kill—or even penetrate the skin of—the target. However, its force will knock the target down—useful for capturing a target alive. Other than that, there are very few reasons to use this type of ammunition.

Equipment

Demolitions Kit

This kit speeds both the placing and disarming of explosives. It contains basic electrical diagnostic equipment along with the essential mechanical tools needed to perform the job. Extra primer, detcord, and a variety of adhesives complete the kit.

Notes
Take this along only if explosives will be placed or disarmed. Assign it to a demolitions specialist.

Electronics Kit

This kit speeds up placing bugs, rewiring security cameras, and related electrical tasks. It contains a high precision multimeter, miniature power supplies, a breadboard, and digital analyzer. A full complement of jumpers, clips, and miscellaneous electrical parts rounds out the kit.

Notes
This kit is vital for getting through security systems. Assign it to electronics specialists.

Lockpick Kit

This kit speeds the picking of locks. Its primary component is a highly sophisticated auto-pick capable of opening most mechanical locks in a few seconds. Electrical keycard or swipe locks are handled using a classified system containing presets for all major keycard variations.

Notes

Your team will need lockpick kits to get through some doors quickly, especially without making a lot of noise, as a shotgun breach or breaching charge would.

Fragmentation Grenade

The M61 fragmentation grenade is the standard issue offensive grenade used by infantry throughout the world. While its blast radius is small, an overhand throw is still necessary to safely clear the blast radius in the open.

Notes

These can clear a small room with a single blast. Take care when you use them during hostage rescues, unless you're certain the targeted room contains no hostages.

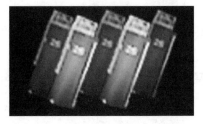

Flashbang

Capable of stunning observers with a combination of bright flash and loud report, flashbangs are commonly tossed into rooms to "prepare" rooms prior to entry. The valuable seconds gained while potential hostiles recover from the stun effects can mean the difference between life and death to a tactical team. They're also known as distraction devices or stun grenades.

Notes

At least one member of each team should carry flashbangs. In fact, it's preferable for all to carry some, because clearing a large building may require a number of these devices. As a rule, use a flashbang if there's a chance an enemy occupies any room you're about to enter.

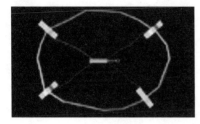

Breaching Charge

Breaching charges are used to explosively remove doors for rapid entry. Flashbangs do not need to be used in conjunction with breaching charges as they stun, wound, or even kill anyone nearby.

Notes

These are great for entering a room quickly. Use them when breaching a door to a room containing both hostages and terrorists. Often terrorists will try to kill hostages as soon as a door is opened. The breaching charge will stun them, giving your team valuable seconds to enter and take down the hostiles.

Heartbeat Sensor

The heartbeat sensor is capable of tracking a human heartbeat even through thick layers of concrete. It works by detecting the characteristic ultra-low-frequency electric field given off by a beating heart. When in use, the heartbeat sensor scans in a small circle around the user as well as a larger cone straight ahead.

Notes

The heartbeat sensor is very valuable. If the character you control carries one, select it as his or her active item. Then, when you hold down the left mouse button, the sensor will scan at a longer range down a narrow arc, instead of the standard short range in all directions. Terrorists show up on the minimap as red dots and hostages as white dots. Use this sensor to see if a room is occupied before you enter it and help determine the type of force or restraint to use.

Binoculars

These compact, lightweight binoculars are specially constructed to withstand the rigors of CT operations. A built in range finder and choice of 4x and 8x zoom factors make these the item of choice for RAINBOW recon missions.

Notes

Binoculars are great for recon teams. They allow you to scout out an area at long range and observe the enemy while your men are out of their sight. While not needed for indoor missions, they are a must for most outdoor missions.

Primary Mags

These are extra magazines for your primary weapon.

Secondary Mags

These are extra magazines for your secondary weapon.

Uniforms

RAINBOW operatives have access to a number of different uniform patterns, each designed for a certain environment (for example, urban, desert, woods). The patterns help make the team as inconspicuous as possible so they can take down the enemy before they're seen.

Each pattern is available in three weights. Light uniforms are basically for recon or other teams uninvolved in firefights. They're quieter and allow the wearer to move about stealthily. Heavy uniforms (a.k.a. "breaching" uniforms) incorporate the most body armor. However, they're bulky and make some noise, limiting wearer mobility and stealth. Breaching and demolitions teams should wear these. The medium-weight uniform is the standard. It's appropriate for assault and other teams that need a balance between protection and ease of movement. As the commander, you must outfit your team members appropriately for the tasks they must perform.

Weights

Light

This class is perfect for night-time missions and recon specialists. It consists of a lightweight Level IIa tactical vest capable of stopping low-powered pistol rounds and is rounded out with the standard soft-soled rubber boots, Nomex balaclava, and Nomex/Kevlar gloves.

Medium

This class consists of a Level II waist-length tactical vest and a Kevlar helmet, soft-soled rubber boots, Nomex balaclava, and Nomex/Kevlar gloves. The vest is capable of stopping most pistol fire and some submachine gun fire as well.

Heavy

This class consists of Level III body armor extending to the groin and is capable of stopping all but the most high-powered rifle rounds. This is the preferred uniform of demolitions experts, as the faceplate on the Kevlar helmet offers excellent protection from flying debris. The desert, camo, and woods heavy uniforms do not include the helmet with faceplate and the body armor extends only to the waist since these uniforms are mainly used on outdoor missions.

Patterns

RAINBOW uses seven different uniform patterns. Each is specially designed for a specific environment or lighting condition.

Arctic 1

This all-white uniform is great for missions in the snow.

Arctic 2

An alternative arctic uniform, this one has dark splotches on white and is best used when operating in snow and brush where an all-white uniform would stand out.

Desert 1

This desert camo uniform is used for desert operations and is issued to RAINBOW operatives for desert type operations.

Desert 2

This darker desert camo uniform is good for low-light operations and is issued to RAINBOW operatives for this purpose.

Black

This black uniform is perfect for nighttime missions.

Blue

This blue uniform is good for nighttime missions as an option to black.

Euro

An excellent uniform choice for those operating in mixed forest environments, it uses a European woods camouflage pattern.

Green

This uniform is used primarily in general outdoor environments.

Gray

This gray uniform is the standard for urban operations.

Street 1

This grayish street camo uniform is one of RAINBOW's choices for urban assault operations.

Street 2

This pattern is similar to Street 1, but with more earth tones and less gray. Useful when operating is less developed towns with dirt and vegetation.

Wood

This uniform is used for operations in forests and rural areas, usually in European and North American operations. The woodland uniforms are a personal favorite of Santiago Arnavisca.

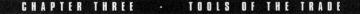

It's time to practice the operations skills you need to complete your real-world missions. The following tactics include breaching doors, room entry and clearing, hostage rescues, and other actions that later missions may call for, such as defusing bombs and planting surveillance devices.

Breaching and Clearing

Most missions require your teams to enter buildings to rescue hostages, defuse bombs, or neutralize terrorists ("tangos"). Entering a room is one of the most dangerous things you'll do during a mission. You may not know what lies on the other side of the door, but those inside the room behind it will be waiting with weapons ready.

Behind the closed door lies uncertainty. Breaching a door and entering a room is one of the most dangerous actions you'll perform.

Unless you're absolutely sure a room is clear, always enter with caution. The heartbeat sensor is a great device for determining whether a room is occupied; it can even distinguish between hostages and tangos in both the recruit and veteran difficulty levels. If your team isn't carrying one, always assume a room contains tangos. During hostage rescues, assume a hostage is inside, as well.

Tip *Before entering a room, use a heartbeat sensor to see what lies on the other side of the door.*

Your team is at a disadvantage as it enters a room. You need an edge: as soon as you breach a door, throw in a flashbang to stun the occupants. (Take care not to stun yourself in the process.) The stun grenade gives you a few precious seconds to enter the room and take down enemies before they can react. A breaching charge also works, blowing the door off and stunning the room's occupants at the same time. You can carry three flashbangs in place of one breaching charge, but save the flashbangs for rooms with hostages.

Tip *Take care when using fragmentation grenades—they can kill hostages as well as your own people. As a rule, avoid using them during hostage missions.*

You also can throw fragmentation grenades to "prepare" a room for entry. Be very careful, however, because they can kill team members and hostages as well as tangos. Avoid using them in hostage missions unless reconnaissance or a heartbeat sensor tells you a room is hostage-free.

Throw a flashbang into the room to stun the tango before entering.

After you enter a room, you must clear it of enemies. If your team receives a "clear" order, it will spread out and do so automatically. Be wary of the room's other doors; more tangos may enter through them to investigate the gunshots.

The Kill Houses give you an opportunity to practice breaching and clearing.

A tango is out in the open. Shoot quickly before he turns and fires at you!

Double-Room Kill House

The Double-Room Kill House contains two rooms containing tangos. There are three exercises for this Kill House. The first uses you alone, the second gives you command of a team of four operatives, and the third uses two teams of four operatives each (you control Blue Team).

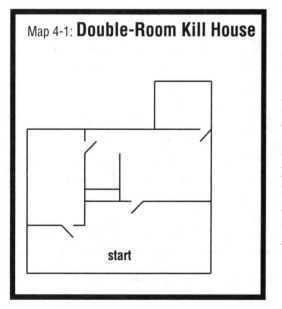

Map 4-1: **Double-Room Kill House**

start

In the first exercise, it's easier to enter the left door first. The tango is usually in the corner to the left of the door; you can drop him before he has a chance to react by sidestepping through the door so your weapon is pointed at him as soon as he comes into sight. Advance into the room and approach the other doorway carefully. The second tango is in the other room. If you can't see him through the doorway, he may be behind the wall to your right. Throw in either a frag grenade to kill him or a flashbang to stun him so you can rush in and use your submachine gun. Watch the closet at the other end of the room. As soon as a grenade goes off, a third tango will run out to investigate. Be ready to drop him.

There's no tango in sight as you open the door. That means he waits in ambush to the left or right.

The second exercise uses the same strategy as the first. Try going through the door on the right this time. Also, try giving orders to your team during the exercise. Stand in front of one of the doors and press [U] to bring up the Orders menu and then select either Frag Room or Flashbang Room. One of the operatives on your team will then move forward, open the door, and toss a grenade inside. Be sure to cover the operative while this order is carried out. There are four tangos in this exercise.

Order one of your operatives to throw a grenade into the room ahead of you.

The final exercise puts you in command of Blue Team. Red Team awaits Go code Alpha. Press [J] to get them moving. They enter the right door while your team goes through the left. Take care not to shoot the other team once you're in the first room. There are six tangos in this exercise.

You command two teams for the third exercise. Give Go code Alpha to order Red Team through the right door while Blue Team goes through the left.

Rescuing Hostages

Missions where you must rescue hostages require extra caution. Often hostages are held in rooms guarded by at least one tango. Although the recon information you get prior to a mission may give locations for the hostages, they may have been moved. The heartbeat sensor is the best way to identify a room's occupants before you rush in.

Hostages will stay put unless your Rule of Engagement mode is set to Escort. Then they'll follow you around like puppies—hopefully to safety.

Don't use frag grenades when entering a room that contains hostages. You'll kill the hostages as well as the tangos. Instead, either throw in a flashbang to stun everyone or, better, use a breaching charge. The charge blows the door open and stuns the room's occupants at the same time.

Tip

Whenever you open a door to a room containing a hostage and a tango, the tango usually moves to kill the hostage, so you must act quickly. You can't just stand in the doorway looking around, or you'll be too late.

After breaching a door, exercise caution as you enter. Avoid firing your weapons at full-automatic; the spread could hit a hostage. Instead, use the three-round burst (or the single shot if the three-round isn't a choice). Things move fast in *Rogue Spear*, and it's easy to develop an itchy trigger finger. Learn to use caution and to pick your targets with care.

Office Kill House

This is a very difficult Kill House to clear. You begin in the outside hall. Two doors provide entry to the office area, which contains six small rooms. What makes this particularly deadly is the way all the offices are lined up across from each other with open doorways. As you enter one office, a tango across the hall can shoot you in the back.

The first of the three exercises gives you a single team of four operatives; the second, two teams of two operatives; the third, one team of two and two teams of three. Two tangos wait in interior hallways and the other two in offices.

For the first exercise, enter the right-hand door. There should be a tango right in front of you or just around the corner. Take him down, and then look around the corner. Shoot the second tango at the far end of the long hall. If he's not there, go back into the outside hall: he's sneaking up behind you. Look through each of the rooms to locate the hostage and the exercise is complete.

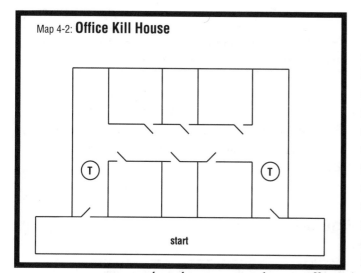

Map 4-2: **Office Kill House**

start

For the second exercise, enter the right door while the other team enters the left door. There are six tangos in this exercise. You command Blue Team, on the right. Red Team on the left, enters the door and then waits for Go code Alpha. Press J to give them the go, and they advance into the offices to search for the hostages. You must lead Blue Team through the right door and do the same. You will probably take out the first as you enter the office. Start at one end and check the two rooms, throwing in a flashbang before entering each. If you hear a groan when the stun grenade goes off, you know there's someone inside. After clearing both rooms at one end, do the same at the other end. You should have found some more terrorists and a hostage. Leave the hostage until all terrorists have been eliminated.

TIP *Use flashbangs to determine where tangos are hiding. If you hear a groan when the flashbang goes off, someone's in that room. Either rush in immediately or throw another flashbang in first.*

The third exercise puts you in control of Blue Team, with two operatives, near the right door. Red Team, with three, is next to you, and Green Team is at the left door. Red and Green teams enter their respective doors, taking out the tangos in the hall. They then wait for Go codes before searching the offices for the hostage. Blue Team's job is to escort the hostages to safety.

The facing, open doorways create a death trap unless you're smart and use caution. Remember to use flashbangs to stun waiting tangos before entering the rooms.

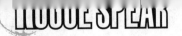

The third exercise has three teams. Red and Green clear the rooms, while Blue waits to escort the hostages to safety.

Your other teams probably will take casualties. If you watch them, you can see why. They don't use their flashbangs before entering the rooms, so any tangos present can fire before the operatives even know they're there.

Two-Story Kill House

Right as you open the door, a tango is waiting to die.

If you can get through this "graduation" Kill House without losses, you're ready to go operational. The Kill House is a two-story building with an accessible roof. There are several tangos inside and one hostage on the second floor.

In the first exercise, you have a single team of four. The second gives you two teams of four. The third exercise has three teams with a total of eight operatives.

In the first exercise, there are only three tangos. One usually patrols downstairs with the other two upstairs. Go up the stairs to the left. As you sidestep up the stairs, keep your weapon aimed down the hallway and take out any tangos you see on your way up. Once upstairs, throw flashbangs into the rooms to stun the tangos before you enter. Be careful to not kill the hostage in the process.

The second exercise sends your team up the left stairs while the other goes up the right stairs. Be careful to not shoot the other team when you get to the second floor hallway. There are five tangos in this exercise.

The final exercise in this Kill House uses three teams to converge on the hostage's position from different directions. There are seven tangos opposing you in this exercise.

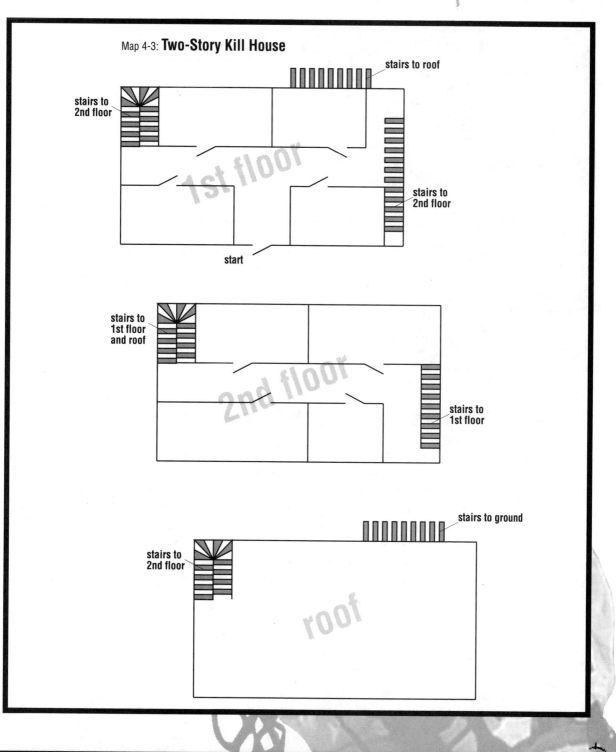

Map 4-3: **Two-Story Kill House**

stairs to roof

stairs to
2nd floor

1st floor

stairs to
2nd floor

start

stairs to
1st floor
and roof

2nd floor

stairs to
1st floor

stairs to ground

stairs to
2nd floor

roof

Sidestep up the stairs to surprise the tango at the top.

Act quickly to take out the tangos upstairs. Try sidestepping and then shooting as they just come into view. This tango is half-hidden by the door frame, but can still be taken down.

Other Types of Actions

Your missions may require special actions, anything from disarming a bomb or deactivating a security system to downloading computer files or tapping a phone. These may sound difficult, but all you need to do is walk to the object and press [SPACEBAR].

If you want the action performed by a team that's not under your control or by a specialist on your team who's not the leader, place a waypoint next to the object in the planning phase and assign an action to the waypoint. Then, when you approach it, the specialist will walk to the object and do what needs to be done. Or you can use the Orders menu by pressing [U] during the mission. Select the order you want the operative to carry out.

Open Training

You can come back and go through all the Kill Houses again in Open Training. However, in these exercises, you can choose your operatives, assign them weapons and equipment and then plan the mini-mission. Before beginning a campaign of operational missions, try planning out mini-missions in Open Training. This will give you practice planning and using different types of equipment such as heartbeat sensors.

The adage "If you fail to plan, you plan to fail" applies to this game more than to any other. The planning stage is the most important, and that's where you'll spend the most time during operations. Most missions take only a few minutes to execute but can take an hour or more to plan and fine tune. The planning stage is broken down into seven screens. Each contains important information or requires you to do something to prepare for the mission.

Briefing

This is the first screen in the planning stage, where you receive valuable information regarding your current mission. Your objective—what you must accomplish to complete the mission—lies in the center of the screen. In Recruit campaigns, you need achieve only the primary objective. The Veteran level requires a secondary objective and the Elite, a third. The higher the level of gameplay, the more terrorists you'll face and the harder they'll be to kill.

The Briefing Screen

On the left side of the screen are quick briefings by Control and other useful information. Your mission orders display below the briefings. Study them carefully to learn what you must do and what you're up against.

Intel

The Intel Screen

Although the Intel screen isn't vital for achieving your particular mission, it provides background and story line for the campaign. It displays your past mission success and shows how it affects the campaign. The four categories of information this screen displays are people, organizations, newswire, and miscellaneous.

Roster Selection

The Roster Selection screen

You choose operatives for the current mission from the Roster Selection screen. It displays background information on each member of RAINBOW, including his or her abilities and health status. When you select your operatives, you needn't pick them in order or by team. You can organize them later.

Kit

The Kit screen

You arm your team from the Kit screen. For each operative, you can select a primary and secondary weapon, additional items to carry (these fit into slots one and two), and a uniform. Although you can assign everyone the same things, you'll probably need to customize individual kits for specific jobs.

Team Assignment

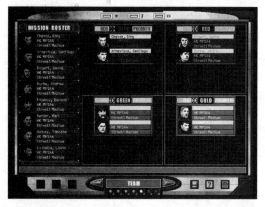

The Team Assignment screen

You'll organize your operatives into teams from this screen. You can take only eight people with you, divided into a maximum of four teams. Teams can comprise no more than four operatives each. You can create two teams of four or four teams of two or anything in between.

Plan

The Plan screen

You'll spend the most time at the Plan screen. It provides a recon report of probable locations of hostages, terrorists, and landmarks. You plot waypoints for each of your teams here and give them special orders or commands. Once the action starts, you control only your team. At each waypoint you can change Rules of Engagement regarding speed and mode—how fast the team moves to the next waypoint and how they respond to others on the way. You can give breaching instructions at waypoints, as well.

You can acquire some control over other teams by using the four Go codes. When a team reaches a waypoint with a Go code, it will wait for you to issue that code before advancing. This way you can synchronize your teams' activities. For example, if all teams get the same Go code near a building's entry point, they'll wait for the code to enter at the same time. The section "Planning a Mission" covers the Plan screen in greater detail.

Execute

The Execute screen

From the Execute screen you choose a team to control, and then start the mission.

Planning a Mission

Mission planning can be difficult and time consuming.
If you fail a mission or are unhappy with the results, you may return to the planning stage and try it again. Rarely will you execute a perfect mission your first time through. However, the better your plan, the better the execution.

Take the following steps when you plan a mission, though not necessarily in this order.

Briefing

First, read through all the briefings to learn what the situation is and determine the nature of your job. You'll find the latter in the mission orders and objective. Listen to Control and to John Clark. They may offer some insights. Next, go to the Intel screen to get background information on the mission.

Recon

At the next screen, pick a team member at random. (You must select one to advance to the next screen.) Continue past the Kit screen, assign the operative to a team, then move on to the Plan screen. It doesn't matter which team you place your operatives in. You'll reassign them later.

At the Plan screen, go to the box in the lower left and select Recon to learn the actual or probable locations of hostages and terrorists in the mission area. The Landmarks category will provide important information about terrain and structures—whether a trellis is climbable or an entrance barricaded, for example. Learn as much as you can about what you face. Then decide how many teams you'll need to accomplish the mission and what their tasks will be.

Set Waypoints

Change the Recon box to Orders, select a team, and begin plotting waypoints. The first must be within an insertion zone and the last within an extraction zone. Determine the team's entry into a building, their route to that spot, how they'll reach their objective, and, finally, how they'll get out. To better understand the space that you'll be operating in use the 3D Map feature.

Tip *Each of the four Go codes has a corresponding key: Alpha* [J]*, Bravo* [K]*, Charlie* [L]*, and Delta* [M]*. You may use each Go code more than once. For example, you may want to assign all Alpha codes to Blue Team, Beta codes to Green, and so forth.*

Go Codes

Use Go codes to coordinate team activity. For example, it's usually a good idea to have all teams enter a building at the same time. But in some cases, one team may have to complete a task before another team can continue.

Orders

In addition to Go codes, you can give teams orders at each waypoint. For example, you can order them to use a flashbang or frag grenade, or even a breaching charge. They require a waypoint near a doorway. Such orders are important, because computer-controlled teams won't do these things unless they're instructed to. Set these for your own team, as well. If you want a demolitions specialist on your team to breach a door a certain way, order it at that waypoint. if you don't, you'll have to either do it yourself using the equipment you're carrying or issue an order to the team during the mission. You can also order teams to disarm bombs, deactivate security systems, and other mission-related tasks.

Cover and Defend

When you assign a Go code to a waypoint, you can also give an order to the team instructing them how to act at that point. "Defend" orders the team to set up a 360 degree defensive perimeter around the point. This is good if your team is stopped in an open area. "Cover" limits the defensive arc to 180 degrees in the direction you choose. This is better than Defend because each team member covers a narrow arc. Use this when you team can back up against a wall or when they don't have to worry about being attacked from a certain direction.

Snipe

"Snipe" is the final order you can assign at a Go code. While it is usually given to a team containing a sniper, it can be given to any team. The sniper, or the team member with the best sniping skill, will aim at the point you designate on the planning map with Sniper view activated. This is a narrow arc, so do not expect a sniper to cover a large area. Meanwhile, the other team members will assume a posture similar to Defend, providing protection for the sniper.

Rules of Engagement

Rules of Engagement tell your teams how to behave as they advance to the next waypoint. There are two types of ROE—speed and mode.

Speed tells the team how fast to move and how careful to be when targeting and firing weapons. "Blitz" instructs the team to move as quickly as possible and to fire at just about anything that moves. Use Blitz only when there are no friendlies in the area. "Normal" speed is a basic walk; the team exercises a bit more caution before firing. Teams assigned "Safety" speed will move slowly, pausing every so often, and take deliberate aim at well-identified targets before firing, perhaps even risking their own safety. When approaching areas where hostages are located, change the speed to Safety.

Mode tells a team how to act and react. Teams with the "Assault" order move along their path while attacking targets of opportunity. In areas such as small rooms, they attempt to clear the area before advancing to the next area. "Recon" orders the team to move stealthily and only return fire. They use silenced weapons if available. Heartbeat sensors are used only by teams with Recon orders. "Infiltrate" orders a team to move as quickly and quietly as possible. If they come across enemies, they'll fire, preferring silenced weapons if available. Their main task is to get to a point rather than clearing areas of terrorists. "Escort" mode tells the hostage to follow the team (if approached in any other mode, hostages will stay put). Hostages will not follow your operatives unless you set their ROE mode to ESCORT. When escorting a hostage, the team should follow a secure route cleared of tangos to the end point.

After planning waypoints for all teams, consider making a few short notes on what each Go code does for quick reference later.

Building Teams

You know how many teams you'll have and the tasks for each. Now it's time to choose operatives from the Roster Selection screen.

Delete the members you chose earlier and start from scratch. First, choose an operative with good leadership ability for each team. Teams that must breach their way in need a demolitions specialist. Next, assign specialists, such as electronics, if the mission calls for them. Finally, fill in the teams with assault specialists. Place those with poor self-control values with stronger leaders. With the operatives and their assignments fresh in your mind, go to the Team Assignment screen and place them into teams, with the leader at the top of each list.

Pass the Ammo

Distribute firearms and equipment to your assembled teams. RAINBOW is well funded, so you have as many of each weapon or item as you need. Equip your teams appropriately for their tasks. For example, if they must breach a door with a charge, at least one member of the team must carry a breaching charge. The same goes for flash-bangs and frag grenades.

Finally, suit your operatives in appropriate uniforms. Choose inconspicuous patterns and weights appropriate for the task. Breachers should wear heavy uniforms; recon teams will don light ones to stay quiet. Most team members should wear medium-weight uniforms that provide a balance of protection and mobility.

Start the Mission

Your teams are ready, so go to the Execute screen next. You've invested a lot of time into planning this mission, so it's a good idea to save it here. If you must start over, you can make small adjustments to your plan instead of going back to the beginning. Finally, select the team you'll lead, and then begin the mission.

Good luck!

Mission Failure?

If you fail a mission or get a lot of your people killed in a successful mission, go back to planning and try again. Study who got killed and where to determine the planning changes you need to make. For example, if a team was massacred entering a room, order them to throw a frag grenade before going through the doorway. You may also need to change a team's ROE for a certain waypoint. Think of each failure as a learning experience.

Tip *After every mission—successful or not— take time to watch the replay. See how the operatives followed the orders you gave them. Study what worked well and what needed improving. No mission will ever go perfectly. Try to learn as much as possible so future missions will go more smoothly.*

Tip *Consider replaying the mission if even one team member dies, especially in the early missions. Losing one member per mission will leave you short of trained, experienced professionals for the last few.*

The *Rogue Spear* campaign comprises 18 missions. You must complete each to advance to the next. This chapter provides all the information you'll need to get through the missions.

The strategies are for the Veteran (medium) difficulty level, requiring you to complete both the primary and secondary objectives before advancing to the next mission. The Recruit level has fewer terrorists with slower reaction times, while Elite has more terrorists with quicker reaction times.

The mission strategies include orders and objectives, who to take, what they should carry, how to organize them, and, finally, how your teams can go about accomplishing the mission, with instructions for each. Use these instructions during the planning phase to set waypoints and issue special instructions and Go codes.

These strategies aren't set in stone. You may find something to add or change to fit the plans to your playing style. Experiment. The best plan is the one that succeeds.

Mission 1—Operation: Pandora Trigger

08.04.01   **0130**
New York

Mission Orders

A group of Egyptian extremists has stormed the Museum of Art in New York City during the opening festivities of a new exhibition of Egyptian antiquities. Your mission is to retake the building with minimal loss of life.

NYPD has established a secure perimeter and set up heartbeat surveillance so you'll be able to track the positions of the hostiles once you're inside. There are two ways in— the main door and a secondary entrance in the rear. According to the blueprints there are a lot of balconies in the main exhibit halls, so watch out for snipers.

Objectives

1. Rescue the Hostages

The Metropolitan Art Museum is hosting an Egyptian exhibit. However, there is more than a mummy's curse to worry about inside.

Mission Data

DIFFICULTY LEVEL	TERRORISTS	HOSTAGES	OTHER
Recruit	10	2	None
Veteran	15	2	None
Elite	22	2	None

Team Assignments

Blue Team

OPERATIVE	PRIMARY	SECONDARY	SLOT 1	SLOT 2	UNIFORM
Chavez	MP5SD5	.45 Mark 23	Flashbang	Flashbang	Street Medium
Yacoby	MP5SD5	.45 Mark 23	Flashbang	Flashbang	Street Medium

Red Team

OPERATIVE	PRIMARY	SECONDARY	SLOT 1	SLOT 2	UNIFORM
Price	MP5SD5	.45 Mark 23	Flashbang	Flashbang	Street Medium
McAllen	MP5SD5	.45 Mark 23	Breaching Charge	Flashbang	Street Heavy
Arnavisca	MP5SD5	.45 Mark 23	Flashbang	Flashbang	Street Medium

Green Team

OPERATIVE	PRIMARY	SECONDARY	SLOT 1	SLOT 2	UNIFORM
Novikov	MP5SD5	.45 Mark 23	Flashbang	Flashbang	Street Medium
Filatov	MP5SD5	.45 Mark 23	Flashbang	Flashbang	Street Medium
Walther	MP5SD5	.45 Mark 23	Flashbang	Flashbang	Street Medium

Strategy

Lots of tangos are running around in the building. Both hostages are located in room 1-D. However, one of them may run into room 1-E once she sees one of your operatives. The insertion zones are located in the front of the museum as well as at a back door. Most of the large ground floor halls have balconies overlooking them. Watch for snipers. While there are none overlooking room 1-A for this mission at the Veteran level, there are a few at the Elite level.

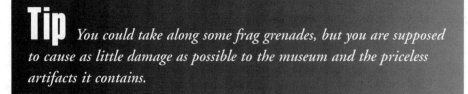

Tip *You could take along some frag grenades, but you are supposed to cause as little damage as possible to the museum and the priceless artifacts it contains.*

The key is to approach room 1-D from two different angles so you can eliminate all tangos at the same time. Be sure to clear the ground floor as well as the balconies above before actually rescuing the hostages. Once you have them secured, escort them quickly out through the front door to safety.

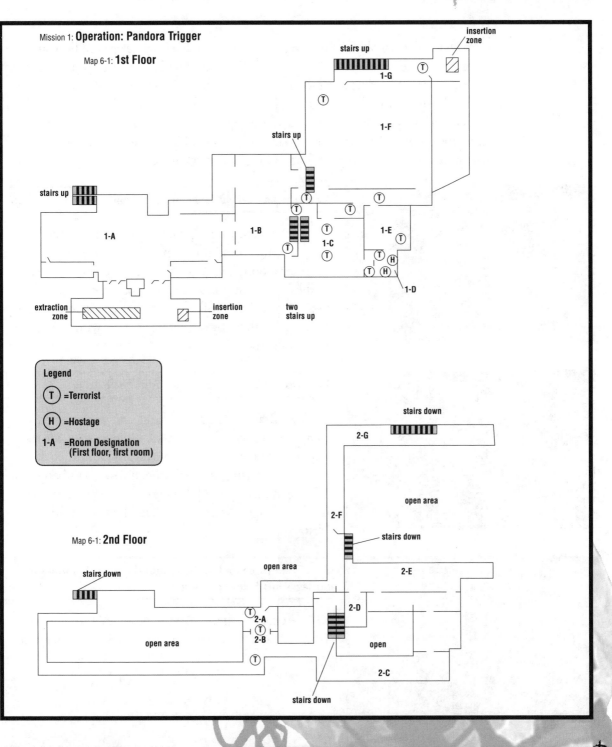

Mission 1: **Operation: Pandora Trigger**

Map 6-1: **1st Floor**

insertion zone

stairs up
1-G

stairs up
1-F

stairs up

stairs up

1-A

1-B

1-C

1-E

1-D

extraction zone

insertion zone

two stairs up

Legend

(T) =Terrorist

(H) =Hostage

1-A =Room Designation (First floor, first room)

Map 6-1: **2nd Floor**

stairs down
2-G

open area

2-F
stairs down

2-E

open area

stairs down

2-A
2-B

2-D

open

open area

2-C

stairs down

Blue Team

You should choose to play as Blue Team. Its job is to help clear the ground floor and then rush in to save the hostages. Once all is clear, Blue Team will escort the hostages to safety.

Blue Team should begin at the insertion zone by the back door. After Red Team breaches the door, rush in and head to the door at the end of the hall. Look at the map to see where the tango in hall 1-F is located. Once you have, open the door and enter 1-F so your weapon is aimed at him, ready to take him down. Hold near the base of the stairs and wait for code Alpha. Cover while waiting and face toward room 1-C

Ease into hall 1-F and take out the tango there as you enter.

After receiving Alpha, take the tango out behind the stairs, then head up them to area 2-D. This balcony overlooks room 1-C. Crouch and waddle up to the edge of the balcony and shoot any tangos below. Be careful because Red Team will be on the balcony across the room. Don't shoot them by mistake. Stay here with Cover orders until code Bravo.

Blue Team overlooks room 1-C from the balcony.

At Bravo, head down the closest stairs and cross room 1-C, moving toward 1-D. Hold just outside the door of 1-D for code Charlie while in Defend position.

After getting code Charlie, throw a flashbang into 1-D, then rush in and kill all tangos, being careful not to hit the hostages. Maintain a Defend posture until code Delta.

Blue Team throws a flashbang into the room holding the hostages just before rushing in.

At code Delta, escort the hostages through rooms 1-C, 1-B, and 1-A, then out the door to the extraction zone.

Red Team

Red Team has a lot of ground to cover. Their job is to clear most of the second floor, then help in the final assault to free the hostages. Finally, they will lead Blue Team and the hostages out to the extraction zone.

Red Team begins at the insertion zone by the back door. Right at the beginning, order McAllen to place a breaching charge on the back door and detonate it. If you are lucky, the tango inside will be walking by the door when it goes off and will be killed. Otherwise, he'll still be stunned. Drop him and head up the stairs. Follow hallway 2-G to the door near 2-F. Continue toward 2-A. Watch out for tangos below. Take out any you see along the way. Before entering room 2-A, throw a flashbang inside. There can be up to three or even four tangos in this area, so the more you stun, the better your chances of dropping them all before they know what hit them. Hold here with Defend orders until code Alpha.

Red Team blows in the back door.

Room 2-A holds several tangos. Try to throw a flashbang inside before entering.

Once you receive code Alpha, advance along the balcony overlooking the main entrance 1-A and clear it. Then advance through 2-B to 2-C and take out any tangos in the room below. Cover here until you get code Bravo.

Red Team takes out a tango trying to sneak up the stairs to get Blue Team on the opposite balcony.

At Bravo, head down the nearest stairs to room 1-C, then through the hallways to just outside of room 1-E. Hold for code Charlie.

Code Charlie is the signal to throw a flashbang into room 1-E, then rush in and take out the tangos inside. Watch out for one of the hostages, who may run into room 1-E. Enter 1-D, then hold for code Delta.

Red Team rushes into room 1-E. Note that one of the hostages has run into this room as Blue Team flashbangs room 1-D.

At Delta, blitz through rooms 1-C, 1-B, and 1-A, and out to the extraction zone, clearing the way for Blue Team and the hostages.

Green Team

Green Team's job is to clear and cover the route out of the museum. They must enter the museum through the front entrance and guard the main hall until the hostages are secure and ready to evacuate.

Start Green team off at the insertion zone at the front of the museum. Move them toward the front doors and hold for code Alpha.

Green Team holds at the front doors.

At code Alpha, enter room 1-A and head to the lower right corner of the room and wait for code Delta. While waiting, maintain a Cover order while facing the center of the room. Red Team will be advancing along the balcony, so be careful not to shoot them while assisting in clearing the area.

While the other teams are preparing to rescue the hostages, Green Team covers the main entrance hall so the escape route will be secure.

At code Delta, move slowly toward the doors (Safety speed), then out to the extraction zone. Make sure no tangos can ambush the other teams as they come out with the hostages.

Notes

For this mission, you should control Blue Team. Green Team is not really necessary for the Veteran level, but it has been included for the practice. At the Elite level, it is a must to help clear room 1-A.

At the beginning of the mission, all teams approach the entrances near their insertion zones. While Green holds, Red and Blue enter the back door and begin clearing a small section of the museum. Code Alpha sends Red Team around the balcony over the entrance while Green Team enters room 1-A below. Blue Team heads up the stairs to the second floor to its position overlooking room 1-C, across from Red Team. There are a lot of tangos moving in and out of 1-C. By having the two teams upstairs and across from each other, every angle is covered. Once a minute has passed with no tangos entering 1-C, give code Bravo, sending both Blue and Red Teams downstairs to positions near the room holding the hostages. Once both are in position, give code Charlie and both will throw flashbangs and rush in to rescue the hostages. Once the hostages are safe, give code Delta and begin the evacuation to the extraction zone.

In most cases, by the time you rescue the hostages, you'll have eliminated all tangos in the museum. In that case, the mission will end as a success without having to evacuate the hostages.

Mission 2—Operation: Arctic Flare

02.07.00   **1700**
London

Mission Orders

Japanese terrorists have seized a PetroMech oil tanker off the coast of Japan and are threatening to destroy it with explosives. Your mission is to board the vessel and neutralize the aggressors before they can trigger the explosive devices.

      The hostages are held in two groups in the stern of the ship. The leader is on the bridge—he'll blow up the ship if he finds out you're on board. You'll be inserted near the bow to minimize the likelihood of detection. No heartbeat surveillance this time, I'm afraid—you'll have to locate the hostiles the old-fashioned way.

Objectives

1. Rescue all hostages
2. Prevent bomb detonation

If this tanker blows up, the resulting oil spill will cause a lot of damage to the Japanese coastline.

Mission Data

DIFFICULTY LEVEL	TERRORISTS	HOSTAGES	OTHER
Recruit	10	4	1 bomb
Veteran	14	4	1 bomb
Elite	17	4	1 bomb

Team Assignments

Blue Team

OPERATIVE	PRIMARY	SECONDARY	SLOT 1	SLOT 2	UNIFORM
Chavez	MP5SD5	.45 Mark 23-SD	Primary Mag	Flashbang	Gray Light
Yacoby	MP5SD5	.45 Mark 23-SD	Heartbeat Sensor	Flashbang	Gray Light
Maldini	MP5SD5	.45 Mark 23-SD	Primary Mag	Flashbang	Gray Light

Red Team

OPERATIVE	PRIMARY	SECONDARY	SLOT 1	SLOT 2	UNIFORM
Bogart	MP5SD5	.45 Mark 23-SD	Primary Mag	Flashbang	Gray Light
Burke	MP5SD5	.45 Mark 23-SD	Heartbeat Sensor	Flashbang	Gray Light
Rakuzanka	MP5SD5	.45 Mark 23-SD	Primary Mag	Flashbang	Gray Light

Green Team

OPERATIVE	PRIMARY	SECONDARY	SLOT 1	SLOT 2	UNIFORM
Hanley	MP5SD5	.45 Mark 23-SD	Primary Mag	Flashbang	Gray Light
Johnston	PSG-1	.45 Mark 23-SD	Primary Mag	Primary Mag	Gray Light

Strategy

This is a very tough mission because it requires extreme stealth and split-second timing. The hostages are located in two groups on two different levels. In addition, the detonator for the bomb is located in a third compartment—on the bridge of the ship. You must simultaneously secure both sets of hostages and at the same time prevent the enemy from detonating the bomb. This requires three separate teams. Blue and Red are tasked with rescuing the hostages while Green, the sniper team, prevents the terrorists from blowing up the ship.

Note *If you can't select a suggested RAINBOW operative due to death or wounds, choose a comparable replacement.*

It is imperative to remain quiet. Light uniforms, as well as silenced weapons, help reduce the noise. If an alarm is sounded, the tangos will begin killing hostages and then blow up the ship. You must also keep the sniper team on hold until the other teams are in position or the sound of the gunshot will alert the guards.

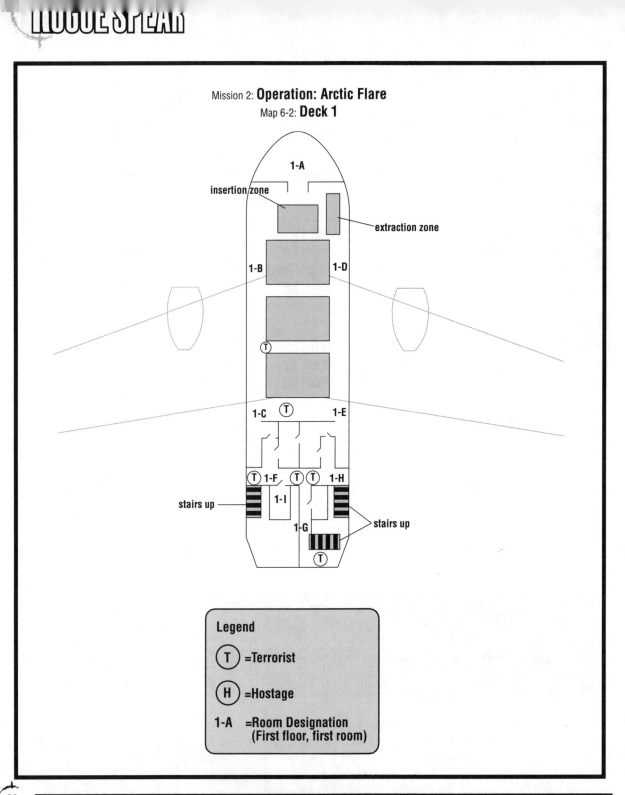

Mission 2: **Operation: Arctic Flare**
Map 6-2: **Deck 1**

1-A

insertion zone

extraction zone

1-B   1-D

1-C   1-E

1-F   1-H

stairs up   1-I

1-G   stairs up

Legend

(T) = Terrorist

(H) = Hostage

1-A = Room Designation
(First floor, first room)

Mission 2: **Operation: Arctic Flare**

Map 6-2: **Deck 2**

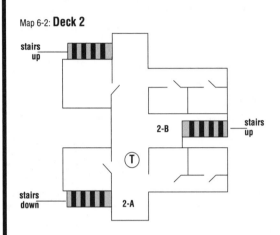

Map 6-2: **Deck 3**

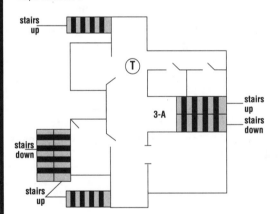

Map 6-2: **Deck 4**

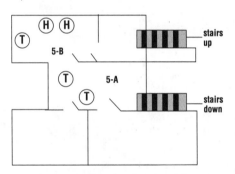

Map 6-2: **Deck 5**

Map 6-2: **Deck 6**

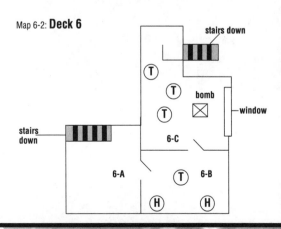

Blue Team

Blue Team is your advance recon team. They will quietly clear out the lower level of the tanker and then move up the superstructure to rescue one set of hostages. All members of this team have some of the highest stealth ratings and great assault skills so they can kill tangos quietly.

From the insertion zone, send Blue Team along the port side of the tanker from point 1-B to 1-C. One tango is patrolling about half way down and a second is near 1-C. Shoot them before they can get off a shot and warn the others. Hold at 1-C for code Alpha. While waiting, switch to Recon mode to bring out the heartbeat sensor and see where the enemy is located.

Blue Team advances up the port side of the tanker, taking out a tango along the way.

At Alpha, carefully enter the door. There are three tangos inside. Two are usually in room 1-I with the third patrolling near 1-F. However, all three could be patrolling. Watch the stairs at either end. A fourth tango will often come down one set of stairs once the shooting starts. When the area is clear, advance out the door to 1-G and drop the tango guarding the outside stairs. Head all the way up the stairs to deck 6 and hold at 6-A for code Charlie.

Blue Team clears out the main deck level. Because they advanced quietly, they'll find two of the tangos still in room 1-I. Drop them as they walk out.

Blue Team heads up the outside stairs. Except for the guard at the base, there are no others along the way to the top.

At Charlie, open the door and kill the guard in 6-B before he can kill the hostages. Then rush in and set up in Cover position facing the door leading into 6-C. Hold for Delta.

Blue Team must kill the tango guarding the hostages before he can execute them. Then rush in and make sure no tangos come from the bridge to do the job themselves.

At Delta, escort the hostages back down to the main deck via the outside stairs, then back to the extraction zone.

Red Team

Red Team's task is to rescue the second group of hostages. They wait for Blue Team to clear out the main deck before heading up stairs on their own.

At the beginning of the mission, head along the starboard side of the tanker from 1-D to 1-E. Hold at 1-E for code Bravo.

While Red Team can usually advance up the starboard side of the tanker without running into any tangos, it's still always a good idea to use caution.

After receiving Bravo, enter the superstructure and then move up the stairs at 1-H. On deck two, use caution. There's usually a tango at 2-A. Drop him quietly and then head up the stairs at 2-B. Keep going up these stairs to deck four, then hold for code Charlie.

RUUUE SPEAR

Red Team holds on deck four.

When Charlie is given, blitz up the stairs to deck five. Kill the two tangos in 5-A, then rush in to 5-B to kill the tango guarding the hostages. Assume a Cover stance facing out the doors of 5-B until you receive code Delta.

Red Team cautiously advances up the stairs to deck five, taking out the enemy tangos as soon as they are visible.

At Delta, escort the hostages back down the way you came up and all the way back to the extraction zone.

Green Team

Green Team is your sniper team. The sniper's job is to watch the area around the bomb detonator and prevent any of the tangos from blowing up the ship.

At the start of the mission, move to point 1-A at the bow of the ship. There, hold for code Delta and assume a Snipe position. Target the area near the detonator on the bridge of the ship on deck six. The sniper team will not fire until the sniper activation code is given as the other teams are rushing in to rescue the hostages.

At code Delta, move to the extraction zone.

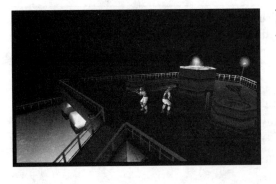

Green Team takes up position at the bow of the tanker.

A tango is in the sniper's sights. As soon as you order sniper to fire at will, no one will get near the detonator and live to press the button.

Notes

As mentioned earlier, split-second timing and stealth are extremely important to this mission. At the beginning of the mission, you should control Blue Team. Once both Blue and Red Teams are holding near the superstructure, give code Alpha and send Blue Team inside to clear deck one. After killing the tango at 1-G guarding the outside stairs, give code Bravo to send Red Team rushing into the superstructure. Both teams will head up to decks four and six respectively to wait for code Charlie. Here is one of the toughest parts of the mission. Take control of Red Team here. Slowly walk backwards up the stairs to deck five so your weapon is trained on the tangos at 5-A. Fire full automatic to take them both out as you give code Charlie and activate the snipers by pressing ⒧ and Ⓨ in quick succession. Continue into 5-B to take out the guard. The sniper team drops any tangos on the bridge that get close to the detonator. After all hostages are secure, wait a few seconds to see if any other tangos rush in to try and kill them, then give code Delta and all teams will head to the extraction zone.

Mission 3—Operation: Sand Hammer

10.04.01   0545
Oman

Mission Orders

Gunmen have seized a seawater treatment plant in Oman and are threatening to release a neural toxin into the local water supply if their demands are not met. Plant workers have also been taken hostage. Your mission is to liberate the plant and halt the release of the toxin.

    The hostages are being held in a different building from the nerve gas—both locations are marked on your map. If the terrorists realize you're in the area they'll release the toxin early, so stealth is essential. Do not attempt to disarm the gas canister yourself—leave that to the mop-up team.

Objectives

1. **Rescue all hostages**
2. **Prevent the release of the toxin**

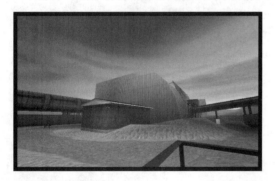

The hostages and the toxin bomb are in separate buildings.

Mission Data

DIFFICULTY LEVEL	TERRORISTS	HOSTAGES	OTHER
Recruit	10	2	1 Toxin Bomb
Veteran	14	2	1 Toxin Bomb
Elite	18	2	1 Toxin Bomb

Team Assignments

Blue Team

OPERATIVE	PRIMARY	SECONDARY	SLOT 1	SLOT 2	UNIFORM
Chavez	UMP 45SD	.45 Mark 23	Frag Grenade	Flashbang	Desert 2 Medium
Raymond	UMP 45SD	.45 Mark 23	Heartbeat Sensor	Flashbang	Desert 2 Medium

Red Team

OPERATIVE	PRIMARY	SECONDARY	SLOT 1	SLOT 2	UNIFORM
Bogart	UMP 45SD	.45 Mark 23	Frag Grenade	Flashbang	Desert 2 Medium
Haider	UMP 45SD	.45 Mark 23	Frag Grenade	Flashbang	Desert 2 Medium

Green Team

OPERATIVE	PRIMARY	SECONDARY	SLOT 1	SLOT 2	UNIFORM
Noronha	UMP 45SD	.45 Mark 23	Frag Grenade	Flashbang	Desert 2 Medium
Hanley	UMP 45SD	.45 Mark 23	Flashbang	Heartbeat Sensor	Desert 2 Medium

Gold Team

OPERATIVE	PRIMARY	SECONDARY	SLOT 1	SLOT 2	UNIFORM
Price	UMP 45SD	.45 Mark 23	Frag Grenade	Flashbang	Desert 2 Heavy
Noronha	UMP 45SD	.45 Mark 23	Breaching Charge	Heartbeat Sensor	Desert 2 Heavy

Strategy

The seawater treatment plant consists of two large buildings and two smaller buildings. The hostages are located in the topmost large building while the toxin bomb is in the other large building. Stealth is vital. If the tangos hear any gunfire, they'll release the toxin into the water supply. Therefore, stay as quiet as possible until the toxin bomb has been secured.

After you have prevented the toxin bomb from being detonated, go after the hostages. Both large buildings have catwalks with tangos patrolling them. Send one of your teams up on the catwalks to clear them so the other teams will not be sniped at.

The small building attached to the lower large building contains a few tangos. Take them out. The other small building is empty.

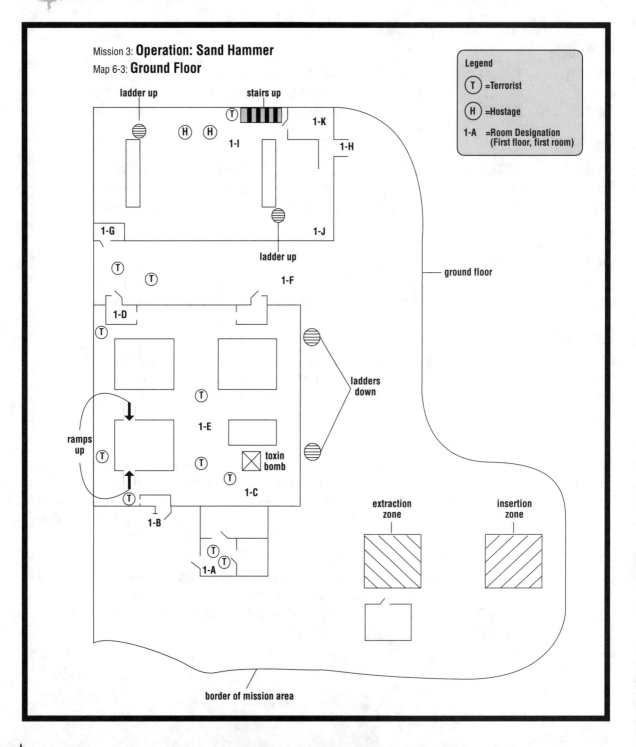

ROGUE SPEAR

Mission 3: **Operation: Sand Hammer**
Map 6-3: **Catwalks**

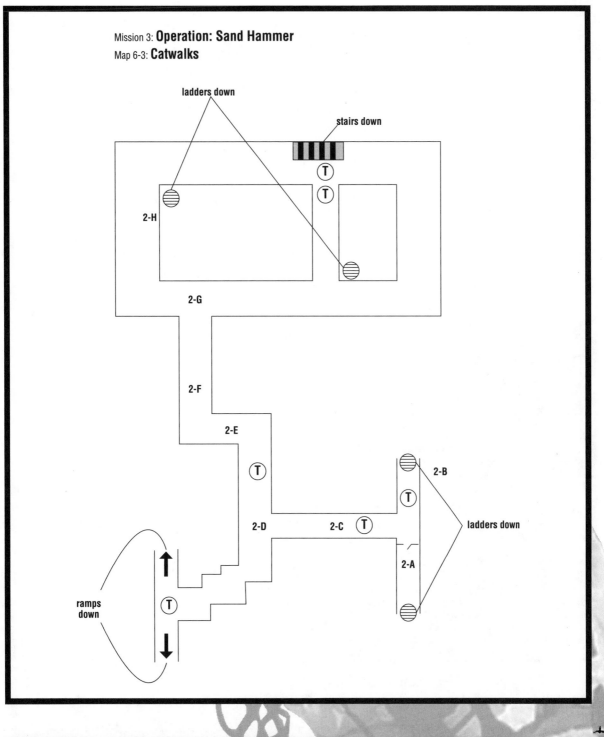

Blue Team

Blue Team is the back-door team. Their job is to sneak in the back door and kill the tango who can set off the toxin bomb. When this first objective is achieved, they will then lead the assault to rescue the hostages and escort them to safety.

From the insertion zone, advance toward area 1-F, between the two large buildings. Along the way, take out the tango up on the catwalk at 2-B. Near 1-F, you find two tangos patrolling. Drop them both before they can return fire or sound an alarm. In addition, a tango is in the walkway overhead at 2-F. Eliminate him as well or he could fire down at your team. Advance carefully through the door into the lower large building. Crouch and use Sniper view as you sidestep facing 1-D. There is a tango crouched down near 1-D facing you. Put him in your sights and shoot first or he'll kill your team and alert the other tangos. Once he is down, stand up and rush into the building. You must take out the tango who begins near 1-E. As soon as he sees you, he begins running to the toxin bomb at 1-C to set it off. Drop him and then set up a Defend position near 1-E until you receive code Bravo.

Blue Team takes out the tango guarding the outside catwalk.

Blue Team sneaks up on the tangos patrolling the area between the two large buildings.

At Bravo, withdraw back through the door you entered and head to the second large building. Enter via the door at 1-H and then hold for code Charlie in room 1-K.

After receiving code Charlie, rush into area 1-I, taking out the tango by the stairs. Set up a Defend position near the hostages and wait for code Delta.

The tango by the stairs is in the sights of Blue Team.

At code Delta, escort the hostages out the door at 1-H and all the way back to the extraction zone.

Red Team

Red Team's job is to secure the toxin bomb, then assist in the rescue of the hostages.

At the beginning of the mission, head toward the door at 1-B and hold there for code Alpha.

When Alpha is given, blitz through the door and head to area 1-C to secure the toxin bomb and prevent it from being detonated. Set up a Defend position there while waiting for code Bravo.

Red Team begins the assault on the first building.

Red Team sets up a Defend position near the toxin bomb.

At code Bravo, move out of the building through door 1-D and then across to 1-G and hold outside for code Charlie.

After receiving code Charlie, rush in through door 1-G and make your way to the hostages at 1-I. Set up a Defend position to protect them until code Delta.

At code Delta, return to the extraction zone.

Green Team

Green Team clears and covers the high ground for this mission—namely the catwalks.

At the start of the mission, head over to and climb the ladder near 2-A. Continue to the door and hold outside of the building until you receive code Alpha.

Green Team holds outside the first building on the catwalk.

When Alpha is given, rush through the door and toward 2-C where one of two tangos are patrolling. Drop them and continue on to 2-D where Green Team assumes a Defend position. From here the team can prevent tangos from using the catwalks to attack the other teams. Hold there for code Bravo.

Green Team enters the building and clears the catwalks.

At Bravo, move toward the walkway connecting the two large buildings and hold at point 2-E for code Charlie.

After code Charlie, rush across the walkway and into the second building. Set up a Cover position at point 2-G aiming toward the hostages and clear the catwalks in this building. Hold here for code Delta.

Green Team rushes across the walkway into the second building.

At Delta, climb down the ladder at 2-H and then make your way back to the extraction zone.

Gold Team

Gold Team acts as a backup and cover team for the other three during this mission. Its job is to prevent tangos from sneaking up behind the other teams as they perform their tasks.

At the beginning of the mission, advance to a point to the left of room 1-A and assume a Cover position while aiming at the door of 1-A. A couple of tangos are inside and may come out if they hear your teams moving around. If they do, Gold Team will have the drop on them. Hold for code Alpha.

Gold Team is in position when the tangos in room 1-A decide to come outside for a look.

At code Alpha, head over to the door of 1-A and if the tangos are still inside, place a breaching charge on it and detonate it before rushing in and clearing the room. The charge either kills or stuns those in the room. Next, go back outside and make your way to the door at 1-H. Go inside just enough so you can see point 1-J and set up a Cover position facing this point. Hold for code Charlie.

When Charlie is given, rush toward 1-J and then around to 1-I to help clear the ground floor of the building. Finally, head out the door at 1-H and move back to the extraction zone.

Notes

The tangos in the two large buildings are scattered about. Therefore, by assaulting from a number of different directions, you can quickly clear each building before the tangos can react.

Take command of Blue Team since they require some fine control at several points in the mission. As soon as Blue enters the first building and goes after the tango at 1-E, give code Alpha to bring the other teams into the assault. Once the toxin bomb is secure, wait for a minute to see if any hidden tangos try to attack before giving code Bravo. This sends all teams to their start points for the assault on the next large building. As Blue Team, put the tango near the stairs at 1-I in your sights and fire as you give code Charlie, which sends all teams in to secure hostages. Once the building is clear, give code Delta and all teams will head to the extraction zone with the hostages

Mission 4—Operation: Lost Thunder

10.24.01   **1915**

Djakovica

Mission Orders

A helicopter containing NATO officials has been shot down over the city of Djakovica in Kosovo. The officials have been taken hostage by Serbian army irregulars. Your mission is to enter the contested area of the city and safely extract the hostages.

The NATO hostages are being held in the back of an abandoned church a few blocks from the insertion zone. Try to avoid the major streets—they're crawling with patrols. Be careful around tall buildings as well—they're ideal locations for snipers. The heavy rain will make hearing and seeing your enemy just that much more difficult, so don't let down your guard even for an instant.

Objectives

1. Rescue all hostages

The ruins of this town hold many dangers. Enemy troops are everywhere. Watch out for the sniper in the tower.

Mission Data

DIFFICULTY LEVEL	TERRORISTS	HOSTAGES	OTHER
Recruit	14	3	None
Veteran	21	3	None
Elite	24	3	None

Team Assignments

Blue Team

OPERATIVE	PRIMARY	SECONDARY	SLOT 1	SLOT 2	UNIFORM
Walther	UMP 45-SD	.45 Mark 23	Frag Grenade	Flashbang	Euro Medium
Maldini	UMP 45-SD	.45 Mark 23	Frag Grenade	Flashbang	Euro Medium
Sweeney	UMP 45-SD	.45 Mark 23	Frag Grenade	Heartbeat Sensor	Euro Medium

Red Team

OPERATIVE	PRIMARY	SECONDARY	SLOT 1	SLOT 2	UNIFORM
Novikov	G3A3	.45 Mark 23	Frag Grenade	Flashbang	Euro Heavy
Murad	G3A3	.45 Mark 23	Frag Grenade	Heartbeat Sensor	Euro Heavy
Loiselle	G3A3	.45 Mark 23	Frag Grenade	Flashbang	Euro Heavy

Green Team

OPERATIVE	PRIMARY	SECONDARY	SLOT 1	SLOT 2	UNIFORM
Narino	PSG-1	.45 Mark 23	Frag Grenade	Flashbang	Euro Medium
Hanley	M16-A2	.45 Mark 23	Frag Grenade	Heartbeat Sensor	Euro Medium

Strategy

The hostages are being held in the church at the opposite end of the map. There are two ways to get there—the front entrance and the back. You will actually send teams both ways and clear the town as you approach the church. Sound is not really an issue in that the hostages will not be killed if the guards hear gunfire. However, your recon team will use silenced weapons as they advance up the back way while the other teams can use anything.

Tip *For this mission, each team uses a different Go Code. Blue uses Alpha, Red—Bravo, and Green—Charlie.*

The first part of the mission is eliminating the sniper in the tower. Following that, comes the approach to the church and finally the assault on the church to rescue the hostages.

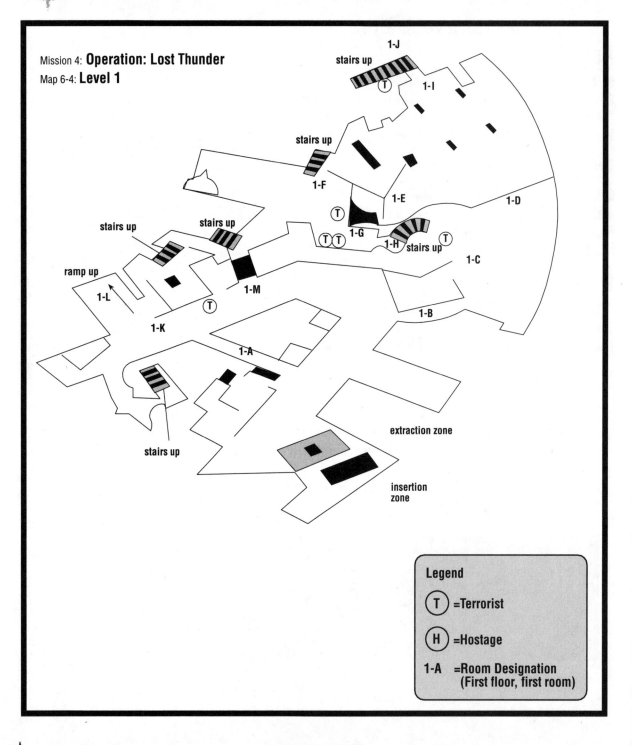

Mission 4: **Operation: Lost Thunder**
Map 6-4: **Level 1**

1-J

stairs up

1-I

1-D

stairs up

1-F

1-E

1-G

stairs up

1-H

stairs up

1-C

stairs up

stairs up

ramp up

1-L

1-M

1-B

1-K

1-A

stairs up

extraction zone

insertion zone

Legend

(T) =Terrorist

(H) =Hostage

1-A =Room Designation
(First floor, first room)

Mission 4: **Operation: Lost Thunder**

Map 6-4: **Level 2**

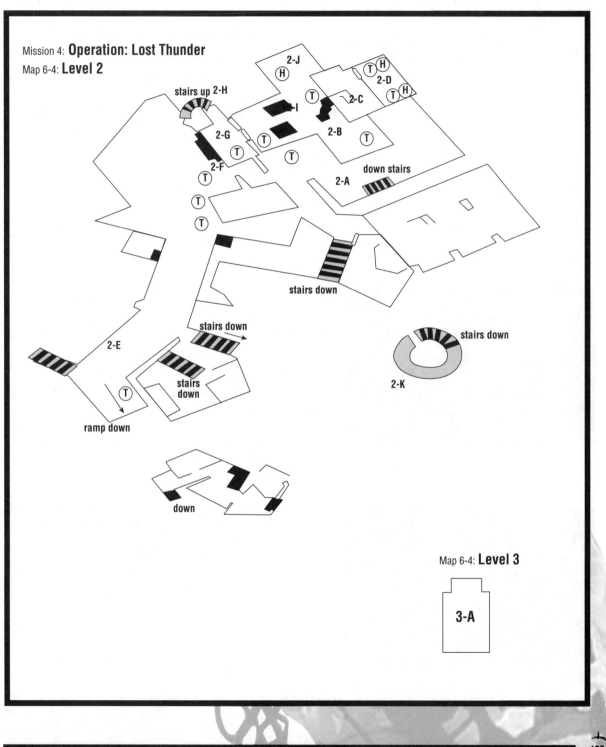

stairs up 2-H

2-J

2-D

2-C

2-I

2-G

2-B

2-F

down stairs

2-A

stairs down

2-E

stairs down

stairs down

2-K

stairs
down

ramp down

down

Map 6-4: **Level 3**

3-A

Blue Team

Blue is your recon team. Take command of this team and try to keep it as quiet as possible. However, feel free to use grenades if the opportunity arises.

From the insertion zone, quickly advance to the alley at point 1-B. From there, carefully continue to 1-C. There is a tango in this area. Put your team in Recon mode so the heartbeat sensor will be used. Use either a flashbang or frag grenade if the tango is difficult to approach for a shot. Just be careful wWhen using a frag grenade make sure that it does not fall too close to your team. After clearing this area, hold for Alpha.

The next phase is tricky. Move through 1-D and 1-E towards 1-F. There are two tangos are located in 1-G. Use a frag grenade to get them both. However, be ready for them should they run out when they see the grenade. When 1-G is clear, return to 1-F and hold for code Alpha while assuming a Cover position facing towards 2-E. There is a patrol and some other enemies which will walk by. However, by staying crouched, you can take them out before they even know you are there.

Blue Team sneaks up on the two tangos guarding the stairs leading to the sniper.

At the next Go code, return to 1-E, then on to 1-I. A lone tango is guarding the stairs at 1-J. Throw a flashbang around the corner. It will kill him if it hits close enough. Otherwise, rush and use your firearm. Sidestep up the stairs while facing 2-A. There is usually a tango in the area, so be ready to shoot as soon as he comes into sight. Hold at 2-A and set up in Cover position facing 2-I. Shoot any tangos who come into your sights.

The tango is waiting for Blue Team at the stairs. Throw a flashbang around the corner.

Side step up the stairs to the second level, watching out for tangos on patrol.

At the next Alpha, rush into the church through 2-B to 2-C. Two hostages are located in 2-D along with two guards. Use the heartbeat sensor to see where they are, then throw in a flashbang. Rush in as soon as it goes off and drop both tangos before they can shoot the hostages. Hold here for code Delta.

Blue Team rushes in after a flashbang detonates to take down the tangos before they can kill the hostages.

At code Delta, escort the hostages back to the extraction zone via the way you came.

Red Team

While Blue Team uses stealth, Red uses raw firepower. Red Team will advances up the streets to the church, taking out all opposition along the way.

At the beginning of the mission, immediately advance to 1-A and hold for code Bravo. Set up a Cover position facing 1-K. Several tangos will come into your sights from 1-L during the first few minutes. Be ready for them.

Red Team's position in the alley gives them a great line of sight to the advancing tangos.

At the next Go Ccode, advance through 1-L to 2-E. Again hold and set up a Cover position facing 2-F.

When given the go, advance up the street to 2-F. The street should be clear by now. At 2-F, use the heartbeat sensors to locate the tangos inside the church. There are usually one or two in or near room 2-G. Throw a frag grenade at them, then rush into 2-G and on up the stairs at 2-H to the balcony at 3-A. Hold here and Cover, facing 2-I. This is a good vantage for clearing out the main area of the church.

Red Team fires into the church after throwing a grenade inside.

The balcony offers a great vantage for clearing out the interior of the church.

At code Bravo, rush down the stairs and over to 2-J where a hostage is located. You will usually have killed the guard in this area by now; however, if he's there, be alert and ready to shoot him if he's there before he kills the hostage. Hold for code Delta.

At code Delta, follow Blue Team back to the extraction zone via the back way.

Green Team

Green Team contains your sniper. Hold at the insertion zone for code Charlie. Then head through 1-B to 1-C and hold again for Charlie.

At the Go code, advance through 1-D, 1-E, and 1-G to the stairs at 1-H. Climb up them and take out the sniper at 2-K. His back is to you, so you can sneak up with no problem. Hold at 2-K and set up in Snipe position, aiming at point 1-M.

Green Team sneaks up on the enemy sniper in the tower.

Green Team's sniper clears the street below of any enemies foolish enough to come out in the open.

When you receive the final code Charlie, head back down the stairs and return to the extraction zone.

Notes

Timing is not as important in this mission as the order in which each team performs their assigned tasks. Since teams Blue and Red are usually not performing at the same time, you can take command of whichever is advancing. Green Team can remain under computer control for the entire mission.

Begin in command of Blue Team. Once area 1-C is clear, give code Charlie so Green Team will advance, then code Alpha to release Blue to continue on. Once 1-G is clear, give code Charlie again and Green team will advance to the top of the tower and begin sniping. Blue will hold for now. Once Green Team is set for sniping, take control of Red Team and give code Bravo. Lead them to 2-E and hold while making sure the street ahead is clear.

Now switch to Blue Team. Give code Alpha and lead them to their next hold at 2-A. Return to Red Team, give code Bravo and then continue up the street to the church. While Blue Team covers the flank, Red Team rushes in to the balcony and holds. Now give code Alpha and take control of Blue Team. Lead them all the way in to rescue the hostages. Once the main area of the church is clear, give code Bravo and Red Team will rush to the third hostage. When all hostages are secure, give code Delta to send Red and Blue back to the extraction zone. Once they are nearly there, give code Charlie and Green team will leave its sniping post and return to the extraction zone as well.

Mission 5—Operation: Perfect Sword

11.13.01   1845
Brussels

Mission Orders

Three days ago, Middle-Eastern terrorists gained control of an Aolian Airlines airliner. The airplane is now stranded without fuel at Brussels Airport. Several hostages have already been executed. Your mission is to retake the airliner before further killings occur.

Getting to the plane without being seen will be your biggest challenge. Be ready to use the fuel truck to cover your approach. The terrorist guarding the plane's main door is using one hostage as a human shield, while the rest of the passengers are being held in the main cabin. You may be able to get on board through the rear cargo door, but watch for guards patrolling the cargo bays.

Objectives

1. Rescue the hostages

The tangos on the 747 are waiting to be refueled. Use this opportunity to sneak operatives aboard.

Mission Data

DIFFICULTY LEVEL	TERRORISTS	HOSTAGES	OTHER
Recruit	10	5	None
Veteran	10	5	None
Elite	11	5	None

Team Assignments

Blue Team

OPERATIVE	PRIMARY	SECONDARY	SLOT 1	SLOT 2	UNIFORM
Chavez	MP5-SD5	.45 Mark 23-SD	none	none	Black Light
Yacoby	MP5-SD5	.45 Mark 23-SD	Heartbeat Sensor	none	Black Light

Red Team

OPERATIVE	PRIMARY	SECONDARY	SLOT 1	SLOT 2	UNIFORM
Bogart	MP5-SD5	.45 Mark 23-SD	none	none	Black Light
Filatov	MP5-SD5	.45 Mark 23-SD	Heartbeat Sensor	none	Black Light

Green Team

OPERATIVE	PRIMARY	SECONDARY	SLOT 1	SLOT 2	UNIFORM
Price	MP5-SD5	.45 Mark 23-SD	none	none	Black Light
Maldini	MP5-SD5	.45 Mark 23-SD	none	none	Black Light
Raymond	MP5-SD5	.45 Mark 23-SD	Heartbeat Sensor	none	Black Light

Gold Team

OPERATIVE	PRIMARY	SECONDARY	SLOT 1	SLOT 2	UNIFORM
Petersen	PSG-1	.45 Mark 23-SD	Primary Mag	none	Euro Light

Strategy

This is a very tough mission. While the tangos are not numerous, the operational area inside the aircraft is quite limited. Stealth is important. Once the tangos know you are after them, they will begin shooting the hostages. This also means you must coordinate the efforts of all teams so they all strike at the same time.

The area around the aircraft is wide open and a tango is standing at the door with a hostage. Use the fuel truck to hide your teams' advance to the cargo entrance of the aircraft.

Blue Team

Blue Team's task is to rescue the hostages on the main level of the aircraft. Start off by heading to 1-A and holding for Alpha.

At Alpha, walk alongside the fuel truck, using it to shield you from the view of the tangos on the plane. Once you get past the right side of the tail of the aircraft, head to the cargo ramp at 1-C, climb inside and hold at 2-A for code Bravo.

Mission 5: **Operation Perfect Sword**
Map 6-5: **Airport**

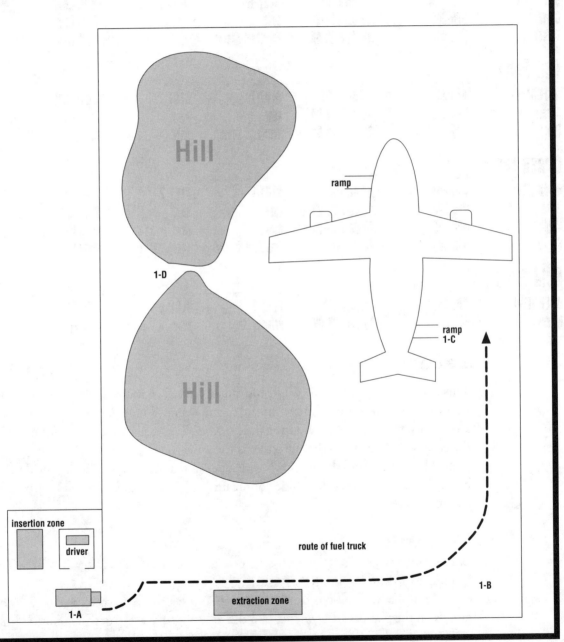

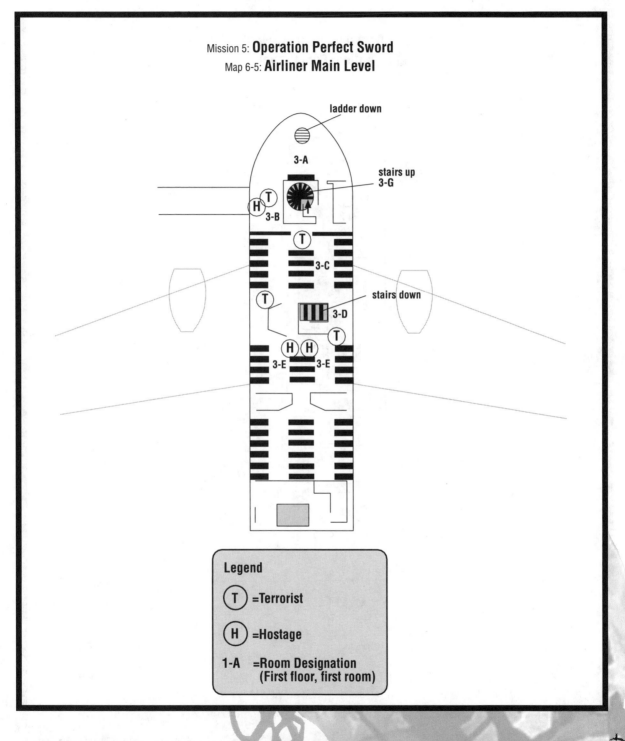

Mission 5: **Operation Perfect Sword**
Map 6-5: **Airliner Main Level**

ladder down

3-A

stairs up
3-G

H T
3-B

T

3-C

stairs down

T

3-D

T

H H
3-E   3-E

Legend

(T) =Terrorist

(H) =Hostage

1-A =Room Designation
(First floor, first room)

Mission 5: **Operation Perfect Sword**
Map 6-5: **Airliner Cargo Level**

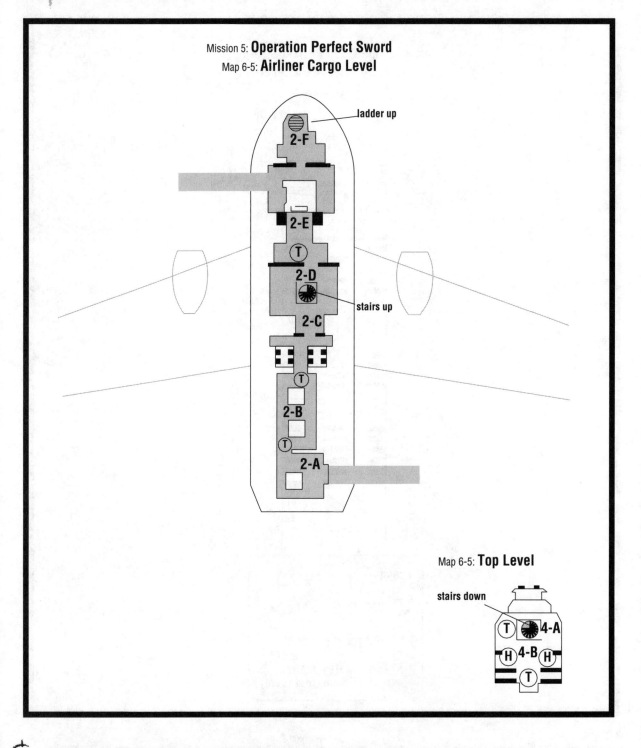

ladder up

2-F

2-E

T

2-D

stairs up

2-C

T

2-B

T

2-A

Map 6-5: **Top Level**

stairs down

T 4-A

H 4-B H

T

The three assault teams advance alongside the fuel truck.

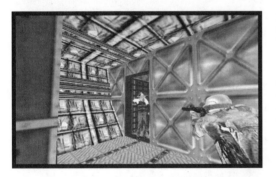

The assault teams climb aboard the aircraft using the cargo ramp.

When you receive code Bravo, advance through the cargo hold to the stairs at 2-D. Start to climb up them a bit, then hold for code Charlie.

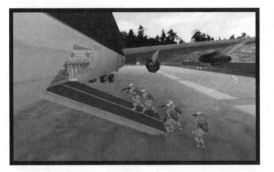

Blue Team takes out a tango patrolling the cargo level.

At Charlie, blitz the rest of the way up the stairs to 3-D, then on to 3-E. Watch out for the tango guarding the stairs. Kill all the tangos in the area, then hold for code Delta. Assume a Defend position while holding.

Blue Team rushes up the stairs and out into the main level, taking out all the tangos guarding the hostages.

At code Delta, escort the hostages to the door at 3-E, picking up the hostage by the door, then down the ramp and to the extraction zone.

Red Team

Red Team will works in support of Blue Team and clears out the front of the aircraft on the main level. Start off by heading to 1-A and holding for Alpha.

At Alpha, walk alongside the fuel truck, using it to shield you from the view of the tangos on the plane. Once you get past the right side of the tail of the aircraft, head to the cargo ramp at 1-C, climb inside, and hold at 2-A for code Bravo.

At Bravo, rush through the cargo level to the ladder at 2-F. There are three tangos in the cargo level; so be careful to kill all them quietly, so those above do not know what is taking place. Hold at 3-A for code Charlie.

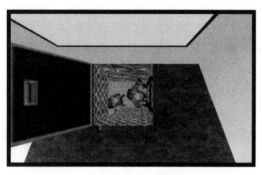

Red Team uses the ladder at the front of the aircraft to climb up to the main level from the cargo level.

When Charlie is given, rush to 3-C and then 3-F, taking out the one or two tangos patrolling this level. Hold at 3-F for code Delta and set up in Defend position.

At Delta, lead Blue Team and the hostages out the door at 3-B, down the ramp and to the extraction zone.

Green Team

Green Team's assignment is to rescue the hostages at the top level of the aircraft. Start off by heading to 1-A and holding for Alpha.

At Alpha, walk alongside the fuel truck, using it to shield you from the view of the tangos on the plane. Once you get past the right side of the tail of the aircraft, head to the cargo ramp at 1-C, climb inside, and hold at 2-A for code Bravo.

After receiving code Bravo, make your way through the cargo level to the ladder at 2-F. Climb up it, then enter the stairway at 3-G. Hold in the stairway for code Charlie.

At Charlie, rush the rest of the way up the stairs to 4-A, then blitz to 4-B, taking out all the tangos near the hostages. Circle around the stairs to make sure the level is secure, then hold in Cover position, facing the stairs, while waiting for code Delta.

Green Team rushes into the top level of the aircraft to rescue two hostages.

At Delta, escort the hostages down the stairs to the main level, then out the door at 3-B. Go down the ramp and to the extraction zone.

Gold Team

Gold Team consists of your sniper. His job is to take out the tango in the doorway of the aircraft and any other tangos who appear in his sights.

At the beginning of the mission, advance carefully to 1-D, crouch and hold for code Delta. Assume a Snipe posture with the tango at 3-B your aiming point. Keep his head in your sights until the other teams begin their main assault at code Charlie, then take the tango down. Be careful not to hit the hostage.

At code Delta, move to the extraction zone.

Gold Team moves into position near the hills.

The sniper of Gold Team blends in with the surrounding terrain.

With the tango in the crosshairs, Gold Team must waits to fire until the other teams are ready to begin the assault.

Notes

As mentioned earlier, this mission requires precise timing. Try playing this mission while commanding Gold team. This lets you monitor the status of the other three teams while having to cover only a single tango.

When the driver of the fuel truck climbs in and begins driving towards the aircraft, give code Alpha to send Blue, Red, and Green Teams to the cargo ramp. Meanwhile, Gold team takes up a Sniping position. Press Ⓖ to change to the four-map view and watch the movements of the three assault teams. When all are at 2-A, give code Bravo to send them through the cargo level. When all are holding at their jump- off points, give code Charlie and immediately take out the tango at the door of the aircraft. If you are controlling one of the three assault teams, order the sniper to fire by pressing Ⓨ, which allows the sniper to fire at will. If one of the teams begins engaging tangos on the main or top levels before all are in position, give code Charlie immediately since your element of surprise is already blown. When all the hostages are secure, give code Delta to get them and your teams back to the extraction zone.

Mission 6—Operation: Crystal Arc

02.07.00   **1700**
London

Mission Orders

An anonymous informant has revealed the location of Vezirzade's dacha in the Caucasus. Your mission is to infiltrate the area, plant surveillance devices within the building, and escape undetected.

This is a pure recon mission. USE OF DEADLY FORCE IS NOT SANCTIONED ON THIS OPERATION. If Vezirzade's guards detect you while you are in the house or on its grounds, the mission will be a failure. You must disable the security system in the guardhouse before entering the main house or the security alarm will be triggered. Check your map for the locations where the two bugs are to be placed. Any of your operatives can plant the devices.

Objectives

1. Deactivate security
2. Bug phone
3. Place camera

The dacha is well guarded. While it would be easy to assault, you have to avoid detection and cannot kill anyone.

Mission Data

DIFFICULTY LEVEL	TERRORISTS	HOSTAGES	OTHER
Recruit	7	0	3 Electronics
Veteran	10	0	3 Electronics
Elite	11	0	3 Electronics

Team Assignments

Blue Team

OPERATIVE	PRIMARY	SECONDARY	SLOT 1	SLOT 2	UNIFORM
Sweeney	none	9mm 92FS 9mm-SD	Heartbeat Sensor	Lockpick Kit	Euro Light

Strategy

This mission is unlike any others you have been assigned previously in this campaign. You must place surveillance gear inside this dacha. However, in order for it to be effective, the tangos must not know you were there. Therefore, not only can you not kill anyone, you cannot be seen by any of the tangos.

This is a solo mission. You need only one operative under your control. Kevin Sweeney is the best choice. He has high ratings in both stealth and electronics. Stealth will help him get around unnoticed, while electronics will help him pick locks and place the surveillance gear faster.

Tip
You can take along a second operative in a separate team if desired. Give this operative a heartbeat sensor and some binoculars. Use him or her for keeping an eye on tangos at different levels where Sweeney's heartbeat sensor will not pick them up.

Tangos climb up and down stairs. If they are not on the same level as your operative, they will not be detected by the heartbeat sensor.

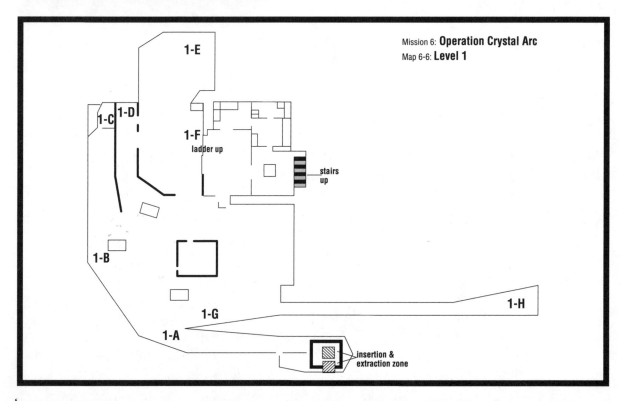

Mission 6: **Operation Crystal Arc**
Map 6-6: **Level 1**

1-E

1-C 1-D

1-F
ladder up

stairs up

1-B

1-H

1-G

1-A

insertion & extraction zone

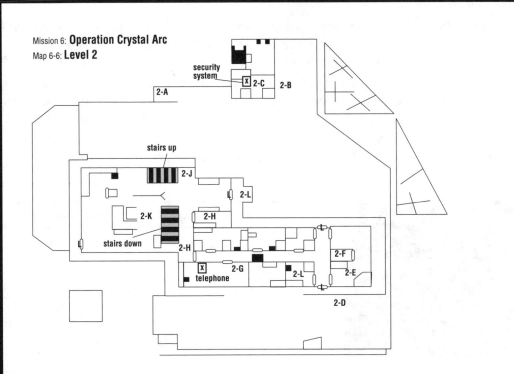

Mission 6: **Operation Crystal Arc**
Map 6-6: **Level 2**

security system

X 2-C   2-B

2-A

stairs up

2-J

2-L

2-K

2-H

stairs down

2-H

2-F

X   2-G

2-E

telephone

2-L

2-D

Map 6-6: **Level 3**

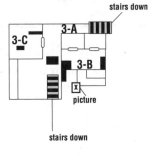

stairs down

3-A

3-C

3-B

X

picture

stairs down

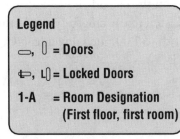

Legend

⬭, ▯ = **Doors**

⬰, ⬿ = **Locked Doors**

1-A = **Room Designation**
           (First floor, first room)

Blue Team

From the insertion zone, go to point 1-A. Crouch here and run to point 1-B, then on to 1-C. Here climb up the ledge and then hide by 1-D. Wait until the tango on your level walks past you towards 1-E and the tango on the balcony passes you headed the other direction. Then rush through 1-E to hide at 2-A. Hold here until the patrolling tango walks past you again and the tango on the balcony begins moving away from you. Then carefully move to point 2-B. Use the heartbeat sensor to see if the tango inside the small building is downstairs. Wait until he heads back up the stairs, then enter the building and go to room 2-C and deactivate the security system by pressing and holding SPACEBAR.

The little alcove behind the wall makes a good hiding spot.

Sweeney deactivates the security system.

Stay crouched by the security console until the tango outside comes in and then leaves and the tango inside goes back up the stairs (in that order). Then move out the door and head back to 2-A. Hide here until the patrolling tango walks past you again toward the small building and the tango on the balcony is walking away.

Then rush to 1-F and hide under the balcony. Listen to the tango above. As the footsteps pass by over you, wait a few seconds, then rush to 1-D, then down to 1-C. From there, carefully head to 1-G and then on to 1-H.

> ## Tip
> *When moving outside, always stay crouched. Run while giving movement commands so your operative will move faster.*

Hide under the balcony until you hear the tango above pass by you.

By using the third- person view, you can watch the tango by the dacha while your operative stays hidden out of sight.

Hold there and watch the tango patrolling near 2-D. When he walks away from you, move carefully, but quickly, to the door at 2-D. Use the heartbeat sensor to make sure there is no tango on the other side or one headed toward the door with the heartbeat sensor. Then switch to the lockpick kit and open the door. Enter and close the door behind you. Don't alert the tangos to your presence by leaving a door supposedly armed with an alarm system open. Immediately go into 2-E and then to 2-F. Don't go into 2-L because the tangos will sometimes go in there.

Use the heartbeat sensor to watch the hallway leading to 2-G. There are two tangos patrolling it. Wait until one heads down the stairs at 2-H and the other walks towards 2-J, then rush into 2-G and plant the bug on the phone. Hold by the phone until one of the tangos goes back down the stairs and the other is headed down the hallway toward-toward 2-F, then rush into 2-H. Hide between the toilet and the counter, crouching. The tangos will not be able to see you as they walk by. You must now watch the regular two tangos as well as three near 2-K. When no one is looking, move quickly to 2-J and up the stairs.

Bug the phone to complete the second objective.

Sweeney hides between the toilet and the counter as tangos pass by the restroom.

Hold at the top at 3-A. If no tangos are upstairs, quickly enter room 3-B and place the camera in the painting. Do not go into 3-C because a tango often checks there. Wait until the tango heads back downstairs, then go to 3-A. As he comes back up again, go down to 2-J. Hold while using the heartbeat sensor to locate the tangos on the second level. When it is clear, head back to 2-H and hide by the toilet. Then when clear, return to 2-D. Wait until the guard outside is walking away, then head out the door to 1-H. From there, make your way back to the extraction zone and the mission is complete.

Sweeney places a camera in the painting.

Notes

This is a very difficult mission. Chances are you will have to play it several times before getting it right. After each try, take time to watch the replay and to see which tango saw your operative— and avoid the same mistake next time.

Mission 7—Operation: Silent Drum

12.19.01   **1745**
London

Mission Orders

Terrorists have stormed a television studio in London during a broadcast debate on European fiscal policy. Senior officers from the central banks of France, Spain, and the Netherlands have all been taken hostage. Your mission is to recapture the station with minimal loss of life.

The hostages are being held in Studio A—it's marked on your map and when you're in the building you should be able to follow the signs. You'll be inserted on the roof. Remember that catwalks cut through the upper levels of all the studios—you may be able to use them to move quickly through the building.

Objectives

1. Rescue all hostages

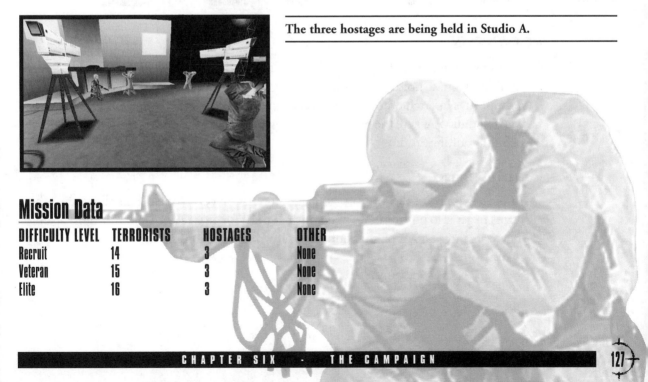

The three hostages are being held in Studio A.

Mission Data

DIFFICULTY LEVEL	TERRORISTS	HOSTAGES	OTHER
Recruit	14	3	None
Veteran	15	3	None
Elite	16	3	None

Team Assignments

Blue Team

OPERATIVE	PRIMARY	SECONDARY	SLOT 1	SLOT 2	UNIFORM
Chavez	MP5/-10SD	.45 Mark 23	Frag Grenade	Flashbang	Black Medium
Yacoby	MP5/-10SD	.45 Mark 23	Frag Grenade	Flashbang	Black Medium

Red Team

OPERATIVE	PRIMARY	SECONDARY	SLOT 1	SLOT 2	UNIFORM
Walther	MP5/-10SD	.45 Mark 23	Frag Grenade	Flashbang	Black Medium
Loiselle	MP5/-10SD	.45 Mark 23	Frag Grenade	Flashbang	Black Medium

Green Team

OPERATIVE	PRIMARY	SECONDARY	SLOT 1	SLOT 2	UNIFORM
Novikov	MP5/-10SD	.45 Mark 23	Frag Grenade	Flashbang	Black Medium
Arnavisca	MP5/-10SD	.45 Mark 23	Frag Grenade	Flashbang	Black Medium

Gold Team

OPERATIVE	PRIMARY	SECONDARY	SLOT 1	SLOT 2	UNIFORM
Noronha	MP5/-10SD	.45 Mark 23	Frag Grenade	Flashbang	Black Medium
Rakuzanka	MP5/-10SD	.45 Mark 23	Frag Grenade	Flashbang	Black Medium

Strategy

This mission is not ats tough as some of the previous ones. Many of the walls inside are soundproofed, so noise is not as much of an issue. However, still use silenced weapons. Your team is inserted onto the roof of the building. From there, you must make your way to Studio A where the hostages are being held. Clear out the rest of the building before assaulting Studio A.

Blue Team

At the beginning of the mission, hold at point 3-A for code Alpha. This allows the other teams to get into position. At Alpha, rush to the door at 3-D and hold for Alpha again. There are three tangos on the roof. Shoot any that come into sight.

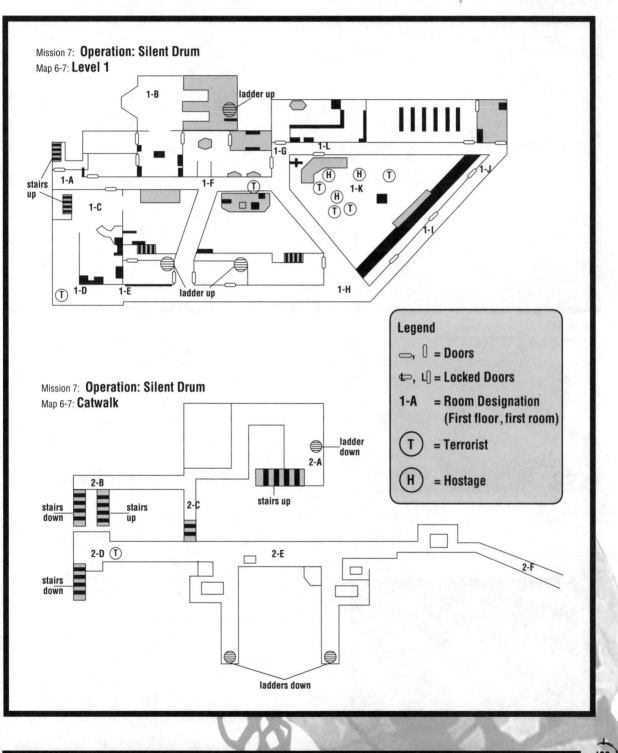

Mission 7: **Operation: Silent Drum**
Map 6-7: **Level 1**

1-B

ladder up

1-A

stairs
up

1-C

1-F

1-G

1-L

1-J

1-K

1-I

1-D   1-E

ladder up

1-H

Mission 7: **Operation: Silent Drum**
Map 6-7: **Catwalk**

Legend

⌐, ▯ = **Doors**

⇐, ◲ = **Locked Doors**

1-A = **Room Designation**
(First floor , first room)

(T) = **Terrorist**

(H) = **Hostage**

ladder
down

2-A

2-B

stairs
down

stairs
up

2-C

stairs up

2-D (T)

2-E

2-F

stairs
down

ladders down

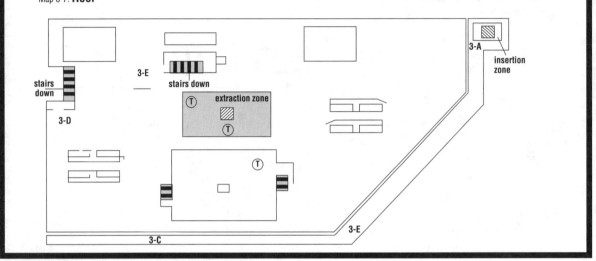

Mission 7: **Operation: Silent Drum**
Map 6-7: **Roof**

3-A
insertion zone

stairs down

3-E
stairs down

extraction zone

3-D

3-C

3-E

The teams move into position on the rooftop.

After the second code Alpha, rush through the door at 3-D, down two flights of stairs and through another door to 1-A. Use caution when entering the hallway. There can be one or more tangos down toward 1-F. Use full automatic to hose them all down. Hold at 1-A for code Bravo and assume a Cover posture facing down the hallway.

At Bravo, run up the stairs near 1-C to 2-D. Clear out any tangos between there and 2-D. Then go back down the stairs to 1-F. Hold there for code Charlie and assume a Defend posture.

Blue Team climbs up the stairs at 1-C to help clear the catwalks.

At Charlie, move through 1-G to 1-J and hold for Delta. When you get this code, rush into the studio at 1-K, being careful not to hit the hostages. Hold at 1-K for code Alpha, assuming a Defend posture. Then head back to the extraction zone on the roof via the stairs at 1-A.

Blue Team enters Studio A ready for action.

Red Team

At the start of the mission, hold for code Alpha. When you receive it, rush to the door at 3-E and hold for a second code Alpha.

At the second Alpha, go through the door and down the stairs to 2-A. Then climb down the ladder and advance to 1-B. Hold here fore code Bravo and assume a Cover posture facing 1-E.

Red Team assumes Cover posture on the first level.

When your receive Bravo, advance to 1-G and assume a Defend posture while holding for Charlie. At Charlie, move next to the door at 1-L and hold for Delta.

Red Team patiently waits for code Delta and the start of the assault on the studio.

At Delta, rush through the door and blitz into 1-K. Once all the tangos are down, hold for Alpha and take up a Defend position. When Alpha is given, return to the extraction zone via the stairs at 1-A.

Green Team

At the beginning of the mission, advance to 3-B and hold for Alpha. If you can see tangos during this time, go ahead and take the shot. At Alpha, rush to the door at 3-E and hold for a second Alpha.

When you receive the second Alpha, rush down the stairs to 2-A and then follow the catwalks to 2-C. Hold here for Charlie and assume a Cover posture facing the main catwalk ahead of you. Several tangos will walk by. Take them down as they do.

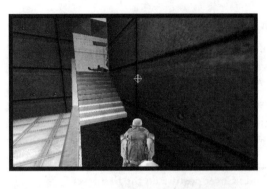

Green Team shoots several tangos as they walk past on the catwalks.

At Charlie, rush to 2-E and hold for Delta, assuming a Defend posture. When you receive Delta, rush out onto the catwalk above the studio, clear it, and hold at 2-F for code Alpha with a Defend posture. At Alpha, head up the stairs at 2-A and then continue on to the extraction zone.

While the other teams enter the studio below, Green Team takes care of any tangos on the catwalks above.

Gold Team

At the beginning of the mission, move along the edge of the building through 3-B to 3-C. Hold there for code Alpha. Take out any tangos you see along the way. At Alpha, rush to the door at 3-D and hold again for a second Alpha.

When you receive the second Alpha, head down the stairs to 1-A, then on in to 1-C. Hold there for code Bravo, assuming a Cover posture facing 1-D.

Gold Team covers Blue Team as it climbs up the stairs at 1-C.

At Bravo, rush to 1-D, then on to 1-E. Hold there for code Charlie and assume a Cover posture facing 1-H. At Charlie, head to point 1-I and hold outside the door for code Delta. If the door is open, hold short of it so those inside cannot see you.

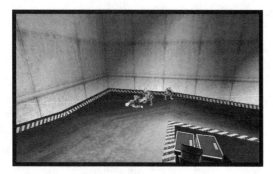

Gold Team clears and secures a hallway while waiting for orders to advance to the studio.

At Delta, rush inside to 1-K and clear the room of tangos. Assume a Defend position while holding for code Alpha. Then return to the extraction zone via the stairs at 1-A.

Notes

While this mission is not too tough, the actual assault on Studio A can be difficult to get right. At the beginning of the mission, take control of Blue Team. When all teams are in their initial jump- off positions, give code Alpha and all will rush across the roof taking out the tangos along the way. After all teams are holding by the stairs, give the second code Alpha and all will enter the building and head down to the first and second levels.

Once all teams are holding and things have quieted down after the initial rush, give code Bravo to send the teams to their next holding positions. There should be little action, and by the time they reach their next position, the building should be nearly clear except for Studio A. Give code Charlie and all teams will move to their jump- off points for the final assault.

The four teams assault the studio in unison.

Take command of Red Team now. Use the map to see where the tangos are located in Studio A. Hopefully there are only two. However, often there will be four. If so, wait a bit to see oif two of them will leave. If they do not, wait until they move away from the hostages before giving code Delta. This code will brings three teams into 1-K and Green team overhead on the catwalks. When the area is secure, issue code Alpha and all teams will return to the extraction zone.

Mission 8—Operation: Feral Burn

01.14.02   2330
St. Petersburg

Mission Orders

Intelligence gathered from Vezirzade's dacha has revealed that criminal elements are illegally buying weapons from sources within the Russian military. Another purchase is scheduled to take place tonight at dockside in St. Petersburg. Your mission is to prevent this exchange.

When the shooting starts the arms dealers will bolt like rabbits. You'll need to guard all the escape routes—both boat and car. Be careful. These guys are desperate and they won't hesitate to run you down if you get in their way. And remember: a few well-placed rounds to the tires or engine can totally disable a vehicle.

Objectives

1. Neutralize all terrorists

Members of the Russian Mafia are meeting with military leaders at this chop shop.

Mission Data

DIFFICULTY LEVEL	TERRORISTS	HOSTAGES	OTHER
Recruit	8	0	None
Veteran	11	0	None
Elite	14	0	None

Team Assignments

Blue Team

OPERATIVE	PRIMARY	SECONDARY	SLOT 1	SLOT 2	UNIFORM
Chavez	UMP45SD	.45 Mark 23	Frag Grenade	Heartbeat Sensor	Green Medium
Maldini	UMP45SD	.45 Mark 23	Frag Grenade	Frag Grenade	Green Medium

Red Team

OPERATIVE	PRIMARY	SECONDARY	SLOT 1	SLOT 2	UNIFORM
Bogart	G3A3	.45 Mark 23	Frag Grenade	Frag Grenade	Green Heavy
Burke	G3A3	.45 Mark 23	Frag Grenade	Frag Grenade	Green Heavy

Green Team

OPERATIVE	PRIMARY	SECONDARY	SLOT 1	SLOT 2	UNIFORM
Price	M16A2	.45 Mark 23	Frag Grenade	Frag Grenade	Green Heavy
Pak	M16A2	.45 Mark 23	Frag Grenade	Frag Grenade	Green Heavy

Gold Team

OPERATIVE	PRIMARY	SECONDARY	SLOT 1	SLOT 2	UNIFORM
Hanley	M16A2	.45 Mark 23	Frag Grenade	Frag Grenade	Green Heavy
Filatov	M16A2	.45 Mark 23	Frag Grenade	Frag Grenade	Green Heavy

Strategy

This mission is a bit different than the previous ones. There are no hostages to rescue or bombs to disarm. All you have to do is clear the area of tangos before they can escape. Russian Mafia and military leaders are meeting in one of the buildings.

> **Tip** *The three assault teams should wear heavy uniforms. They will be engaged in a major firefight, so give them all the protection possible.*

You must eliminate them and all of their guards. Once the shooting starts, the Mafia men will run down to the boat while the military men will head for the car and truck. If any get away, the mission is a failure.

Blue Team

Blue Team is your recon team, which clears the way for the other teams and then begins the action. From the insertion point, move to point 1-A. Crouch and carefully peek around the corner. A lone sentry is patrolling between points 2-C and 2-G. Wait until he is walking away from you to take him out. Don't fire if a metal door is behind him. If a bullet hits the door, it will alert the others to your presence and the mission will fail. Once the sentry is down, wade to 1-B and climb up on to the dock by pressing [SPACEBAR]. Continue to 1-C. While still behind the wall, face 1-E, crouch and peek to the right so the tango at 1-E is in your sights. Take him out silently, then move to 1-E. Hold there for Bravo.

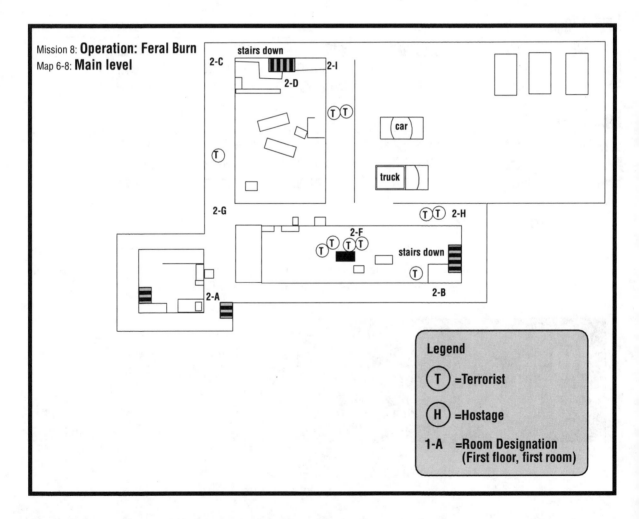

Mission 8: **Operation: Feral Burn**
Map 6-8: **Main level**

stairs down

2-C   2-I
2-D

car

truck

2-G   2-H

2-F
stairs down

2-A   2-B

Legend

(T) = Terrorist

(H) = Hostage

1-A = Room Designation
(First floor, first room)

Mission 8: **Operation: Feral Burn**
Map 6-8: **Lower level**

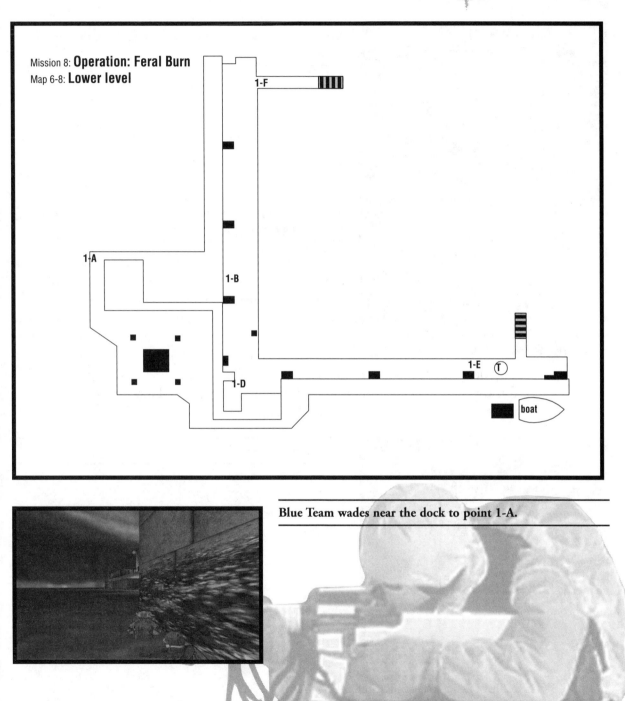

1-F

1-A

1-B

1-E (T)

1-D

boat

Blue Team wades near the dock to point 1-A.

While still in the water, Blue Team takes down the first sentry.

A Blue Team operative peeks around a corner and takes out the Mafia guard by the boat.

At Bravo, head up the stairs near 1-E. Before you get to the top, take out your heartbeat sensor and see where everyone is located in room 2-F. There will be four men in the center with the Russian truck driver somewhere else in the room. If he is near the top of the stairs at 2-E, it will make the job tougher. If he is somewhere else in the room, edge up to the door and take out a frag grenade. Pull the pin, peek to the right and then throw is as far as possible in the room. Quickly pull up your submachine gun and enter the room after the grenade goes off, taking out any survivors.

Blue Team readies a frag grenade.

A Blue Team member peeks through the doorway and throws a frag grenade right into the middle of the meeting.

If the driver is by the stairs, you'll have to shoot him first, then rush in with guns blazing. There isn't enough time to use the frag grenade before everyone leaves the building.

Red Team

Red Team is one of the heavy assault teams tasked with preventing anyone from leaving the area. Hold at the insertion zone for code Alpha. Then advance as quickly as possible through 1-A, 1-B, and up the stairs at 1-D. Hold near 2-A for code Charlie.

Red team holds and prepares for the assault.

At Charlie, blitz to 2-G and hold for code Delta while setting up in Cover posture facing 2-H. Kill any guards patrolling in your view as well as anyone coming out of the building at 2-F. Stay here until the mission ends.

Red Team fires at the guards and those heading for the get-away vehicles.

Green Team

Green Team is also tasked with preventing anyone from escaping. Hold at the insertion zone for code Alpha. Then advance through 1-A and 1-B to the stairs at 1-F. Climb up them and enter the building at 2-D. Go out the door at 2-C and hold for code Charlie.

At Charlie, blitz to 2-I and hold for code Delta while assuming Cover posture facing 2-H. Kill all the guards in your sights as well as anyone going for the car or truck. Stay in this position until the end of the mission.

Green Team holds and prepares for the assault.

Green Team takes out the Russian truck driver before he and get into the truck of weapons.

Gold Team

Gold Team is the third team tasked with preventing anyone from escaping. Hold at the insertion zone for code Alpha. Then advance through 1-A and 1-B to the stairs at 1-D. Climb up them and continue to point 2-B. Hold there for code Charlie.

At Charlie, blitz around the corner to 2-H and hold for code Delta. Assume a Cover posture while facing 2-G. Take out any tangos in your sights, especially any coming out of building 2-F and heading for either the car or truck. Stay at this point until the end of the mission.

Notes

While getting your operatives into position is not too difficult, the timing of the assault can be touchy. Take control of Blue Team. It's the most important team, especially in taking out the first two sentries so the rest of your team can get into position for the assault. Just before you shoot the second sentry located at 1-E, give code Alpha. That will get the other teams moving. After you have scouted out the meeting room at 2-F with the heartbeat sensor, pull out the grenade and get ready to throw. However, before releasing it, give code Charlie to send the other three teams running into position. If you have good aim, the frag grenade will take out all five in the room. Most of the time you will take out three or four. The two Mafia men will head toward Blue Team to get to the boat while the military men will head out the door to the car and truck. Worry about the Mafia first. The six assault rifles outside should take care of the rest. When all tangos are dead, the mission will be a success.

Mission 9—Operation: Diamond Edge

01.21.02   0030
Murmansk

Mission Orders

Nuclear weapons–grade plutonium has been recovered during a RAINBOW interdiction operation in St. Petersburg. The material has been traced to a weapons storage facility near Murmansk. Your mission is to raid the facility and take control of any remaining fissile material.

Your objective is to locate the colonel and escort him back to the extraction zone. If the alarm is raised Rudenko and his bodyguards will try to escape by car—keep all the escape routes covered. Be aware that the guards at the front gate can contact the main complex by telephone.

Objectives

1. Capture the Russian colonel

Your team must infiltrate this Russian nuclear installation and capture a colonel.

Mission Data

DIFFICULTY LEVEL	TERRORISTS	HOSTAGES	OTHER
Recruit	14	0	1 Captive
Veteran	20	0	1 Captive
Elite	25	0	1 Captive

Team Assignments

Blue Team

OPERATIVE	PRIMARY	SECONDARY	SLOT 1	SLOT 2	UNIFORM
Chavez	UMP45SD	.50 Desert Eagle	Frag Grenade	Flashbang	Street 1 Medium
Arnavisca	UMP45SD	.50 Desert Eagle	Frag Grenade	Flashbang	Street 1 Medium
Yacoby	UMP45SD	.50 Desert Eagle	Frag Grenade	Heartbeat Sensor	Street 1 Medium

Red Team

OPERATIVE	PRIMARY	SECONDARY	SLOT 1	SLOT 2	UNIFORM
Noronha	UMP45SD	.50 Desert Eagle	Frag Grenade	Flashbang	Street 1 Medium
Loiselle	UMP45SD	.50 Desert Eagle	Frag Grenade	Flashbang	Street 1 Medium
Woo	UMP45SD	.50 Desert Eagle	Frag Grenade	Heartbeat Sensor	Street 1 Medium

Green Team

OPERATIVE	PRIMARY	SECONDARY	SLOT 1	SLOT 2	UNIFORM
Galanos	Barrett Model 82A1	.45 Mark 23-SD	Primary Mag	Frag Grenade	Desert 2 Medium

Gold Team

OPERATIVE	PRIMARY	SECONDARY	SLOT 1	SLOT 2	UNIFORM
Weber	Barrett Model 82A1	.45 Mark 23-SD	Primary Mag	Frag Grenade	Desert 2 Medium

Strategy

This mission is somewhat similar to the last one. You must prevent the colonel from escaping. However, instead of killing him, you must capture him. For the purposes of the game, the colonel will act as a hostage.

The Russian installation is well guarded. You must first get through the front gate and make your way to the building at the rear of the installation. If any alarms are set off, the colonel and his bodyguards will move to the armored car and escape.

Blue Team

Blue Team leads the others through the Russian installation, captures the colonel, and escorts him to the extraction zone.

At the beginning of the mission, move toward the door at 1-B. It's locked, so pick the lock, then enter the room and take out the tango inside. Exit the room at 1-C and head over to the door at 1-D. Open it and kill the tango in 1-E. Now move through 1-G to hold at 1-H for Bravo.

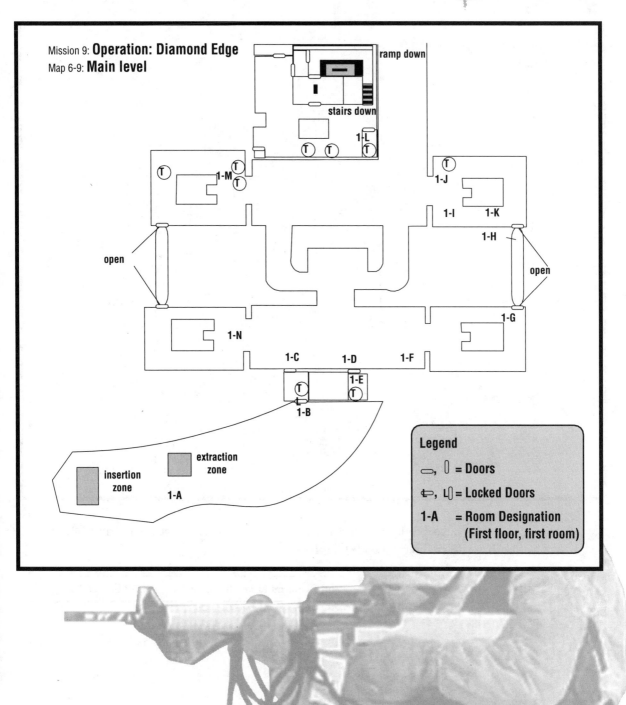

Mission 9: **Operation: Diamond Edge**
Map 6-9: **Main level**

ramp down

stairs down

1-L

1-M

1-J

1-I

1-K

1-H

open

open

1-G

1-N

1-C

1-D

1-F

1-E

1-B

extraction
zone

insertion
zone

1-A

Legend

⬭, ▯ = **Doors**

⬅, ◪ = **Locked Doors**

1-A = **Room Designation**
(First floor, first room)

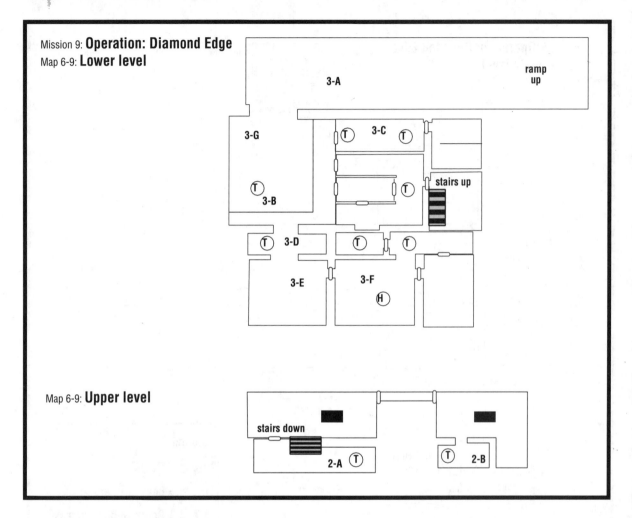

Mission 9: **Operation: Diamond Edge**
Map 6-9: **Lower level**

Map 6-9: **Upper level**

At Bravo, crouch and advance to 1-I, taking out the tangos at 1-L and 1-J. Once both are down, hold for code Charlie.

Blue Team takes out the tango in the building at 1-L.

Blue clears the area around 1-I by taking out this tango on sentry duty.

When Charlie is given, advance down the ramp at 1-N to 3-A. Crouch and sidestep out into the opening of the motor pool and kill the tango at 3-B. Then move toward 3-C and take out the two tangos in the booth quickly. If they see you, they'll sound the alarm. Now move toward 3-D. Be careful. These doors are automatic and will open on their own as you approach. There is a tango in 3-D. Advance to 3-E and then rush 3-F to secure the colonel. You must kill the two bodyguards that are with him. Finally, escort him back to the extraction zone following the same path you took into the installation.

Blue Team drops the tango guarding the armored car.

Blue Team must move quickly to kill both tangos in the guard booth before they can sound the alarm.

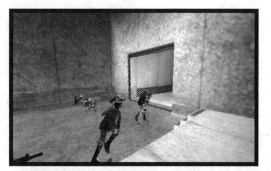

Blue Team escorts the colonel back to the extraction zone.

Red Team

Red Team supports Blue Team. Hold at the insertion zone for code Alpha. Then advance to 1-B, through to 1-C, and hold at 1-G for code Charlie.

Tip *Use the heartbeat sensor to keep track of what's going on inside the other rooms by setting the mode to Recon. If the colonel begins moving, rush back to 3-B and shoot the bodyguards as they approach the armored car. Be careful not to shoot the colonel.*

At Charlie, rush through 1-H, 1-I, and down to 1-N. Go down the ramp and hold at 3-A for code Alpha. When you receive this code, enter the motor pool and hold at 3-G for code Delta. Assume a Cover posture facing the door to the side of the armored car. If the alarm sounds, Red Team must kill any tangos coming out the door to get into the armored car. Be careful not to kill the colonel.

At Delta, return to the extraction zone following the same path you took into the installation.

Red Team takes out the bodyguards as they try to escort the colonel to the armored car.

Green Team

Green Team is one of the sniper teams. At the start of the mission, move to point 1-A and hold for code Alpha. Assume a Snipe posture and aim at 2-A.

At Alpha, advance through 1-B, 1-C, and 1-G and then hold at 1-H for another code Alpha. When you receive this code, carefully move to point 1-K and hold for code Delta. Assume a Snipe posture while aiming at point 1-M. Three tangos can be taken out from this vantage.

At Delta, return to the extraction zone following the same path you took in.

Gold and Green Teams take aim at the front gate towers.

Green Team takes out one of the tangos in the guard towers.

Green Team clears out the area around 1-M.

Gold Team

Gold Team is the other sniper team. At the beginning of the mission, move to point 1-A and hold for Alpha. Assume a Snipe posture and aim at 2-B.

At Alpha, move through 1-B and 1-C to 1-G. Hold there for code Delta. Assume a Snipe posture and aim at point 1-N.

At Delta, return to the extraction zone following the same path you took in.

Notes

This mission has a lot of different Go codes, which can make it somewhat confusing. However, they help keep your teams under control. Take command of Blue Team at the beginning. Slowly head toward the front gate. Once the sniper teams are in position, give them the order to fire by pressing Y. After clearing out 1-E, give code Alpha so the rest of the teams start moving into the installation. When you get to 1-H, give code Bravo so Blue team can continue.

After Blue has cleared the area around 1-I and is holding, switch to Green Team and give code Alpha again to get the team moving. At 1-K, shoot the tangos at 1-M. The first two are fairly easy. However a third may run past and crouch down at the entrance of a bunker, out of your sight. When the area is clear, switch back to Blue Team.

Now give code Charlie, which sends Blue and Red Teams down the ramp to the lower level. Once Blue has cleared the motor pool and taken out the guards at 3-C, give code Alpha again so Red Team will enter the area.

When the colonel has been captured and is being escorted by Blue Team, give code Delta and send all teams back to the extraction zone.

Mission 10—Operation: Silver Snake

02.02.02   0615
Georgia

Mission Orders

RAINBOW's Russian informant has revealed that a major meeting of Vezirzade's men will take place at his Georgian dacha. Your mission is to raid the meeting and obtain a set of computer files that are believed to contain details of Vezirzade's nuclear weapons purchases.

The files you need to recover are located in a computer in the upstairs bedroom. Any member of your team can download the files. This computer has been wired with a self-destruct device that can be set off by a switch on the opposite wall. If you alert the guards the first thing they'll do is trigger the self-destruct.

Objectives

1. Download computer files
2. Get everyone to the extraction zone

When you return to the dacha, snow is falling. Get out the Arctic uniforms.

Mission Data

DIFFICULTY LEVEL	TERRORISTS	HOSTAGES	OTHER
Recruit	17	0	Computer Files
Veteran	17	0	Computer Files
Elite	20	0	Computer Files

Team Assignments

Blue Team

OPERATIVE	PRIMARY	SECONDARY	SLOT 1	SLOT 2	UNIFORM
Woo	UMP45SD	.45 Mark 23-SD	Frag Grenade	Flashbang	Arctic 2 Medium
Pak	UMP45SD	.45 Mark 23-SD	Frag Grenade	Heartbeat Sensor	Arctic 2 Medium

Red Team

OPERATIVE	PRIMARY	SECONDARY	SLOT 1	SLOT 2	UNIFORM
Price	M4 Carbine	.45 Mark 23-SD	Frag Grenade	Frag Grenade	Arctic 2 Medium
Filatov	M4 Carbine	.45 Mark 23-SD	Frag Grenade	Frag Grenade	Arctic 2 Medium
Murad	M4 Carbine	.45 Mark 23-SD	Frag Grenade	Heartbeat Sensor	Arctic 2 Medium

Strategy

This mission should look very familiar. You had to plant surveillance devices here before. However this time your hands are no longer tied. Feel free to use as much force as necessary to get the job done. While this mission can be completed by a single team if everything goes correctly, a second team has been included in case you have some problems. The key is to get to the computer as stealthily as possible. Otherwise more tangos will be near the computer.

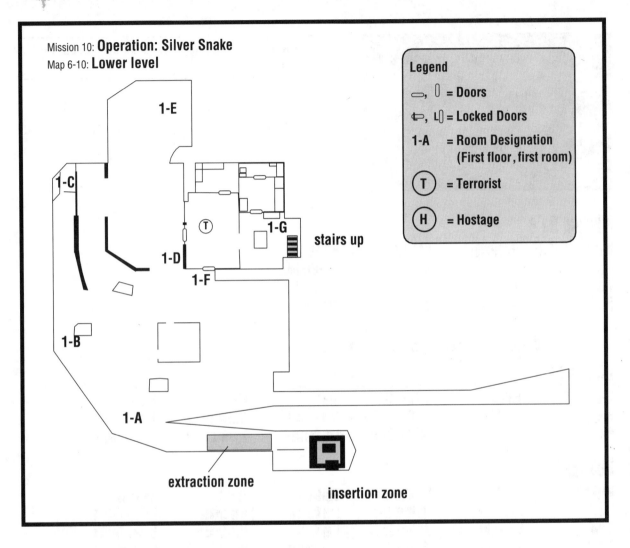

Mission 10: **Operation: Silver Snake**
Map 6-10: **Lower level**

1-E

Legend

⌐, ▯ = Doors

⇐, L▯ = Locked Doors

1-A = Room Designation
(First floor, first room)

Ⓣ = Terrorist

Ⓗ = Hostage

1-C

Ⓣ

1-G

stairs up

1-D

1-F

1-B

1-A

extraction zone

insertion zone

Blue Team

Blue Team is your main team for this mission. In fact, you can try performing the mission using only Blue Team.

At the beginning of the mission, advance through 1-A and 1-B to point 1-C. From here, shoot the tango patrolling the balcony at 2-D. Once he is down, climb up the ledge and head over to 1-D. Crouch and peek right around the corner, aiming at 2-A. Shoot the tango patrolling as soon as he appears.

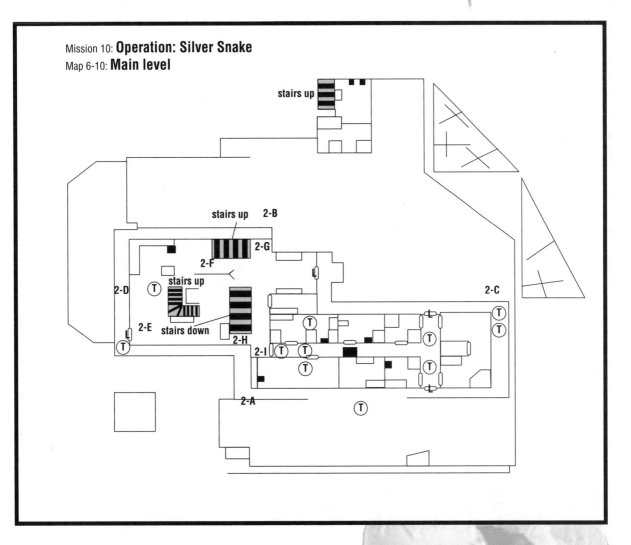

Mission 10: **Operation: Silver Snake**
Map 6-10: **Main level**

stairs up

stairs up   2-B

2-G

2-F

stairs up

2-D

T

stairs down

2-E

2-H

2-I

2-C

T

T

T

T

T

T

2-A

T

Blue Team advances along the wall, out of the sight of the patrolling tangos.

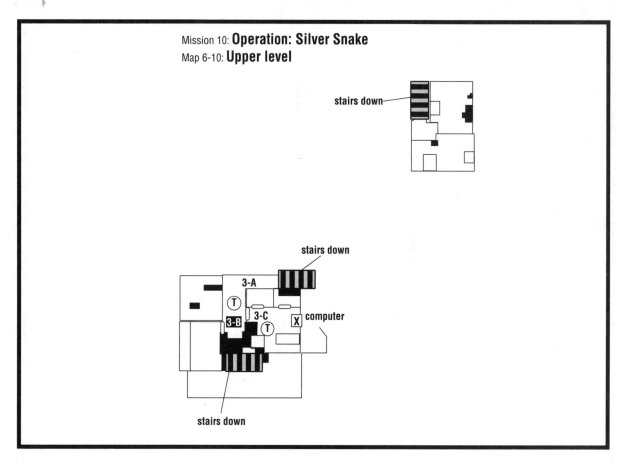

Mission 10: **Operation: Silver Snake**
Map 6-10: **Upper level**

stairs down

stairs down

3-A

T

3-B   3-C
        T   X   computer

stairs down

A tango is patrolling along the balcony. Take him out.

Blue Team peeks around the corner at 1-D.

Blue Team takes a tango down just as he comes into view.

Next, move up to 1-E, then to 2-B. Hold here for code Alpha and assume a Cover posture facing 2-C. Use the crouching and peeking tactic to take out the two-man patrol when it appears near 2-C. Once all of the outside guards have been taken care of, head inside.

The two-man patrol at 2-C is a long shot, but with the submachine gun set to full automatic, you should be able to take them both before they can get off a shot.

When you receive code Alpha, advance to 2-D on the balcony and hold for Bravo. Move right next to the door and switch to Recon mode so the second operative in the team will use the heartbeat sensor. A single tango patrols inside. Wait until he is near 2-E and walking away from the door, then enter at code Bravo and take him down. Move through 2-F to 2-G. Slowly go up the stairs, watching the mini-map to see where the tango at the top is located. He'll be patrolling around 3-B. Halt at 3-A until he is facing away, then peek around the corner and drop him.

Blue Team opens the door to the dacha and takes out the tango patrolling downstairs.

By peeking around the corner at the top of the stairs, Blue Team is able to take out the tango in the hallway.

The next step is tough. You must neutralize the tango in 3-C before he can get to a button on the wall across from the computer. He'll rush for the button as soon as he sees you. The open door partially blocks your view. There are two ways to accomplish this task. The first is to rush in with a full magazine and your submachine gun blazing. The other way is to throw a frag grenade in through the open doorway. The latter is the best choice. Even if the grenade doesn't kill the tango (which it almost always does), the door will be blown away, which gives you a better shot at the tango. Don't throw the grenade near the computer or you may blow it up.

The tango in the computer room must be killed quickly before he can destroy the computer.

After the room is clear, move over to the computer and press (SPACEBAR) while aiming at the keyboard. This downloads the files. When you are done, hold near the door for code Delta and assume a Cover posture facing the door. Now you must get your team back to the extraction zone. At Delta, head down the stairs, out the door you used to enter the dacha and along the balcony to 2-A, then rush to the extraction zone.

Downloading the computer files

Red Team

Red Team serves as a backup to Blue Team in case something goes wrong and the stealthy approach is blown.

At the beginning of the mission set the mode to Infiltrate so the team members will use their silenced pistols, then advance to 1-A and hold for code Alpha. When you receive it, rush to the door at 1-F. Hold there for code Charlie.

> **Tip** *Even if Blue Team makes it to the computer without alerting the rest of the dacha, you can kill a few more tangos as Red Team by lobbing frag grenades down the hall at 2-I. Since the leader of Red Team is carrying six frag grenades, you can cause a lot of destruction.*

After receiving Charlie, rush through the door and take out the tango in the garage area. Rush up the stairs and hold at 2-H for code Delta. Assume a Cover posture facing 2-I. Any reinforcements rushing toward Blue Team must pass through your sights.

At code Delta, head back down the stairs, out the door at 1-F and back to the extraction zone.

Notes

Take control of Blue Team at the start. After they kill the tango patrol at 2-C, give code Alpha which sends Blue team along the balcony and Red Team to the door to the garage. Issue code Bravo to send Blue Team into the dacha. Once the tango patrolling the area near the door is down, give code Charlie and send Red Team into the garage. After Blue Team has the computer files and there is no opposition, give code Delta and both teams will leave the dacha and head to the extraction zone.

Mission 11—Operation: Oracle Stone

02.12.02   0100
Smolensk

Mission Orders

Intelligence gathered from the raid on Vezirzade's dacha has revealed that Kutkin is assembling nuclear weapons at an unknown location in Siberia. Your mission is to infiltrate Kutkin's private spa, plant surveillance devices, and escape without being detected.

This is a pure recon mission. USE OF DEADLY FORCE IS NOT SANCTIONED ON THIS OPERATION. Your mission is to plant a bug and a surveillance camera in strategic locations within the house—both locations are clearly marked on your map. Any of your operatives can plant the devices, but be aware that if any of Kutkin's guards or guests detect your presence your mission will be a failure.

Objectives

1. Bug phone
2. Place camera
3. Get everyone back to the extraction zone

The spa contains several of Kutkin's guests—and their escorts. Stay out of their sight or they will call for the guards and the mission will be a failure.

Mission Data

DIFFICULTY LEVEL	TERRORISTS	HOSTAGES	OTHER
Recruit	7	0	2 Electronics
Veteran	9	0	2 Electronics
Elite	9	0	2 Electronics

Team Assignments

Blue Team

OPERATIVE	PRIMARY	SECONDARY	SLOT 1	SLOT 2	UNIFORM
Maldini	none	.45 Mark 23-SD	Heartbeat Sensor	Binoculars	Street 1 Light

Strategy

This mission, while tough, is not as difficult as the recon mission at the dacha was. You will only need a single operative to stealthily infiltrate the spa and plant the surveillance devices. Do not let anyone see you—including guests. If you are detected, the mission will be a failure. Once the bug and camera have been planted, get back out of the spa and to the extraction zone.

Blue Team

At the start of the mission, you are behind a small berm. Crouch and carefully move forward so you can see the garage at 1-C. Use the binoculars to watch for the tango patrolling there. As soon as he walks back into the garage, rush to 1-B, then to 1-C. Enter the door and close it behind you. Head up the stairs and wait at the top.

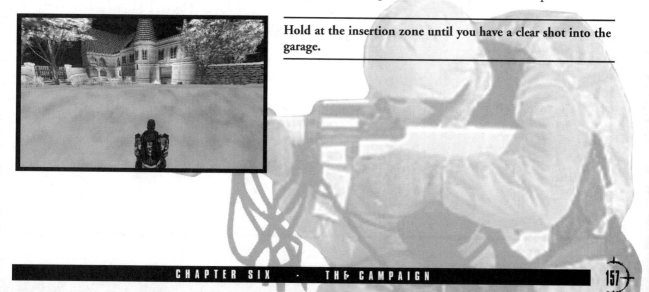

Hold at the insertion zone until you have a clear shot into the garage.

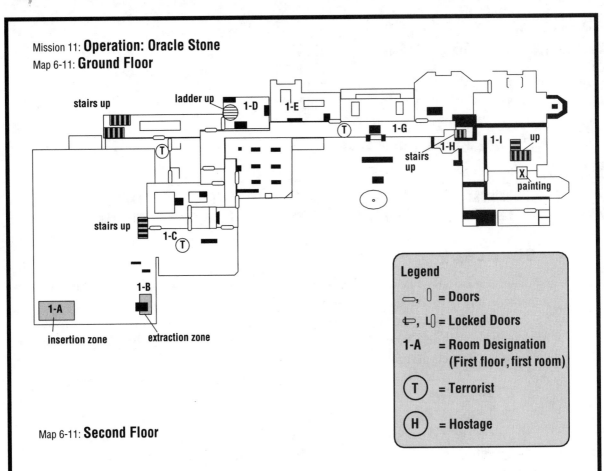

Mission 11: **Operation: Oracle Stone**
Map 6-11: **Ground Floor**

stairs up

ladder up

1-D

1-E

T

1-G

1-H

stairs up

1-I

up

X

painting

stairs up

1-C

T

1-B

1-A

insertion zone

extraction zone

Legend

⊂, ▯ = Doors

⇐, ▯ = Locked Doors

1-A = Room Designation
(First floor, first room)

(T) = Terrorist

(H) = Hostage

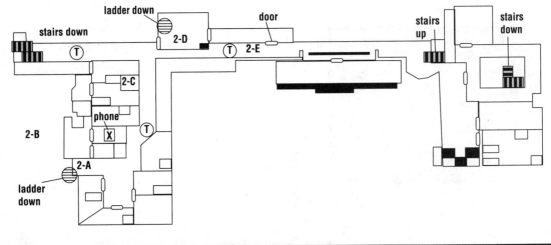

Map 6-11: **Second Floor**

ladder down

stairs down

2-D

door

stairs up

stairs down

T

2-E

T

2-C

phone

2-B

X

T

2-A

ladder down

The operative runs along the wall toward the garage. Notice the footprints he leaves in the snow.

Hold at the top of the stairs and check the area out with the heartbeat sensor. If a tango approaches the stairs, head back down.

Use the heartbeat sensor to locate persons in the hallway. When it is clear, rush toward room 2-B. Enter it and close the door. Walk over to the phone and plant the bug by pressing (SPACEBAR). Now walk back to the door. Before opening it, check for tangos. When it is clear, rush to 2-C and hide in this restroom. While moving, always use the heartbeat sensor and keep an eye on the mini-map for tangos. If one begins coming toward you, duck into the closest room and hide. By the time you get to 2-C, you will probably have to wait while a tango and a guest pass by heading toward 2-A. After they are out of sight and the guard at 2-E is walking away from you, rush across the hall and into room 2-D.

Plant the bug in the phone to complete one of your objectives.

The restroom serves as a good hiding spot if tangos begin coming toward you.

A ladder in this room leads back down to the ground floor. Climb down to 1-D and move through 1-E to the door at 1-F. If it's open, hug the wall near the hallway and wait for the tango patrolling the hall to walk outside. Now rush through 1-G to 1-H and hold up while you use the heartbeat sensor to check around. If it's clear, advance into 1-I and over to the painting at 1-J. Press SPACEBAR to plant the camera. Then quickly move to the door. You must move quickly in here. A guest and his companion will walk around the balcony above 1-I. If they see you, the mission is a failure.

Climb down the ladder to the ground floor.

Hold in this little alcove while checking the heartbeat sensor.

Quickly place the camera in the painting and get out of the library.

Check the map and when the tango at 1-G is heading outside again, rush to 1-F and then on to 1-D. Climb back up the ladder and make your way back to the stairs at 2-A, hiding in the rooms along the way if necessary. As you approach the stairs, be careful. A guest may come walking up as you are going down.

After placing the surveillance devices, get out of the spa as quickly and carefully as possible.

At the base of the stairs, use the heartbeat sensor to check the garage area. When the tango on patrol walks past you and away from the extraction zone, open the door and leave the spa. The mission will end a success as soon as you make it to the extraction zone.

Notes

The above walkthrough does not contain any Go codes. The codes are not necessary because you control the only operative.

Mission 12—Operation: Temple Gate

02.23.02   0230
Prague

Mission Orders

Terrorists have stormed the Prague Opera House during a command performance. The Czech president has been taken hostage, along with several prominent diplomats. Your mission is to liberate the hostages with minimal loss of life.

Luckily heartbeat surveillance has been established, so you've got accurate positions for both the hostiles and the friendlies. The hostages are in a very vulnerable position—they're being held right in the middle of the stage, exposed to potential gunfire from every direction. The terrorists are escorting them one at a time to the bathrooms, so be sure you don't miss anyone when you initiate the takedown.

Objectives

1. Rescue all hostages

Four hostages are being held inside the opera house.

Mission Data

DIFFICULTY LEVEL	TERRORISTS	HOSTAGES	OTHER
Recruit	17	4	None
Veteran	22	4	None
Elite	22	4	None

Team Assignments

Blue Team

OPERATIVE	PRIMARY	SECONDARY	SLOT 1	SLOT 2	UNIFORM
Chavez	UMP45SD	.45 Mark 23	Frag Grenade	Flashbang	Black Medium
Yacoby	UMP45SD	.45 Mark 23	Frag Grenade	Flashbang	Black Medium

Red Team

OPERATIVE	PRIMARY	SECONDARY	SLOT 1	SLOT 2	UNIFORM
Bogart	UMP45SD	.45 Mark 23	Frag Grenade	Flashbang	Black Medium
Burke	UMP45SD	.45 Mark 23	Frag Grenade	Flashbang	Black Medium

Green Team

OPERATIVE	PRIMARY	SECONDARY	SLOT 1	SLOT 2	UNIFORM
Price	UMP45SD	.45 Mark 23	Frag Grenade	Flashbang	Black Medium
Raymond	UMP45SD	.45 Mark 23	Frag Grenade	Flashbang	Black Medium

Gold Team

OPERATIVE	PRIMARY	SECONDARY	SLOT 1	SLOT 2	UNIFORM
Filatov	UMP45SD	.45 Mark 23	Frag Grenade	Flashbang	Black Medium
Rakuzanka	UMP45SD	.45 Mark 23	Frag Grenade	Flashbang	Black Medium

Strategy

This mission can be quite difficult. The hostages are being held out in the middle of the stage with tangos all around. A direct assault right from the start will only get all the hostages killed as well as your operatives. Tangos are on the stage, out among the lower seats, and in the balconies. They have created a kill zone. Therefore, you have to work at their defenses a bit at a time, working your way toward the hostages.

Blue Team

Blue Team leads the way for the other teams. Start at the insertion zone at the front of the opera house. Move to the door at point 1-A. Check the map to see where the two tangos inside 1-C are located. Then open the door and take them out as best you can without exposing yourself to fire. If they are in the corner of the room, use frag grenades to take them out. Make as much noise as necessary here—it won't carry to the rest of the building.

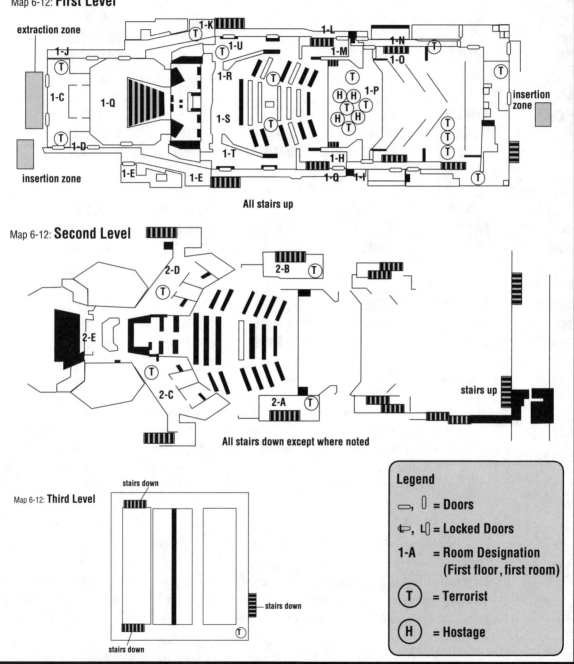

Mission 12: **Operation: Temple Gate**
Map 6-12: **First Level**

extraction zone

1-J

insertion zone

1-C

1-Q

1-D

1-E

1-E

insertion zone

1-K

1-U

1-R

1-S

1-T

1-L

1-M

1-H

1-Q

1-I

1-N

1-O

1-P

insertion zone

All stairs up

Map 6-12: **Second Level**

2-D

2-E

2-C

2-B

2-A

stairs up

All stairs down except where noted

Map 6-12: **Third Level**

stairs down

stairs down

stairs down

Legend

⬭, ▯ = **Doors**

⬅, ◖▯ = **Locked Doors**

1-A = **Room Designation**
(First floor, first room)

(T) = **Terrorist**

(H) = **Hostage**

The teams get ready to enter the building.

Blue Team takes out the tangos guarding the front entrance.

Once the entryway is clear, go to 1-D and wait until you see two tangos and a hostage coming toward you on the map. They are escorting a hostage to the restroom at 1-E. Wait until the hostage moves away from the two, then rush around the corner and take them both down. Leave the hostage in the restroom for now. He'll be safe there. Now head down the hall and hold at 1-G for code Bravo.

Blue Team takes out the tangos by the restroom.

At Bravo, order the rest of the team to hold by pressing ⒭, then crouch and open the door. Move into 1-H and up the stairs to 2-A. Take out the pistol and sidestep to the left along the wall while facing the tango. At soon as he's in sight, drop him, then quietly descend the stairs. Release the team hold and advance to 1-I to hold for code Delta.

A single operative sneaks up into one of the side balconies and takes out a tango sniper.

When Delta is issued, rush the stage and hold for code Alpha out by the hostages. Assume a Defend posture. At Alpha, escort the hostages to the extraction zone following the path you took in. Don't forget the hostage in the restroom on your way out.

Blue Team rushes out onto the stage.

Red Team

Red Team mirrors Blue Team's actions on the other side of the building. Red starts the mission at the insertion zone in the front of the opera house, moves to 1-B, and holds by the door for code Alpha.

At Alpha, rush into 1-C and then through the doors into hallway 1-J. Continue all the way down to 1-L and hold for code Charlie. When you receive it, leave the second operative behind on team hold and advance into 1-M and up the stairs to 2-B. Take out the tango in this balcony using the same tactic as Blue Team did. Return to 1-L, pick up the other operative, and continue through 1-N to 1-O. Hold here for code Delta.

At Delta, rush out onto the stage at 1-P and hold for Alpha. Assume a Defend posture and kill all tangos in sight. When you receive Delta, lead Blue Team out by going through 1-S, 1-F, 1-D, and out to the extraction zone.

Red Team, along with Blue, defends the hostages as they clear out the main hall.

Green Team

Green Team's task is to help clear out the second level and then assist in the assault on the stage. From the front insertion zone, advance to 1-A and hold for Alpha. At the Go code, rush into 1-C, then advance to 1-F and head up the stairs. Continue to 2-C and hold for code Charlie. Assume a Defend posture while holding.

Green Team clears out half of the upper level overlooking the main hall.

At Charlie, head down the stairs you came up and advance to 1-T. Hold there for code Delta. At Delta, rush into the main hall and hold at 1-S for code Alpha. Kill all tangos in sight and assume a Defend posture.

At Alpha, make your way back to the extraction zone using any path of your choosing.

Gold Team

Gold Team mirrors Green Team. From the front insertion zone, advance to 1-J and hold for Alpha. At the Go code, rush into 1-C, then advance to 1-K and head up the stairs. Continue to 2-D and hold for code Charlie. Assume a Defend posture while holding.

At Charlie, head down the stairs you came up and advance to 1-U. Hold there for code Delta. At Delta, rush into the main hall and hold at 1-R for code Alpha. Kill all tangos in sight and assume a Defend posture.

Gold Team picks off tangos in the main hall prior to the assault.

At Alpha, make your way back to the extraction zone using any path of your choosing.

Notes

For this mission, you should take command of Blue Team at the beginning. Take them through their assigned waypoints. Give code Alpha after you kill the two tangos escorting the hostage the restroom. This code will bring the other three teams into the building. When Blue Team gets to 1-G, give code Bravo and use ⓡ to leave the other operative behind while you clear out the balcony. After you get back downstairs, press ⓡ and the other operative will follow. When Blue Team gets to 1-I and holds, switch to Red Team and give code Charlie. This will send Green and Gold Teams down to their positions for the main assault. Use ⓡ again to leave the second operative behind while you neutralize the tango on the balcony. Head back down, release the hold, and continue to 1-O. When you get there, open the door and give code Alpha before rushing out to the stage. Take out the tangos on the stage first. When the main hall is clear, switch to Blue Team and give code Alpha. Escort all the hostages out to the extraction zone and the mission is complete.

All hostages and RAINBOW operatives are safe at the extraction zone.

Tip

This is a hard mission to plan because some of the tangos are in different positions each time you play. If you are having trouble during the final assault, try this strategy. While all teams are waiting for code Delta, take command of Green and Gold Teams and try to pick off the tangos patrolling in the aisles. You can kill them without the hostages being killed as long as no one sees your operatives or hears the shot. However, if anyone sees you, including the tango you are about to kill, the hostages are toast. The more tangos you can kill before the assault, the better your chances for success. You can also use Blue or Red Teams to help clear the stage in advance. Use the map to see where the tangos are facing and what each can see. If you are really good at picking off tangos without being seen, you can even try this mission with a single team or even a single operative.

Mission 13—Operation: Sargasso Fade

03.03.02   **1315**
Siberia

Mission Orders

Intelligence gathered from Kutkin's spa has located his nuclear weapon production facility in an abandoned radar base near the Siberian town of Svetlogorsk. Your mission is to raid the base and shut down its operation.

Your goal is to disable the communications center, cutting off the base from the outside world. Any member of your team can set the demolitions charge—the location where it should be placed is clearly marked on your map. The Russian guards are in radio contact with each other, so you'll need to take them out quickly before they can raise the alarm.

Note that this is the first stage of a two-stage mission. Be aware that you will not have the opportunity to assign new operatives between stages.

Objectives

1. Place the explosives

The communications center is accessed through a couple of narrow paths through the woods and mountains.

Mission Data

DIFFICULTY LEVEL	TERRORISTS	HOSTAGES	OTHER
Recruit	16	0	1 Explosive
Veteran	19	0	1 Explosive
Elite	20	0	1 Explosive

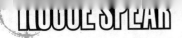

Team Assignments

Blue Team

OPERATIVE	PRIMARY	SECONDARY	SLOT 1	SLOT 2	UNIFORM
Chavez	UMP45SD	.50 Desert Eagle	Frag Grenade	Flashbang	Arctic 1 Medium
Arnavisca	UMP45SD	.50 Desert Eagle	Frag Grenade	Flashbang	Arctic 1 Medium
Sweeney	UMP45SD	.50 Desert Eagle	Frag Grenade	Heartbeat Sensor	Arctic 1 Medium

Red Team

OPERATIVE	PRIMARY	SECONDARY	SLOT 1	SLOT 2	UNIFORM
Walther	M-14	.50 Desert Eagle	Frag Grenade	Flashbang	Arctic 1 Medium
Loiselle	M-14	.50 Desert Eagle	Frag Grenade	Flashbang	Arctic 1 Medium
Filatov	M-14	.50 Desert Eagle	Breaching Charge	Heartbeat Sensor	Arctic 1 Medium

Green Team

OPERATIVE	PRIMARY	SECONDARY	SLOT 1	SLOT 2	UNIFORM
Johnston	PSG-1	.50 Desert Eagle	Frag Grenade	Primary Mag	Arctic 1 Medium
Maldini	M-14	.50 Desert Eagle	Frag Grenade	Flashbang	Arctic 1 Medium

Strategy

This mission is not too difficult. While the orders state to use stealth, the alarms will sound early in the mission no matter how careful you are. When they go off, remote activated mines will detonate and kill any of your operatives who are close by. The mines are marked on the mission map and show up as green on your in game map as well. Stay away from them. Everyone is an enemy in this mission, so don't worry about killing innocents.

Blue Team

Blue Team is your recon team for this mission. Their task is to clear a path and provide cover for the other teams. At the start of the mission, advance to 1-A, then continue to 1-C, and hold for code Alpha. While holding, assume a Cover posture facing 1-E. Two or three tangos on patrol will approach. Take them out before they fire at you.

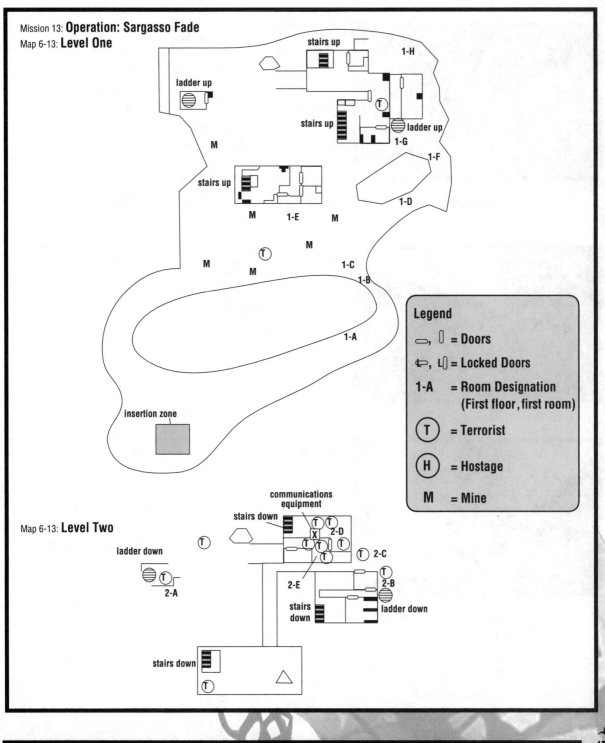

Mission 13: **Operation: Sargasso Fade**
Map 6-13: **Level One**

stairs up

1-H

ladder up

stairs up

T

ladder up

1-G

stairs up

M

1-F

M   1-E   M

1-D

M

M

1-C

T

1-B

M   M

1-A

insertion zone

Legend

⌐, ▯ = **Doors**

⇐, ▯ = **Locked Doors**

1-A = **Room Designation**
(First floor, first room)

(T) = **Terrorist**

(H) = **Hostage**

M = **Mine**

Map 6-13: **Level Two**

communications
equipment

stairs down

T T
X 2-D

T

ladder down

T   2-C

T

2-E   2-B

T   T

stairs
down

ladder down

stairs down

T

All teams move out at the start of the mission.

At Alpha, move to 1-D and then on to 1-F. Hold there for code Bravo. While holding, assume a Cover posture facing 2-C. Two tangos are near this point. Take them out as soon as they come into sight and cover Red Team as they climb up the ladder and advance to 2-C.

When you receive Bravo, move quickly to point 1-H and hold for code Delta. Again assume a Cover posture, this time facing 2-D. Neutralize any tangos who get too close to the windows. Stay in this position until the mission is complete.

Blue Team rushes to its next Cover position.

Blue Team attacks a tango through the window of the communications room.

Red Team

Red Team is your main assault team. It is armed with heavy rifles capable of punching through the body armor that most of the tangos are wearing.

At the start of the mission, advance to point 1-A and hold for code Alpha. When you receive this Go code, move quickly through 1-C, 1-D, and 1-F to 1-G. Climb up the ladder and hold at 2-B for code Bravo. Don't worry about tangos at the top of the ladder because Blue Team is covering you. While holding for Bravo, assume a Cover posture facing 2-C.

At Bravo, move carefully toward 2-C. As you peek around the corner, looking at 2-D, take out any tangos you can see through the window. If you set your mode to Recon, the operative carrying the heartbeat sensor will use it to show you where the tangos are located. This helps you aim your rifle before looking around a corner. After you shoot out the windows, throw a frag grenade inside to help clear out the room. You will be able to clear 2-D without too much of a problem. However, there are usually three tangos lined up at 2-E behind the metal door. If they do not move out of the door to come after you, move to 2-C and hold for Charlie. Assume a Cover posture facing the door to 2-E.

Red Team takes down a tango as he comes around the corner.

Red Team peeks around the corner and takes out tangos in the communications room.

Red Team throws a frag grenade through the window of the communications room to clear it out.

When you give Charlie, one of your operatives moves forward and places a breaching charge on the door. As soon as he backs away, it detonates. Any tangos right next to it will be killed while the rest are stunned. Take out any survivors then advance into 2-E and then to 2-D.

Walk over to the communications console and place the explosives. Once it is done, the mission is complete.

Red Team fires at the tangos as they come out the door at 2-E.

When the communications room is secure, plant the explosives to complete the mission objective.

Green Team

Green Team is your sniper team. Their job is to take out some of the tangos at long range and then cover the other teams.

At the start of the mission, move through 1-A to 1-B and hold for code Alpha. Assume a Snipe posture facing 3-A and take out the tango patrolling on top of the communications tower.

The sniper in Green Team gets ready to shoot the tango on top of the communications tower.

When you receive Alpha, move to 1-C and hold for Delta. Again assume a Snipe posture; however, this time face 2-A. Try to take out the tango in the guard house. He's very hard to see—only a portion of his body is visible through the firing ports. Stay in this position for the remainder of the mission.

Notes

The strategy for this mission is fairly simple and straightforward. Take command of Green Team at the beginning. When the tango on the communications tower is in sight, take the shot, then aim over at the guard house at 2-A. Once the tangos patrolling the grounds have been neutralized, give code Alpha and take command of Red Team.

As Red, you can advance all the way to the ladder and onto the top unmolested since Blue Team has cleared the way and is covering you. Once at 2-B, give code Bravo to send Blue Team to its next Cover position. Once 2-C and 2-D have been cleared, move to 2-C and hold for a bit to see if the tangos behind the door will come out after you. If not, give code Charlie to begin the breach of the door. When 2-E and 2-D are totally secure, rush in and plant the explosives to end the mission.

Mission 14—Operation: Majestic Gold

03.03.02 **1445**
Siberia

Mission Orders

Communication between the base and the outside world has been cut. Your final objective is to enter the main complex and use explosive charges to destroy the core of the bomb manufacturing facility. None of Kutkin's men must be allowed to leave the base.

Your mission is to destroy both the base's precision machine shop and its electrical generator, effectively putting Kutkin out of the bomb-making business. Any member of your team can set the demolitions charges—the locations of both targets are clearly marked on your map.

Note that this is the second stage of a two-stage mission. Be aware that you will be limited to the operatives you took on the prior mission.

Objectives

1. Place explosives

Your teams must enter a heavily guarded installation and plant two explosives to eliminate Kutkin's ability to build nuclear bombs.

Mission Data

DIFFICULTY LEVEL	TERRORISTS	HOSTAGES	OTHER
Recruit	19	0	2 Explosives
Veteran	22	0	2 Explosives
Elite	22	0	2 Explosives

Team Assignments

Blue Team

OPERATIVE	PRIMARY	SECONDARY	SLOT 1	SLOT 2	UNIFORM
Chavez	UMP45SD	.45 Mark 23-SD	Frag Grenade	Flashbang	Arctic 1 Medium
Arnavisca	UMP45SD	.45 Mark 23-SD	Frag Grenade	Flashbang	Arctic 1 Medium
Sweeney	UMP45SD	.45 Mark 23-SD	Frag Grenade	Heartbeat Sensor	Arctic 1 Medium

Red Team

OPERATIVE	PRIMARY	SECONDARY	SLOT 1	SLOT 2	UNIFORM
Walther	UMP45SD	.45 Mark 23-SD	Frag Grenade	Flashbang	Arctic 1 Medium
Loiselle	UMP45SD	.45 Mark 23-SD	Frag Grenade	Flashbang	Arctic 1 Medium
Maldini	UMP45SD	.45 Mark 23-SD	Frag Grenade	Heartbeat Sensor	Arctic 1 Medium

Green Team

OPERATIVE	PRIMARY	SECONDARY	SLOT 1	SLOT 2	UNIFORM
Johnston	PSG-1	.45 Mark 23-SD	Frag Grenade	Primary Mag	Arctic 1 Medium
Filatov	UMP45SD	.45 Mark 23-SD	Frag Grenade	Flashbang	Arctic 1 Medium

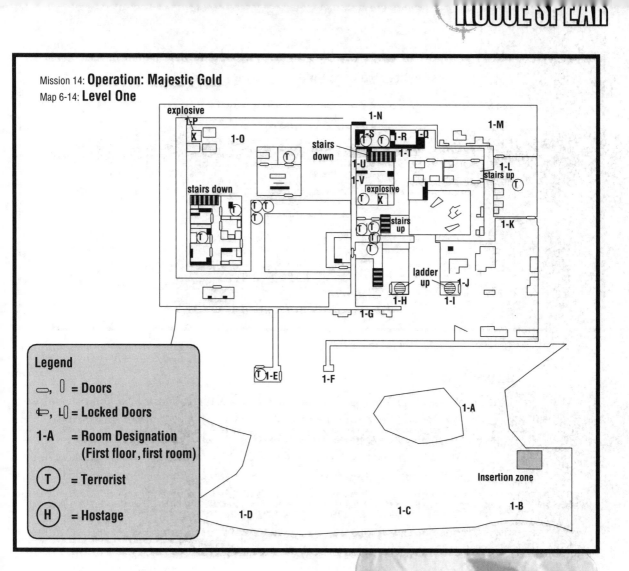

Mission 14: **Operation: Majestic Gold**
Map 6-14: **Level One**

Legend

⬭, ▯ = **Doors**

⬱, ⌐▯ = **Locked Doors**

1-A = **Room Designation**
(First floor, first room)

(T) = **Terrorist**

(H) = **Hostage**

Strategy

This mission is not very difficult as long as you move carefully and take your time. Your teams must infiltrate the former Soviet base. The outside contains mines that can be detonated remotely. Once inside, lots of tangos guard and patrol the installation. Most are former Russian soldiers, so they carry weapons that will penetrate body armor. You must place explosives on the generators and the machining tools. When both are accomplished, the mission is a success.

While you should take heartbeat sensors, do not rely totally on them. The heavy blast doors and thick outside walls can mask tangos on the other side. Even if the map shows the next room as clear, still use caution while entering.

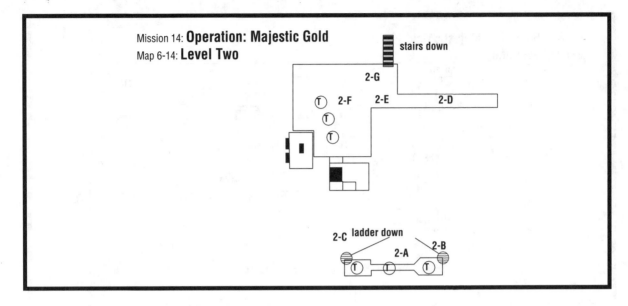

Mission 14: **Operation: Majestic Gold**
Map 6-14: **Level Two**

stairs down

2-G

2-F   2-E   2-D

2-C ladder down

2-B

2-A

Blue Team

Blue Team is one of your assault teams tasked with infiltrating the base and planting one of the explosives. At the start of the mission, move to point 1-A and hold for Alpha. Here you will be safe in case the mines are detonated.

At Alpha, rush to point 1-F and on to 1-B. Peek around the corner and take out the tango at 2-A between the two guard towers. If you can see the tangos inside the towers, take them out. Otherwise crouch and walk to 1-H, then across to 1-I and around the fence to 1-J. By moving right next to the towers, the tangos inside cannot see or fire at you. Don't bother going inside the towers to take out the tangos—it's usually too dangerous. Instead, advance to 1-K. Peek through the door and take out the tango inside. The heartbeat sensor may not work, so you have to use your eyes to locate him. Enter the room and hold at 1-L for Charlie.

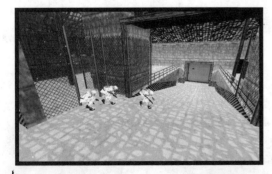

Blue Team sneaks past the guard towers.

Blue Team takes out the tango in room 1-L.

At Charlie, move forward through 2-D to 2-E. Near 2-F is a patrol of three tangos. Again, your heartbeat sensor may not detect them. They may hear you and come to investigate, so be ready to take them down. If after you halt, they do nothing for a while, throw a frag grenade around the corner. That should take at least one out and get the rest coming toward you. Once the area is clear, go through the door at 2-G and down the stairs to 1-Q.

Blue Team gets ready to take out the patrol of tangos at 2-F.

Enter room 1-R and approach the door to 1-S. Use the heartbeat sensor to see where the two tangos inside are located. Move to one side of the door, open it, and throw in a frag grenade. When the room is clear, go back to 1-Q, then on to 1-T. Be careful as you approach 1-U. Some tangos may have come to check out the sound of the grenade going off. Take them out and halt at 1-U. Again, use the heartbeat sensor. There are two scientists and a tango inside. The tango is usually crouched down near the machining tools in the far corner. Sidestep out in front of the door and it will open automatically. If you cannot see the tango, throw a flashbang over the console to where he is hiding and then rush in after it goes off. Neutralize the tango and then plant the explosive on the machining tools. Finally, hold at a point facing the door and hold for Delta. Assume a Cover posture aimed at the door. Stay here until the mission ends.

Blue Team prepares to clear 1-S by throwing in a frag grenade. Be sure to bounce it off the wall so it does not take out you as well.

With 1-V clear, Blue Team plants an explosive on the machining tools.

Red Team

Red Team is the other assault team that must infiltrate the base and plant an explosive. At the beginning of the mission, move to point 1-A and then hold for Alpha.

At Alpha, advance to 1-F, then on to 1-G. Hold for code Bravo. After receiving Bravo, move carefully around the corner to 1-H, then over to 1-I and on to 1-J. Use the same tactic as Blue Team to get past the guard towers. Move to 1-K and then on to 1-L. Hold here for code Alpha.

At the second code Alpha, move through 1-M to 1-N. From there, look toward the generators at 1-P. There may be a patrol of three tangos there or nearby. Carefully move forward while crouched. Take out any tangos as they appear. If you stay crouched in the pathways, the snowbanks will conceal you somewhat. Move to the generators at 1-P and place the explosives on them when the area is clear. Completing this second objective ends the mission.

Red Team takes out the tangos guarding the generators.

Use the snowbanks for cover by crouching while moving.

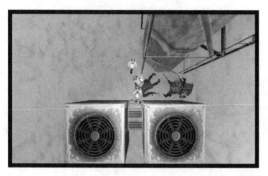

Red Team plants the explosive on the generators.

Green Team

Green Team is your sniper team and has a very limited but important role. They must clear the path for the other teams into the installation and prevent the mines from being detonated.

At the beginning of the mission, advance to 1-B, then crouch and head through 1-C to 1-D. Once there, hold for code Delta and assume a Snipe posture facing the guard room at 1-E. Take out the guard and remain here for the remainder of the mission.

Green Team takes out the tango guarding the front of the installation.

Notes

This mission is fairly straightforward. Begin in command of Blue Team. Move to the jump-off point at 1-A and wait for Green Team to get to 1-D. When their status changes to "Snipe-D" they are in position. Green Team tells you their sights are hot. This means the tango is in their sights. Press Y to release the sniper hold and you will hear a gunshot. Shortly thereafter, Green Team will let you know the tango is down.

Give code Alpha and take Blue Team through its rounds. Once you clear 1-L, give code Bravo to bring Red Team past the guard towers. Or you can put Blue Team on hold and take command of Red Team and move them past the towers if they are having trouble doing it themselves without getting killed. When Red Team is in 1-L, give code Charlie and take Blue Team all the way into the installation and plant the explosive on the machining tools. After they are holding in a Cover posture, take command of Red Team and lead them to the generators to plant the second explosive. When they are done, the mission will end a success.

Mission 15—Operation: Frost Light

03.19.02   1830
Smolensk

Mission Orders

Susan Holt and Lukyan Barsukov have been captured by Kutkin's men and taken to his spa near Smolensk. Barsukov is believed to possess valuable information about Vezirzade's nuclear capabilities. Your mission is to take the spa by force and free both Holt and Barsukov.

They are being held in separate wings of the estate. Their exact locations are unknown, but intel's best guess is marked on your map. Be aware that if Kutkin's men realize the spa is under attack both hostages will likely be moved to safer locations and, possibly, executed.

Objectives

1. Rescue Lukyan Barsukov
2. Rescue Susan Holt

Susan Holt has been kidnapped while she was meeting with Lukyan Barsukov. Rescue both of them.

Mission Data

DIFFICULTY LEVEL	TERRORISTS	HOSTAGES	OTHER
Recruit	22	2	None
Veteran	23	2	None
Elite	24	2	None

Team Assignments

Blue Team

OPERATIVE	PRIMARY	SECONDARY	SLOT 1	SLOT 2	UNIFORM
Price	MP5SD5	.45 Mark 23-SD	Frag Grenade	Flashbang	Black Medium
Hanley	MP5SD5	.45 Mark 23-SD	Frag Grenade	Flashbang	Black Medium
Murad	MP5SD5	.45 Mark 23-SD	Heartbeat Sensor	Flashbang	Black Medium

Red Team

OPERATIVE	PRIMARY	SECONDARY	SLOT 1	SLOT 2	UNIFORM
Noronha	MP5SD5	.45 Mark 23-SD	Frag Grenade	Flashbang	Black Medium
Rakuzanka	MP5SD5	.45 Mark 23-SD	Frag Grenade	Flashbang	Black Medium
Raymond	MP5SD5	.45 Mark 23-SD	Heartbeat Sensor	Flashbang	Black Medium

Green Team

OPERATIVE	PRIMARY	SECONDARY	SLOT 1	SLOT 2	UNIFORM
Novikov	UMP45SD	.45 Mark 23-SD	Frag Grenade	Flashbang	Euro Medium
Woo	UMP45SD	.45 Mark 23-SD	Frag Grenade	Flashbang	Euro Medium

Strategy

This mission takes place at the same location as mission 11, so you should already be familiar with the structure. It is imperative that you be as stealthy and quiet as possible. If any of the tangos are able to get off a shot, it will alert the rest and the hostages will be escorted to room 1-H and executed.

The nice part of this mission is that neither of the hostages have tangos in the same room with them. This makes the mission a bit easier. Two of your teams will infiltrate the structure and rescue the hostages while the third team provides cover outside.

Blue Team

Blue Team is the main infiltrating team. Not only will they clear a path into the spa, but they'll also rescue the hostages and escort them outside. At the start of the mission, advance to 1-C and hold for code Alpha.

At Alpha, rush into the carport at 1-D and go through the door at 1-E. Climb the stairs and pause at 2-A. Crouch at the corner and face 2-B. Two tangos are in the room and the door is open. Sidestep to the edge of the corner and quickly peek around the corner and let it rip with automatic fire. You must take out both tangos before either can get off a shot. When they are down, advance to 2-F and pause. Use the same tactic to

ROGUE SPEAR

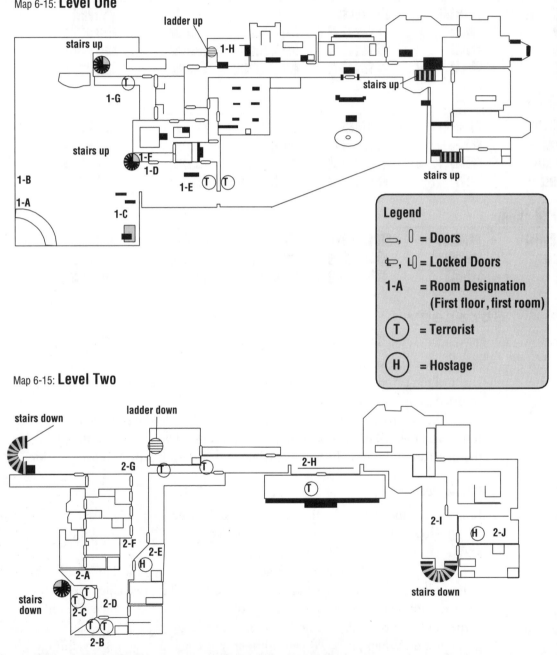

Mission 15: **Operation: Frost Light**
Map 6-15: **Level One**

ladder up

stairs up

1-H

1-G

stairs up

stairs up

stairs up

1-B

1-A

1-E

1-D

1-E

1-C

Legend

⌐, ▯ = **Doors**

◄, ⌐ = **Locked Doors**

1-A = **Room Designation**
(First floor, first room)

Ⓣ = **Terrorist**

Ⓗ = **Hostage**

Map 6-15: **Level Two**

stairs down

ladder down

stairs down

2-G

2-H

2-I

2-J

2-F

2-E

2-A

stairs down

2-D

stairs
down

2-C

2-B

peek around the corner toward 2-G and take out a couple of tangos as they go walking by. If you miss one of them, advance down the hall toward 2-G. Use the team's heartbeat sensor to locate the tango and neutralize him. You are all clear to go after Barsukov. Move through 2-H to 2-I. Open the door to 2-J and escort Barsukov out and back through the hall to 2-E. Inside you will find Holt. Hold for code Charlie.

Blue Team peeks around the corner by the stairs.

Blue Team takes out the two tangos is room 2-B with a burst of automatic fire.

Blue Team takes out a tango patrolling the hallway.

Blue Team locates and rescues Lukyan Barsukov.

At Charlie, escort both hostages down the stairs near 2-A, out into the carport, and to the extraction zone to complete the mission.

Red Team

Red Team supports Blue Team inside the spa. At the beginning of the mission, advance to 1-C and hold for code Alpha.

At Alpha, rush into the carport and through the door by 1-E. Continue up the stairs and hold at 2-A for code Bravo. When you receive Bravo, move to 2-D and hold for Charlie. Assume a Cover posture facing 2-F. Shortly after taking up the position, two tangos will try to leave room 2-C. Red Team is in perfect position to ambush them and take both out before they know what hit them.

Red Team ambushes a couple of tangos as they exit room 2-C.

At Charlie, lead Blue Team and the hostages back down the stairs, through the carport, and to the extraction zone.

Green Team

Green Team is your outside cover team. At the start of the mission, crouch and move to point 1-B and hold for Alpha. Assume a Cover posture facing 1-E. Take out the tango at 1-G as well as the one in the carport at 1-E. When a second tango enters the carport, wait until he advances toward you a bit before dropping him. This ensures that the body will fall out of sight of the tangos patrolling the main entrance of the spa.

Green Team takes out the tango patrolling at 1-G.

Green Team clears out the carport at a distance so the tangos inside cannot detect them.

At Alpha, move into the carport and hold at 1-F for code Delta. Assume a Cover posture facing 1-E. No tangos should come into your sights, but you are there to make sure the other teams have a safe escape route for the hostages. When you receive code Delta, return to the extraction zone.

Green Team covers the exit for the other two teams and the hostages.

Notes

For this mission, you should begin in command of Green Team. Once the three tangos outside have been neutralized, switch to Blue Team and give code Alpha. This sends all the teams into the carport and then on to their next waypoints. Take Blue Team through their tasks. After killing the two tangos in 2-B, give code Bravo to send Red Team to their Cover position before the other two tangos decide to come out.

Continue to lead Blue Team to rescue Barsukov and return to get Holt. Once you are escorting the two hostages out of Holt's room, give code Charlie to send Blue and Red Teams back to the extraction zone. Once they both clear the carport, give code Delta so Green Team can join the rest.

Both hostages make it safely to the extraction zone.

Mission 16—Operation: Hero Claw

03.22.02   2330
Moscow

Mission Orders

Information provided by Barsukov has revealed that Kutkin is planning to personally deliver the two remaining nuclear devices to Vezirzade's men in a train yard in Moscow. Your mission is to raid the site and prevent the exchange from taking place.

If either side gets wind that something's up they'll make a run for it. Be sure to guard all the escape routes and be prepared to take out any individuals or vehicles that try to leave the area—that's the only way to be completely sure you've got the bombs.

Objectives

1. Neutralize all terrorists

None of the tangos can be allowed to escape in the cars.

Mission Data

DIFFICULTY LEVEL	TERRORISTS	HOSTAGES	OTHER
Recruit	9	0	None
Veteran	14	0	None
Elite	16	0	None

Team Assignments

Blue Team

OPERATIVE	PRIMARY	SECONDARY	SLOT 1	SLOT 2	UNIFORM
Chavez	UMP45SD	.45 Mark 23-SD	Frag Grenade	Flashbang	Street 1 Medium
Arnavisca	UMP45SD	.45 Mark 23-SD	Frag Grenade	Flashbang	Street 1 Medium
Haider	UMP45SD	.45 Mark 23-SD	Frag Grenade	Heartbeat Sensor	Street 1 Medium

Red Team

OPERATIVE	PRIMARY	SECONDARY	SLOT 1	SLOT 2	UNIFORM
Walther	UMP45SD	.45 Mark 23-SD	Frag Grenade	Flashbang	Street 1 Medium
Loiselle	UMP45SD	.45 Mark 23-SD	Frag Grenade	Flashbang	Street 1 Medium
Filatov	UMP45SD	.45 Mark 23-SD	Frag Grenade	Heartbeat Sensor	Street 1 Medium

Green Team

OPERATIVE	PRIMARY	SECONDARY	SLOT 1	SLOT 2	UNIFORM
Narino	PSG-1	.45 Mark 23-SD	Frag Grenade	Primary Mag	Street 1 Medium
Pak	UMP45SD	.45 Mark 23-SD	Frag Grenade	Flashbang	Street 1 Medium

Strategy

In this mission, you must move fast, but quietly. If any of the tangos inside the building or by the cars learn of your presence, they will quickly take off. Therefore, you must eliminate the tangos patrolling the rail yard before they can fire a shot or run to inform the others inside. Once all of your teams are in position, take out the tangos as they head to the cars.

Blue Team

Blue Team is your main assault team and is tasked with covering the cars and killing all the tangos as they head to them. At the beginning of the mission, move out to 1-B, then on to 1-C and 1-E. There are four tangos in the rail yard. Two are near 1-C and the others by 1-E. If they see you, they often run toward the main building rather than engage you. All must be killed before they can warn the others. Continue through 1-F and hold at 1-G for Charlie.

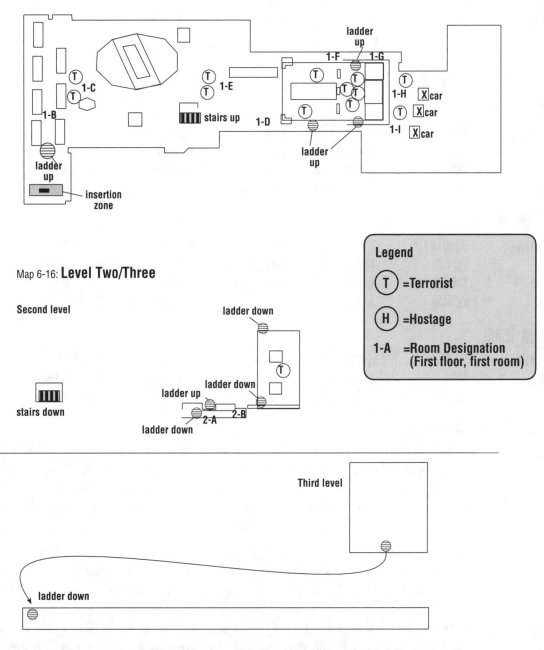

Mission 16: **Operation: Hero Claw**
Map 6-16: **Ground Level**

ladder up

1-F   1-G

1-C

1-E

1-B

stairs up

1-D

1-H   X car

X car

1-I   X car

ladder up

ladder up

insertion zone

Map 6-16: **Level Two/Three**

Second level

ladder down

stairs down

ladder down

ladder up

2-A   2-B

ladder down

Legend

T = Terrorist

H = Hostage

1-A = Room Designation
(First floor, first room)

Third level

ladder down

Blue Team takes out a tango in the rail yard.

Blue Team holds for code Charlie.

At Charlie, blitz toward 1-H, killing all the tangos in sight. If any make it to their cars and begin driving away, run after them while firing your submachine gun. You should be able to take out the drivers if the cars haven't gotten too far away. When all the cars are disabled and no one else is coming out, use the heartbeat sensor to locate tangos still inside and hunt them down. All must be eliminated to complete the mission.

Blue Team blitzes to the cars, taking out tangos as they appear.

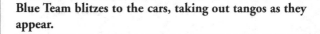

Blue Team runs after a fleeing car and kills the driver.

Blue Team covers the other two cars, ensuring they do not escape either.

Red Team

Red Teams task is to support Blue Team in clearing the rail yard and in covering one of the doors out of the building. At the start of the mission, advance to 1-A and hold for code Alpha.

At Alpha, blitz toward 1-D, taking out any tangos in sight. They will try to run for the door by 1-D, so you must stop them before they can warn the other tangos inside. From 1-D, advance around the outside of the building to 1-F and hold for Delta. Assume a Cover posture facing the door. Kill any tangos who try to come out of it.

Red Team holds for code Charlie.

Red Team takes out a tango as he tries to leave the building for the cars.

When you receive Delta, enter the door and clear out any remaining tangos inside.

Green Team

Green Team is your sniper team. They must cover one of the escape routes to the cars and eliminate all tangos who come into the sights of the sniper scope. At the start of the mission, advance to 1-A and hold for code Bravo.

At Bravo, blitz to 1-D and climb up the ladder. Move forward a bit to 2-A, then hold for code Charlie. When you receive Charlie, move to 2-B and hold for code Delta. Assume a Snipe posture and aim at 1-I, the car with the driver in it. Take out the driver and all tangos headed for the car. The second operative covers the sniper in case the tangos try to sneak up on the team. Stay in this position until the end of the mission.

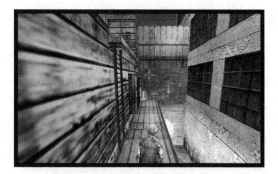

Green Team holds for code Charlie.

Green Team takes out the tangos as they head for the car.

Notes

For this mission, you should command Blue Team. Their task is one of the most important and also susceptible to change. As soon as you advance out past the first rail car, give code Alpha to send Red Team into the fight. Shortly thereafter, give code Bravo to send Green team to its jump-off point. When you get to 1-G, wait until all three teams are holding, then give code Charlie. Rush out and take out the tangos by the cars. Red Team covers your back while Green Team covers the far car. Concentrate on the tango by the car nearest you—he'll be the first to drive away. Once the area around the cars is clear, give code Delta and enter the building to mop up any stragglers.

Mission 17—Operation: Ebony Horse

03.24.02   0545
Azerbaijan

Mission Orders

Upon interrogation, one of Vezirzade's men has revealed the location of his base of operations in Azerbaijan. Your mission is to raid this stronghold, take Vezirzade into custody, and destroy the heart of his terrorist organization.

Vezirzade has made a few modifications to the original Persian fortress. His private quarters are in a bunker cut deep into the mountain behind the old fortifications—that's where you'll find him hiding. His guards are well-armed and fanatically loyal—expect them to defend the stronghold to the last man.

Objectives

1. Neutralize all terrorists

Vezirzade's fortress is well guarded.

Mission Data

DIFFICULTY LEVEL	TERRORISTS	HOSTAGES	OTHER
Recruit	17	0	None
Veteran	21	0	None
Elite	28	0	None

Team Assignments

Blue Team

OPERATIVE	PRIMARY	SECONDARY	SLOT 1	SLOT 2	UNIFORM
Chavez	Enfield L85A1	.50 Desert Eagle	Frag Grenade	Flashbang	Desert 1 Medium
Maldini	Enfield L85A1	.50 Desert Eagle	Frag Grenade	Flashbang	Desert 1 Medium
Yacoby	Enfield L85A1	.50 Desert Eagle	Frag Grenade	Heartbeat Sensor	Desert 1 Medium

Red Team

OPERATIVE	PRIMARY	SECONDARY	SLOT 1	SLOT 2	UNIFORM
Bogart	Enfield L85A1	.50 Desert Eagle	Frag Grenade	Flashbang	Desert 1 Medium
Burke	Enfield L85A1	.50 Desert Eagle	Frag Grenade	Flashbang	Desert 1 Medium
Rakuzanka	Enfield L85A1	.50 Desert Eagle	Frag Grenade	Heartbeat Sensor	Desert 1 Medium

Green Team

OPERATIVE	PRIMARY	SECONDARY	SLOT 1	SLOT 2	UNIFORM
Noronha	Enfield L85A1	.50 Desert Eagle	Frag Grenade	Flashbang	Desert 1 Medium
Sweeney	Enfield L85A1	.50 Desert Eagle	Frag Grenade	Heartbeat Sensor	Desert 1 Medium

Strategy

This mission has a lot of tangos to kill. While overall it is not as difficult as some of the previous missions, some choke points are difficult to get through. You need three teams for this mission. The first infiltrates the fortress through a subterranean passage, enters the citadel, and clears it out, while the other two teams enter through the front gate and clear out the walls and interior grounds. Control asks you to try to capture Vezirzade, but don't even try. He won't surrender, so you'll have to kill him.

Blue Team

Blue Team's task is to infiltrate the citadel inside the fortress and take out Vezirzade and his guards. At the beginning of the mission, head down the mountain path through 1-A, 1-B, and 1-C to the lower level and follow it all the way to the subterranean entrance at S-B. Hold there for code Alpha.

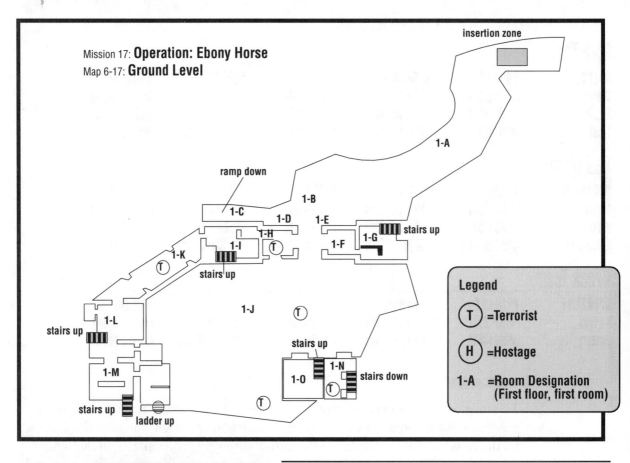

Mission 17: **Operation: Ebony Horse**
Map 6-17: **Ground Level**

insertion zone

1-A

ramp down

1-B

1-C

1-D   1-E

1-H

1-I   stairs up

1-F   1-G

1-K

stairs up

Legend

(T) =Terrorist

(H) =Hostage

1-A =Room Designation
(First floor, first room)

1-L

stairs up

1-J

stairs up

1-N

1-M   1-O   stairs down

stairs up

ladder up

Blue Team prepares to enter the subterranean passage to the citadel.

At Alpha, go inside and follow the corridor until you come to a locked gate at S-C. Use the team's heartbeat sensor to locate the three tangos in S-D. If they're out in the open, try throwing a frag grenade in their midst. You should be able to take out at least one of them. Check the map for their location again, then peek out around the corner of the gate and pick them off with your assault rifle. When the area is clear, go up the stairs at S-E to 1-N. You are now on the ground floor of the citadel. There may be a tango in this room or the next, so advance with caution. When 1-N and 1-O are clear, back up toward the door while aiming at the banister above. There are two tangos on the second level. Take them both out and then head up the stairs to 2-A. Hold here for code Bravo.

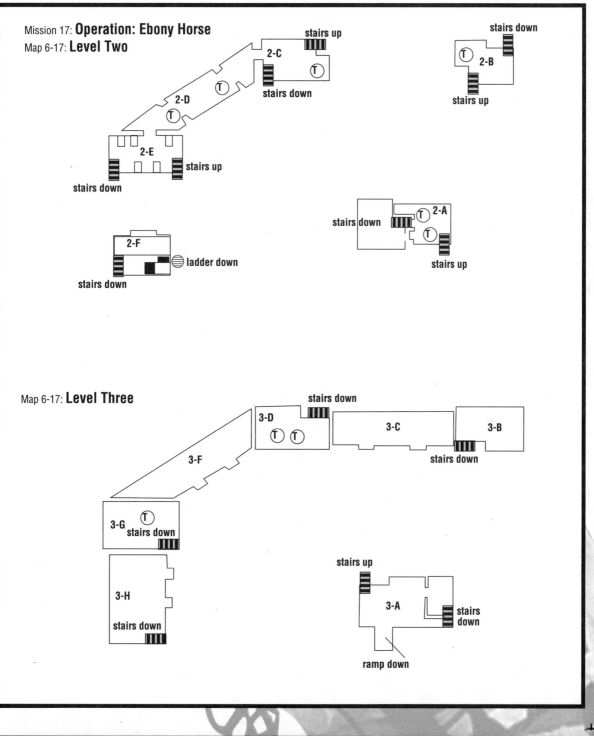

Mission 17: **Operation: Ebony Horse**
Map 6-17: **Level Two**

stairs up

2-C

stairs down

stairs down

2-B

stairs up

2-D

2-E

stairs up

stairs down

stairs down

2-A

stairs down

2-F

ladder down

stairs down

stairs up

Map 6-17: **Level Three**

stairs down

3-D

3-C

3-B

3-F

stairs down

3-G

stairs down

stairs up

3-H

3-A

stairs down

stairs down

ramp down

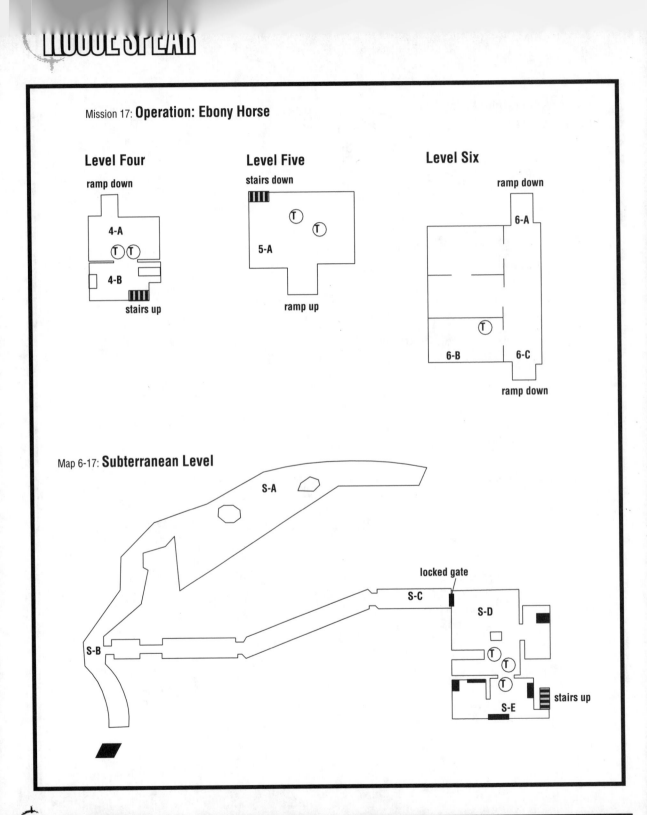

Mission 17: **Operation: Ebony Horse**

Level Four

ramp down

4-A

4-B

stairs up

Level Five

stairs down

5-A

ramp up

Level Six

ramp down

6-A

6-B   6-C

ramp down

Map 6-17: **Subterranean Level**

S-A

locked gate

S-C

S-D

S-B

S-E   stairs up

Blue Team takes out the three tangos at 2-E.

Blue Team sneaks into the citadel and neutralizes the two tangos at the top of the stairs in 2-A.

When you receive Bravo, advance up to 3-A. It should be clear. Move over by the ramp, crouch, and peek around the corner. A couple of tangos should come into view after a bit. Take them both out, then head up the stairs behind you, which take you to 5-A where two more tangos are waiting. Clear this room and go up the ramp to 6-A. Vezirzade retreats to 6-B after you shoot the two tangos from 3-A. Use the team's heartbeat sensor to locate him, then throw a flashbang into the room. Take out Vezirzade if he runs out, otherwise go in after him. Return to the ground floor and hold for Delta.

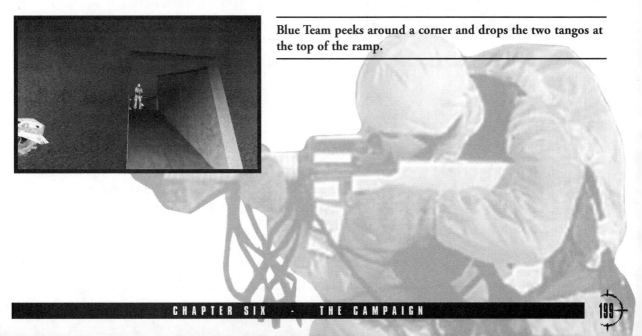

Blue Team peeks around a corner and drops the two tangos at the top of the ramp.

Vezirzade runs out of a room on level six after Blue Team throws a flashbang inside.

At Delta, exit the citadel and help clear out the grounds at 1-J.

Red Team

Red Team is tasked with helping to clear out the walls and fortress grounds. At the start of the mission, advance through 1-A and hold at 1-B for code Alpha. Assume a Cover posture facing the gate of the fortress.

At Bravo, move to 1-E and hold for code Bravo. When you receive this code, blitz to 1-F. Take out the tango above the door while you're moving. Enter 1-G and climb up the stairs to 2-B. Take out any tangos there and then climb up the stairs to 3-B. Hold near the door for code Charlie. Assume a Cover posture facing 3-C.

Red and Green Teams hold at the gate to the fortress, ready to begin the assault.

When code Charlie is given, move across 3-C to 3-D and then 3-F. Clear these areas of tangos before returning to the stairs in 3-B. Go back down the stairs to the ground level and then hold by the door at 1-H leading to 1-J. Hold here for code Delta. At Delta, open the door, go out into the yard at 1-J, and take out any tangos you see.

Red Team clears out the top of the wall.

Green Team

Green Team's job in this mission is to clear out the walls of the fortress. At the start of the mission, follow Red Team to 1-B and hold for Alpha. Assume a Cover posture facing the gate. When you receive Alpha, advance to 1-D and then hold for Bravo.

At Bravo, rush to 1-H, enter 1-I, and then climb the stairs. Take out the tango at 2-C, then hold for code Charlie. Assume a Cover posture facing the doorway to 2-D.

Green Team rushes up to 2-C and takes out the tango guarding the gate to the fortress.

When you receive Charlie, advance through 2-D to 2-E and then go up the stairs to 3-G. Clear out this room, then 3-H, before heading down the stairs to 2-F. Clear it out, then continue down the stairs to 1-M. Head back through the wall to 1-I and hold for Delta. At Delta, join Red Team in clearing out the grounds at 1-J.

Green Team walks through the wall taking out every tango it comes across.

Notes

For this mission, command Blue Team. The other teams can usually take care of themselves. Lead Blue Team to the subterranean passage. When you get to the locked gate, give code Alpha. After you have cleared out the second floor of the citadel, give code Bravo to send Red and Green Teams into the fortress. When you reach the fifth level, give code Charlie so the other two teams can begin clearing the walls. When the citadel is secure and Blue Team is back at the ground floor, give code Delta and all three teams will pour out in 1-J and mop up any remaining tangos. If the mission doesn't end, you'll have to take a team through the fortress again and find the tangos you missed earlier.

Mission 18—Operation: Zero Gambit

Mission Orders

Maxim Kutkin and a small group of his followers have seized the Cherkasy nuclear power plant in Ukraine. They are threatening to shut off its cooling system, triggering a reactor meltdown. Your mission is to retake the plant and neutralize the terrorists before they can initiate this event.

There are two control rooms where the meltdown can be initiated—the locations of both are clearly marked on your map. Kutkin's men appear to have radios and check in with each other on a regular basis, so time your assault carefully to avoid tipping them off. Some plant workers may still be in the area, so watch out for innocent bystanders. Be aware that interference from the generating equipment may disable your heartbeat sensors in some areas of the plant.

Objectives

1. Prevent the terrorists from triggering a nuclear meltdown
2. Neutralize all terrorists

You must stop Kutkin before he can cause this reactor to melt down.

Mission Data

DIFFICULTY LEVEL	TERRORISTS	HOSTAGES	OTHER
Recruit	15	0	2 Triggers
Veteran	29	0	2 Triggers
Elite	28	0	2 Triggers

Team Assignments

Blue Team

OPERATIVE	PRIMARY	SECONDARY	SLOT 1	SLOT 2	UNIFORM
Chavez	MP5/10SD	.45 Mark 23-SD	Frag Grenade	Heartbeat Sensor	Black Medium
Johnston	Walther WA2000	.45 Mark 23-SD	Primary Mag	Heartbeat Sensor	Black Medium

Red Team

OPERATIVE	PRIMARY	SECONDARY	SLOT 1	SLOT 2	UNIFORM
Petersen	Walther WA2000	.45 Mark 23-SD	Primary Mag	Heartbeat Sensor	Black Medium
Maldini	MP5/10SD	.45 Mark 23-SD	Frag Grenade	Heartbeat Sensor	Black Medium

Green Team

OPERATIVE	PRIMARY	SECONDARY	SLOT 1	SLOT 2	UNIFORM
Bogart	M4 Carbine	.45 Mark 23-SD	Frag Grenade	Frag Grenade	Black Medium
Yacoby	M4 Carbine	.45 Mark 23-SD	Frag Grenade	Heartbeat Sensor	Black Medium

Gold Team

OPERATIVE	PRIMARY	SECONDARY	SLOT 1	SLOT 2	UNIFORM
Price	M4 Carbine	.45 Mark 23-SD	Frag Grenade	Frag Grenade	Black Medium
Murad	M4 Carbine	.45 Mark 23-SD	Frag Grenade	Heartbeat Sensor	Black Medium

Strategy

This is the most difficult mission of the entire game. Kutkin and one of his lieutenants are located at opposite ends of the plant. Either one can trigger a meltdown. In addition, the two are in radio contact with each other and some of the guards. Kutkin is hub of the radio network. His lieutenant must check in with him on a regular basis or he will start the meltdown. There are also four other patrols that check in with Kutkin.

Mission 18: **Operation: Zero Gambit**
Map 6-18: **Level One**

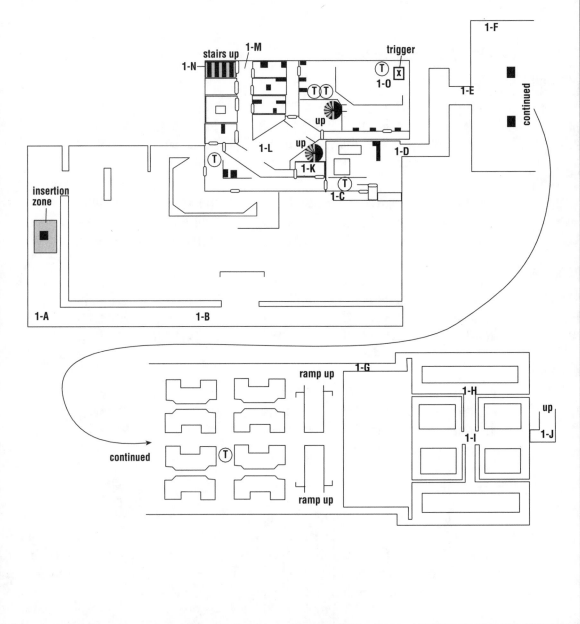

Mission 18: **Operation: Zero Gambit**
Map 6-18: **Level Two**

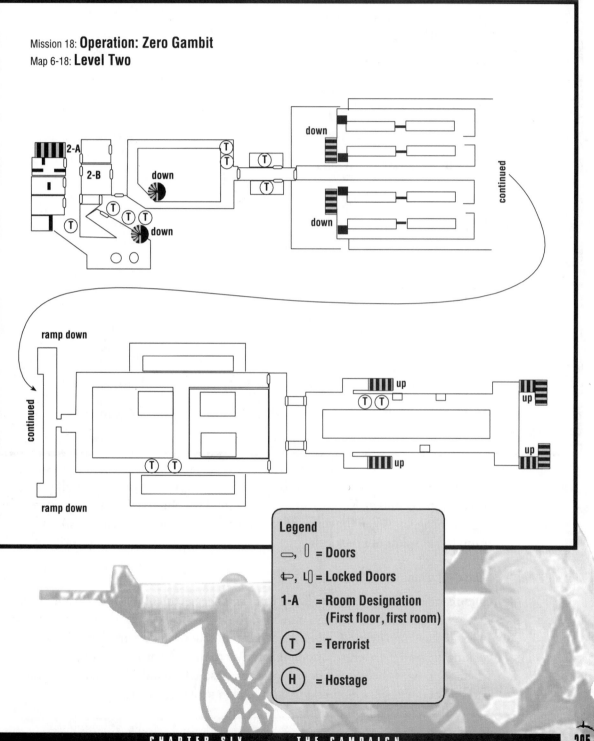

2-A

2-B

down

down

down

down

down

continued

continued

ramp down

up

up

up

up

ramp down

Legend

⬭, ▯ = Doors

⬅, ▯ = Locked Doors

1-A = Room Designation
(First floor, first room)

(T) = Terrorist

(H) = Hostage

Mission 18: **Operation: Zero Gambit**
Map 6-18: **Level Three**

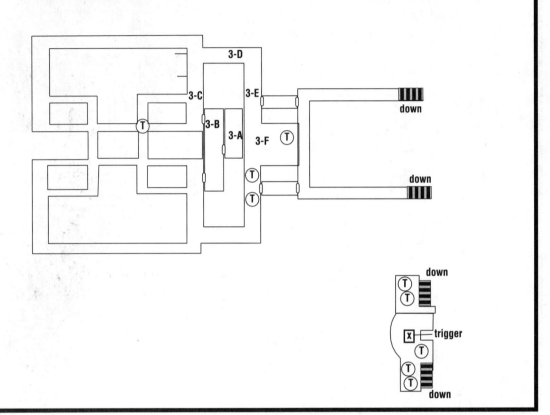

As a result, you must infiltrate one team into the power plant without being detected and eliminate Kutkin, then send a second team in to take out the lieutenant at the other trigger. When the threat of meltdown has been averted, send in two more teams to help clear out the plant.

Blue Team

Blue Team is tasked with neutralizing Kutkin at the far end of the power plant. Start the mission by crouching down and moving through 1-A to 1-B. Use the heartbeat sensor to locate the tango near 1-C. If he is not outside, wait until he comes out, checks the parking lot, and then returns inside. Then rush to the door at 1-C. Again, check to see where the tango is before entering. If necessary, use 1-K to hide. You cannot kill the parking lot tango since he checks in with Kutkin on a regular basis.

Advance to 1-D and then on to 1-E. Move through 1-F to 1-G. Your heartbeat sensors will not work very well in this area, so use your eyes. A single tango patrols down here. If necessary, you can kill him—he's not on the radio network. However, if he fires at you, the mission will fail.

From 1-G, move to 1-H then 1-I. Watch out for the tangos patrolling the catwalks above. When it is clear, rush to the stairs at 1-J and climb them all the way to the top to 3-A. Move out into 3-B. Use the heartbeat sensor to locate the tango patrolling the catwalks around 3-C. Take him out silently and then move to 3-D. Use the heartbeat sensor to detect the two tangos patrolling 3-E. If they start moving toward you, return to 3-C. After they turn around, go after them and shoot them in the back before they can sound an alarm.

Sneak up behind the patrol in the hallway and take them out before they can alert anyone else.

You must now approach 3-F. There is a tango kneeling down by the window. Peek around a corner and take him out. Move to a point near the window and hold for code Delta. Assume a Snipe posture, aiming at 3-G. As soon as Kutkin is in your sights, press [Y] to order the sniper to fire. After firing, move away from the window and set up in Cover posture facing the hallway while holding for a second Delta.

A single tango is guarding the window overlooking the reactor.

Blue sniper takes aim across the reactor.

Kutkin is in the crosshairs.

Red Team

Red Team is the other sniper team tasked with taking out Kutkin's lieutenant in the front part of the power plant. At the start of the mission, move to 1-A and hold for code Alpha. Assume a Cover posture facing away from the building. This will ensure that the team does not fire at tangos patrolling the parking lot.

At Alpha, rush to 1-B and then 1-C. Since Kutkin is dead, go ahead and quietly take out any tangos you come across, including the one at 1-C. Enter the building at 1-C, then continue to 1-L and then to 1-M. Climb up the stairs at 1-N. Use caution when stepping out into 2-A—a tango patrols the hallway. Enter 2-B and close the door behind you. Climb up on the table and aim down at the lieutenant at 1-O. All you can see is his head when you are standing. If crouched, you won't be able to see him at all. Take him out, then move off the table and hold in the corner of the room for code Delta. Assume a Cover posture facing the window and the door.

Red Team takes out a tango as it rushes through the office part of the power plant.

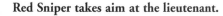

Red Sniper takes aim at the lieutenant.

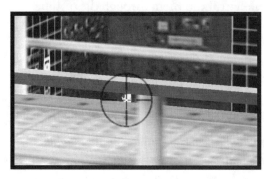

The head of the lieutenant is all that is visible. However, that's all the sniper needs.

Green Team

Green Team is one of the assault teams tasked with clearing out the power plant. By the time they enter, noise will not be a problem, so take along some heavy assault rifles. At the insertion zone, hold for code Bravo. Assume a Cover posture facing away from the plant so the team does not fire prematurely.

At Bravo, move toward the power plant and enter at 1-C. Neutralize any remaining tangos in the office part of the power plant—there are three upstairs and a few in the control room.

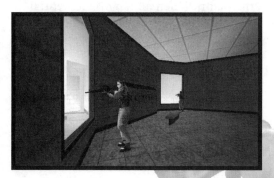

These tango snipers on the upper floor of the office complex cover the accessways to the control room.

Gold Team

Green Team is the other assault team tasked with clearing out the power plant. At the insertion zone, hold for code Bravo. Assume a Cover posture facing away from the plant so the team does not fire prematurely.

At Bravo, move to the plant and enter through the door at 1-C. Continue to 1-E and hold for code Charlie. When you receive Charlie, move into the back part of the plant. Be sure to clear both the ground floor as well as the catwalks. Continue all the way to 3-G. Clear out both rooms to the side of 3-G and your mission should be complete.

Green Team clears out the back part of the power plant.

Notes

As mentioned earlier, this is an extremely difficult mission. The first part of it is similar to the recon missions where you had to avoid being detected. Take command of Blue Team at the start. Lead them through the turbines and such to 3-F. When you get there and clear it out, the sniper should automatically take up a Snipe posture. Press [Y] to order the sniper to fire. After Kutkin is hit, give code Delta so Blue Team can move away from the window. The tangos down in the reactor room start shooting at you. Once Blue Team is covering the halls, switch to Red Team.

Give code Alpha, then head into the plant. Move as quickly as possible. Kill any tangos in your way before they can get off a shot and warn others. Take out the lieutenant, then take cover.

Tip *When clearing the plant, use the maps to see the general area the tangos patrol.*

Now switch to Green Team and give code Bravo. Both Green and Gold Teams enter the plant. Clear out the office complex and then give code Bravo and take Gold Team through the rest of the plant. When all tangos are neutralized, the mission is a success.

CHAPTER SEVEN
MULTIPLAYER AND OTHER TYPES OF GAMES

While the campaign game is a major part of — *Rogue Spear,*— the action does not end when you kill Kutkin and save the Ukraine. *Rogue Spear* contains one of the best multiplayer systems available, using the same realistic model from the campaign game. In addition, you can play on any of the carefully crafted maps. During the campaign missions, you usually moved very quickly through the maps to your objective. However in these other types of games, you can use each and every little room, corner, and balcony.

In addition to multiplayer games, you can also play missions as an individual. Once you have completed a campaign mission, you can go back to that map and play it again in Lone Wolf or Terrorist Hunt modes. This basically triples the number of single-player missions from 18 to 54! After you complete the campaign, the game is not even close to over.

These additional games let you try the campaign maps without the former objectives. The 747 might be more fun to assault when you are not worried about the hostages.

Multiplayer Games

The multiplayer games allow you to use your skills against or with other players over a LAN or on the Internet. If you are looking for other players, use *Rogue Spear*'s ability to go to the MSN or MPlayer sites and find games. In addition, there are many *Rainbow Six* clans that will now be playing *Rogue Spear*. You can find links to some of these at Red Storm Entertainment's website at *www.redstorm.com* or by using an Internet search engine.

You can either join a game or create one yourself. The player creating the game is called the host. The host determines the type of game played as well as several options for the game. At the setup screen, you can divide into teams and equip your operatives.

Unlike some other multiplayer games, death is final during a game. When your operative is killed, he or she does not immediately respawn so you can begin playing again. Instead, you must wait until the current game is over and a new game is started to get back in the action. However, you can still watch the game in progress as an observer. While you cannot communicate with the living, you can see what is going on.

There are two types of multiplayer games—adversarial and cooperative. In adversarial games, all of the players are divided into teams and play against each other. On the other hand, cooperative games put all players on the same team for the purpose of completing the campaign missions.

Adversarial Games

There are 11 different types of adversarial games. Each has its own objectives, which can vary from last man standing to last team standing or even offense vs. defense. Each requires a different style of play. Try them all.

Survival

Survival is a free-for-all game in which the objective is to be the last person left alive in a level. No one should be on anyone else's team.

Team Survival

Team survival is similar to survival. Each person must select one of two teams (Blue or Gold) to join. The winning team is the last one with at least one team member left alive.

Scattered Teams

Scattered teams is team survival except the teams start out scattered all over the map instead of starting out together in team bases. Bases are visible as in standard team survival. As in normal team survival, the game ends when only one team has members still active, or if neither team has anyone still active.

Terrorist Hunt

Terrorist hunt is a team survival game in which terrorists are scattered throughout the level. In addition to the team survival victory condition of being the last team with a member standing, your team can win if it kills more than half of the terrorists on the level (kill 16 terrorists because there are 30 on the level). The terrorists are randomly placed on the level.

Scatter Hunt

Scatter hunt is the terrorist hunt game except members of a team start out scattered over the map

Assassination

Assassination is a team survival variant where each team has a general who they must defend from the other team. In addition to winning by killing the entire other team, a team can achieve victory by killing the other team's general.

Scatter Assassination

Scatter assassination is the assassination game except teams are spread out over the map; each team must find and then defend its general.

Save Your Base

Save your base is another team survival variant. In this version, each team has a base that it starts separate from. The team must race to this base and disarm the bomb there before the other team finds its base and disarms that bomb.

Double Bluff

Double bluff is a team survival game with the added objective of trying to get both hostages back to your base. Each team starts in its base with a hostage. If either team kills a hostage, that team loses.

Stronghold

Stronghold is a team survival game in which the Gold Team must stop the Blue Team from entering Gold Team's base. If the Blue Team gets a team member into the Gold Base for at least three seconds, then the Blue Team wins. If either team can successfully eliminate all the members of the other team, then that team wins.

Double Stronghold

Double stronghold games are the same as stronghold games except that both sides defend their bases. So, in addition to the above victory conditions, if the Gold Team can get a person into the Blue Team's base for at least three seconds, then they will win.

The Maps

You can use 19 different maps for multiplayer *Rogue Spear* games. Each map can be played against the other team alone or tangos can be included to spice up things. Tangos act as a third team hostile to all other teams. Let's take a look at the different maps you can use.

City Street Large

This map is from the training missions. However it has a lot of windows from which to snipe as well as great hiding spots for setting up ambushes.

Kill House Two Story

This is another training map. It's rather small, so it's not good for lots of players. However, it can be useful for training your team. Use it for offense vs. defense type of games.

Kill House Double

This map has two two-story Kill Houses. It is great for double bluff or double stronghold games because each team has the same type of base.

The Met

The Metropolitan Art Museum offers several balconies overlooking the ground floor. These are great for sniping. Watch out for all the open spaces. These can be kill zones if the other players position their operatives correctly.

Oil Tanker

This map has is great for close-quarters battles as it has lots of small rooms and confined space. However, there is also a very big open space out on the deck that you can cover with snipers.

Desalination Plant

With two large buildings, this map is good for double bluff or double stronghold games. Each building has catwalks that provide good coverage of the ground floor. In addition, each building has a limited number of entrances, most of which can be covered from a distance.

Ruined City

This is an awesome map for multiplayer games, especially with lots of players. Besides the main tower, there are several other great sniper positions. In addition, the many holes in the walls of the buildings serve as firing ports, giving your operatives cover while allowing them to fire at the enemy.

747

If you thought the campaign mission with the 747 was tough, you'll find this just as tough for multiplayer games without having to worry about hostages. This map is best for offense vs. defense type games. The confined space of the airliner allows for some up-close combat.

Chalet

You can choose to play this map either during the spring or in the winter with snow on the ground outside. It combines good indoor and outdoor play. Several windows can be used to shoot through, so use them. During winter games, remember that your operative leaves tracks in the snow and then wet footprints inside for a distance. Be careful to not leave a path for the enemy to follow. Or, leave a path to your ambush.

TV Station

This map can be a lot of fun. There are catwalks over most of the ground floor and several dark rooms in which you can hide and set up ambushes.

Docks

This map is better for smaller games because there isn't a lot of room to maneuver. While sniper positions are limited, there are several great hiding spots for ambushes and other surprises.

Nuke Storage Site

This is another good map for large games. There are several entrances and also some great spots for setting up kill zones. The firing ports near the main building can be great for the defender, but are useless against attacks from the sides.

Spa

This map can also be played during spring or winter. The building is filled with lots of small rooms and long hallways. There are also some balconies.

Opera House

The main hall out in front of the stage contains several different balconies and can lead to battles between snipers. In addition, the halls on either sides with small rooms connecting can lead to close-quarters battles as well.

Siberian Base I

This map with the communications center has a lot of open ground outside with small buildings offering close-quarters battle.

Siberian Base II

This map combines the openness of outdoor play with the confines of indoor play. It offers a lot of cover and has good places for setting up ambushes.

Train Yard

The outdoor section of this map offers some great sniper perches as well as good cover for moving behind. While the building is small, it can be defended fairly easily. Don't forget about the skylight on the roof.

Castle

This map is great for large games. Snipers can cover the outdoors area from a number of positions. The main citadel provides a great base because its few entrances can be easily covered.

Nuke Power Plant

This is a huge map and awesome for the games with the most players. While there is a lot of area to cover, there are several choke points that can be more easily defended than the large rooms.

Cooperative Games

In cooperative multiplayer, as you might expect, players work together to complete one of the campaign game's 18 missions. This offers an exciting new way to play the single player campaign missions. However, before you do, use the training facilities to hone your skills and learn to work as a team. I suggest going through the Kill Houses together before embarking on any mission.

The host may select from several options. Players may choose to be any of the RAINBOW operatives, but there can be only one of each personality. A chat window on the Game Creation screen facilitates mission planning. Use it to ensure that team operatives carry appropriate equipment and know their roles in the mission. When everyone's ready, the host can start the mission. Players begin at one of the insertion zones.

Tactics for Multiplayer Games

While all the tactics used for the campaign missions still apply to multiplayer games, there are several additional tactics to use against other players.

Note *I would like to thank Ryan Lynch (Orion Blade), Danny Rentschler (Snowlord), Mike Putnam (Blammo), Jonathan Raflowski (Noj), Paul Jergusen (Kaotic Demeanor), and Jason Wyatt (Darkpup) for their tips and tactics for multiplayer games. Watch out for them if playing against team Warbones..*

Communications

One of the most important parts of team play is communicating with the other players on your team. While you can type out messages using the chat function, *Rogue Spear* is a fast-paced game and the time it takes to type out a message is often too long—you may be killed while typing. Therefore, use the Bound Keys. They allow you to pre-program 10 different messages, which can be sent with a keystroke. These messages are sent audibly so your team members don't have to take their eyes away from their gun sights. You should plan the game before it starts and use the various Bound messages to report in or order an assault to begin.

Teamwork

Teamwork is among the most important tactics in *Rogue Spear*. If you have enough players, group them in pairs or even larger teams. Two people see twice as much and can accomplish different tasks, making the team more effective.

While one team member checks the other side of the door with the heartbeat sensor, the other covers the door in case the enemy decides to come through.

My favorite such tactic involves using the heartbeat sensor: the leader carries a weapon while the second or other team member uses the heartbeat sensor to locate enemies. Everything the sensor picks up is relayed to all team members, so it becomes unnecessary for each to use his or her own.

> **Tip** *Each team should have at least one heartbeat sensor. Only one team member needs to use it, and all players on that team can see what the sensor detects.*

A multiperson team also is useful for breaching a door or clearing a room. One opens the door as the other tosses a frag grenade or flashbang and the rest cover the first two. All then run through the doorway and spread out, going left and right. This prevents anyone getting shot in the back because he or she looked left when the tango was right. (Practice at the training ranges will help teams develop the good timing such tactics require.) Other players also can help prevent surprises from the rear.

While one opens a door, the rest of the team gets ready to fire at anyone on the other side.

Spacing between team members also is something to think about. You want to stay close enough to support one another, but not so close that a single automatic burst could take you both out. Outdoors, you can space team members far enough apart that they can support one another without a single grenade killing both.

Keep a proper spread between your team members. They should be close enough to support one another, but not so close that all are killed by a single grenade.

Every team must have a leader. In this game, you lead from the front, so the leader is usually the point man. In large games where each side has multiple teams, designate an overall commander to help coordinate the actions of the various teams.

Movement

When you're outdoors, it's important to spread out and cover all the angles of threat. An open window, door, corner, upstairs balcony, or any other place an enemy could hide represent points of threat and must be watched. Also, spreading out the team while in the open provides fewer targets of opportunity for the enemy.

When you're indoors, it's important to keep your teammates close. By staying close to the man in front of you, you don't get lost. If you get lost, then everyone behind you is lost. Confusion sets in, and you usually die. If you're in position number two, keep the point man in sight. If you're in position number four, keep the number three man in sight. Staying close to the man in front of you does have its disadvantages though. For instance, frag grenades thrown by the enemy or a burst of automatic fire can get you all killed if your team is bunched up.

When you must go through a narrow choke point, move fast and get through as quickly as possible. The same goes for large open areas. If you cannot cover all angles of threat, run as fast as you can to minimize the chance of the enemy hitting you.

Blitz through open areas to make it harder for the enemy to hit you.

If you have to go up stairs, face the direction where the enemy could be. This may mean going up stairways sideways or even walking backwards. Stairs can be dangerous choke points. Because your heartbeat sensor only works on the level you are currently on, there's no way to see if a tango is at the top until you get there.

Heartbeat sensors are virtually useless on stairways. Don't let another player sneak up on you from a different level while you are concentrating on the map.

Fire Discipline

In multiplayer games, you can quickly run out of ammo. Therefore it is important to use it sparingly in most cases. Because a single shot will often kill, and a three-round burst nearly always will, avoid using full-automatic fire. Firing while moving is highly inaccurate. If you miss a target, you not only let the enemies know you are out there, you also give them the opportunity to fire back. As a general rule, you should stop, drop, fire! All of this will increase your accuracy and also minimize the chance of your being detected if you miss.

In some instances full-automatic fire and movement are acceptable. If you have to get through a choke point or a large open area, running and firing wildly at the enemy may force them to keep their heads down and prevent them from firing accurately at you.

Attacking

You can attack the enemy in several different ways. In most cases, you should advance slowly and carefully as a team, using good fire discipline and covering each other. However, there are also times when rushing the enemy has its benefits.

Some players refer to this as "Rambo-ing." This strategy can be very effective on small maps. At the beginning of the mission, your team blitzes toward the enemy with guns blazing. By catching the enemy before they have a chance to set up or get organized, you gain the element of surprise and can win a game in a matter of a minute or two.

The best way to advance is by using "Bound and Overwatch." This tactic divides a team into two parts. While one advances, the other covers. When the first gets to some cover, it halts and covers the second group as it advances. Practice this tactic so everybody on your team understands his or her role.

Defending

Defending a position can entail setting up firing positions, ambushes, and snipers. This can take time, so at the start of a mission, each player should assume some sort of defensive position in case the enemy tries blitzing you right from the start.

For firing positions, try to choose locations with cover and at a distance from an entrance such as a doorway. This increases your ability to survive grenade attacks and makes it harder for the enemy to shoot you.

Locate the choke points and set up your defenses near them. It is hard to defend a large area, so concentrate on the narrow spots through which the enemy must advance. Use C-4 to blast a hole in an enemy's attack. Grenades can also be useful. Set up heartbeat sensors and jammers to help locate the enemy and conceal your location from them.

More Tips and Hints

- Move decisively and with purpose! You are the hunter, not the victim. Move like a victim, and you'll soon be one. Move with purpose as a hunter, and you will attack your enemy with confidence.
- Put your opponent under duress—if you see your opponent, open fire! With rounds coming at him, he'll panic, giving you—or preferably your partner—the chance to take a good kill shot.
- Teamwork! You have to trust your teammates to cover their zones and do their jobs. Everyone has to do his or her part, even if it's watching a locked door miles from the action. It could save your whole team from being wiped out from behind.
- Never assume a room is cleared simply because you've "already been in there."
- Choose a weapon with some stopping power, not just because it looks cool.
- Remember, fire short, controlled bursts. It doesn't matter how many rounds you fire, just where they land.
- If you aren't using auto-aim, then aim for your opponent's crotch. The head is harder to hit and the chest is usually covered by some type of body armor.
- Never leave your back to an open window or door.
- The enemy may not be able to hear a suppressed submachine gun, but if you are 500 yards away, it won't matter because you won't actually be hitting them.
- When you yell "cover me," make sure someone on your team responds before making your move.
- As a team, secure all doorways coming into your location as quickly as possible. You should do this every time you enter a new room during an advance so you are not surprised by the enemy.
- Be careful when trying to throw a grenade through a window. Some types of glass won't break. Grenades may bounce right back at you.

Additional Equipment for Multiplayer Games

Rogue Spear includes some additional equipment for use only in the multiplayer games. These can add a new twist to games against other players.

HB (Heart Beat) Jammer

This handheld device prevents other players from picking up heartbeat sensor information in a radius from the player holding it. To activate it, make it the current item.

This item can be very useful in setting up ambushes. While some players consider the heartbeat sensor cheating, the jammer is a cheat against a cheat. Only one member of a team needs to carry the jammer because it operates over a small radius. As long as your team stays together, all are invisible to enemy sensors.

SA (Stand Alone) HB Jammer

This is the same as a HB jammer, with the exception that it can be placed on the ground and does not need to be carried. This item can be destroyed. To use this, make it the current item and then press the fire button or key to place it on the ground.

This item is useful for defensive roles. You can place these around an ambush point to prevent the enemy from detecting your defenders. The only problem is that once it is placed, you cannot pick it up and move it to another location.

C-4

This is a small (less than one kg) block of C-4 plastic explosive with a radio detonator in it. The player can place this anywhere on the ground and detonate it from anywhere in a level. It's similar to a frag grenade, but has a smaller radius. To plant the C-4, make it the current item and then press the fire button or key. You can then change to another item if you wish. To detonate the planted explosive, make the C-4 your current item again and press the fire button or key.

Think of C-4 as a land mine that you can remotely detonate. It is great for ambushes and other defensive tasks. Place it along the path you expect the enemy to use to get to you. Then hide. You can use heartbeat sensors to monitor the kill zone or just your eyes. Don't place it out in the middle of a hall where the enemy might be able to spot it. Instead, put it along the side of a wall or around a corner. Because the blast radius is smaller than a frag grenade, wait until the enemy is right next to the C-4 before detonating it.

SA HB Sensor

This is similar to the handheld device except it is placed at a point on the ground and detects within a radius of itself. This item can be destroyed. To use this item, make it the current item, then press the fire button or key to place it on the ground.

This item is useful for defensive missions as it frees up a team member from having to use the handheld sensor. Because it can be destroyed, place it out of the enemy's sight.

False HB Puck

This item can be dropped on the ground. It produces a HB signature that mimics that of the person who dropped it. This item can be destroyed. To use this item, make it the current item, then press the fire button or key to place it on the ground.

This is another useful item for defensive tasks, especially if your opponent relies on heartbeat sensors. Place it in a position away from, but within sight of, your operatives. Use it in conjunction with a heartbeat jammer. When the enemies detect the false heartbeat, they will enter the room or throw a grenade at it, not realizing that you are somewhere else. So while they are going one way, you can hit them from the other.

Lone Wolf

Lone Wolf missions are a bit different than any other in *Rogue Spear*. Because the game relies heavily on teamwork for success, the Lone Wolf missions test your individual skills and abilities. There are no hostages to rescue or bombs to disarm. Your only objective is to move from the insertion zone to the extraction zone without being killed. Thirty tangos have been scattered about the map to try to stop you. You are free to kill as many as you want. However, the success of the game depends only on whether you can get to the extraction zone. Lone Wolf missions can be played on any of the campaign maps after the campaign mission has been completed successfully.

In the Lone Wolf missions, it is just you against 30 tangos.

When you begin a Lone Wolf mission, you go through the planning stage as you would any other mission. However, you are only allowed to choose one operative. Pick one with good assault and stealth ratings—the two skills you'll need the most. As for weapons, it is usually best to go with silenced submachine guns. Because the odds are 30 to 1, you want to maintain the element of surprise for as long as possible. A heartbeat sensor is a must. You need to know the enemies' location before you run into their guns. Finally, take along either frag grenades or an extra primary mag. With no hostages, there's no real need for flashbangs. If you must make noise, kill with the noise. Go with a light- or medium-weight uniform. While the light is quieter, the medium offers you a bit more protection.

Once your operative is outfitted, you can go to the Planning screen and assign waypoints. You should already be somewhat familiar with the map because you have completed the campaign mission on it. First take note of where you begin and to where you must move. Select a path that minimizes moving through wide open areas where multiple tangos can fire at you from different angles. Find back ways to the extraction zone that provide a lot of cover and concealment. Also look for small side rooms that you can duck into and use to ambush patrolling tangos.

During the mission, the key is to use caution and take your time. There is no rush. You should use your heartbeat sensor as much as, if not more than, your weapons. Always use it to check the next room before going around a corner or through a doorway. Even if it was clear a few seconds before, a tango could have entered during that time. Peek around corners to take out tangos once you have determined their positions and facing directions with the heartbeat sensor. Use grenades sparingly. Their noise will often bring more tangos to your position. However, a frag grenade is a great way to clear a room of multiple tangos, especially if you are getting close to the extraction zone.

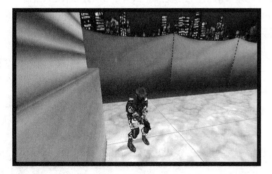

Use the heartbeat sensor often throughout the mission to locate the enemy in advance.

Peeking around corners is the best way to take out tangos and keep yourself partially protected against return fire.

Terrorist Hunt

Like Lone Wolf missions, once you have completed a campaign mission, you can then use the map for Terrorist Hunt missions. Your objective is to neutralize all 30 tangos that are scattered randomly throughout the map. However, for this type of mission, you can take along eight operatives. Plan this type of mission as you would a campaign mission. However, you do not need to worry about hostages being killed or bombs detonated. Divide your operatives into teams and assign each team waypoints so every inch of the map is covered. Tangos can be in the most unlikely places. You may go through a mission that won't end because a single tango is holed up in a closet or the corner of a shack.

For Terrorist Hunt missions, you can choose to be stealthy with silent weapons or as loud as possible with large assault rifles. A good tactic is to use the Cover posture. Order your teams to move to a point, then hold for a Go code while covering a hallway or open area. Leave them there for a bit to catch any patrolling tangos. Then move to the next Cover position and repeat the process.

In the Terrorist Hunt missions, tangos are everywhere, often clustered in small groups.

Because you have to get every last tango to complete the mission successfully, use a sweep strategy. From one position, move out and clear every room or structure as you advance. Don't leave any tangos behind you or allow any to sneak past into the area you already cleared. A good way to do this is to use two teams working together. One covers a hallway or other means of access while the other team searches and clears all the rooms. This prevents a tango from moving past a team while it is clearing a room.

PART II

Tom Clancy's
RAINBOW SIX
ROGUE SPEAR
MISSION PACK: URBAN OPERATIONS

CHAPTER EIGHT

New Features in Urban Operations

The Urban Operations mission pack is filled with lots of new features to make a great game even better. One such feature is the Custom Mission builder, which allows players to create their own missions and set them up just how they want. *Urban Operations* also adds three new weapons to the RAINBOW arsenal. Let's take a look at some of these new features.

Custom Missions

The Custom Mission Menu

When you go to the Custom Mission screen, you're presented with several variables from which you can choose to create scores of different missions. You can pick the map or level on which you want to play, the difficulty of the mission, and select the number of tangos for some missions. You also can choose from six different mission

types. The type of mission determines the objectives and the number of Operatives that can go on the mission. You can play on any of the multiplayer maps and those from the campaigns, so long as you have unlocked them by playing them during a campaign first.

Assault

Take out all the tangos you can find.

Assaults are the basic counterterrorist mission where you must assemble a team and neutralize all tangos on the map. The number of tangos in an assault mission is determined by the difficulty level you set. During the planning phase, select up to eight Operatives and give them orders to cover all parts of the map looking for tangos. They can be anywhere, but usually congregate around or inside the main structures.

Lone Wolf

You're on your own. Either get to the extraction zone safely, or eliminate all the tangos on the map.

This mission type is different from the rest. What makes it tough is that you can take only a single Operative. Choose one with high stealth and assault skills, such as Chavez or Maldini. Your objective is to get your Operative safely from the insertion zone to the extraction zone. However, you also can complete the mission by taking out all the tangos. To help get through this mission safely, take along a heartbeat sensor to locate tangos before they find you. You decide whether you want to take silenced weapons and whether you want to play stealthily. For this mission type, you can set the number of tangos you face from 1 to 50.

Terrorist Hunt

Tangos can be hiding anywhere.

This type of mission is similar to the assault mission. You choose a team of up to eight Operatives and give them orders to neutralize all the tangos on the map. The difference is that the tangos can be anywhere and everywhere. Also, similar to the Lone Wolf missions, you can choose how many tangos your team faces, from 1 to 50.

Hostage Rescue

The mission briefing shows you where the hostages are. However, you still have to get them out safely.

This is the standard RAINBOW mission. Assemble a team of up to eight Operatives, and then locate the hostages, secure them, and escort them to the extraction zone. The number of tangos you face is determined by the difficulty level. This is a good type of mission because it allows you to use maps from the game that didn't have hostage rescue objectives during the campaigns.

Defend

The switch often can be in a bad area, forcing you to cover two or three approaches all at the same time.

This is another solo mission. However, this time your Operative must defend an area by preventing tangos from triggering a switch. If that's not enough, you also must neutralize all tangos on the map. For this mission, make sure you take along something with a lot of firepower.

Right at the start of the mission, find a position from where you can cover the switch and be partially protected from enemy fire. There's also one more challenge in this type of mission—the tangos can throw grenades. Therefore, make sure you're somewhere where you can duck behind an object that will protect you from the shrapnel.

Recon

Get to the phone, bug it, and get out, all without getting caught.

During campaigns, the recon missions can be some of the most challenging. The objectives are to plant surveillance devices at certain spots on the map and get all your Operatives back to the extraction zone. The tough part is that none of your Operatives can be detected by the enemy—or the mission ends in failure. Also, you can't attack any of the tangos. Some of the maps are very tricky. Take along a heartbeat sensor and an electronics kit.

The key to this type of mission is to find a position where you can hide, then use the heartbeat sensor to study the patrol routes of all the tangos. Having more than one team is also helpful. One can be positioned at a distance to observe the enemy through binoculars to determine when it's clear for other teams to make their moves.

The New Weapons

To help you get through some of the new and challenging missions in the campaigns and the custom missions, three new primary weapons have been added to your arsenal.

M249 SAW

The Minimi M249 SAW is a light machine gun firing a 5.56x45mm round. It's is the standard U.S. Army squad support weapon. This gun comes with a 200-round box magazine, and fires only in fully automatic mode. It packs tremendous firepower, but is only accurate from a crouched, stationary position. Used this way, it's an effective covering weapon.

This weapon's firepower can help keep the heads of tangos down, if not take them out altogether. The only drawback is that the firing Operative must be crouched and stationary in order to be accurate. Give this weapon to a team that can place itself in a position and then cover an area. Because it's not effective while you're moving, don't assign it to a team leader and have the other Operatives in the team carry weapons for protection while moving into position.

HK 21E3

Based on the HK G3A3 framework, the HK 21E3 is a light machine gun firing the 7.62x51mm round from a 100-round box magazine. This round packs more punch than the 5.56x45mm round. Also, the HK 21E3 has single-shot and three-round burst options. It's more accurate than the M249 SAW, but harder to control when moving around. As with the M249 SAW, this weapon is best used from a stable firing stance.

If you need accuracy and heavy firepower, this is a better choice than the M249. Although its magazine only holds 100 rounds, the initial load out is two magazines so you have the same total rounds at the M249. Use the HK 21E3 in the same manner as you would the M249.

AW Covert

The AW Covert is a silenced sniper rifle firing the 7.62x51mm subsonic round. This round is less powerful than the standard 7.62x51mm round, making this rifle slightly less powerful and accurate than other sniper rifles in the game. This reduced effectiveness is offset by the silencer. Also, the subsonic round doesn't produce the sonic crack as it leaves the barrel, allowing a sniper to get closer to his target, and still avoid direct detection.

This weapon really is the best of both worlds. It provides the long-range firepower of a sniper rifle with the silence of a submachine gun. This gives you new options when planning a mission and allows you to position your snipers in more threatening positions from where they can strike and still avoid detection. If you need to take out tangos at long range, consider taking along a sniper armed with the AW Covert. It's also awesome for multiplayer missions.

CHAPTER NINE
The Urban Operations Campaign

The *Rogue Spear: Urban Operations* campaign comprises five new missions. You must complete each to advance to the next. This chapter provides all the information you need to get through the missions.

The strategies are for the Veteran (medium) difficulty level, requiring you to complete both the primary and secondary objectives before advancing to the next mission.

The mission strategies include orders and objectives, who to take, what they should carry, how to organize them, and, finally, how your teams can go about accomplishing the mission, with instructions for each. Use these instructions during the planning phase to set waypoints and issue special instructions and Go codes.

Mission 1—Operation: Iron Comet

02.02.03 1850

Istanbul

Mission Orders

Kurdish extremists have raided cease-fire talks in Turkey and kidnapped the UN negotiator and his aide. The Turkish police have tracked the kidnappers to an open-air market in Istanbul. Your mission is to neutralize the terrorists and escort their captives to safety.

There are lots of ways to mess up this one. The police can't put up a cordon without the kidnappers knowing something's up, so the target area will be crawling with civilians. These guys are experienced guerilla fighters—they're well armed and are accustomed to combat—so don't expect them to roll over and play dead just because they take a few casualties. You'll need to be quick, or those hostages are dead meat.

Objectives

1. Rescue the UN Negotiator
2. Rescue the UN Negotiator's Aide

In this mission, you must move through a bazaar filled with innocent bystanders. The only way to determine who the tangos are is the by guns they're carrying.

Team Assignments

Blue Team

OPERATIVE	PRIMARY	SECONDARY	SLOT 1	SLOT 2	UNIFORM
Chavez	MP5-S10SD	.45 Mark 23-SD	Flashbang	Flashbang	Street 2 Medium
Yacoby	MP5-S10SD	.45 Mark 23-SD	Heartbeat Sensor	Flashbang	Street 2 Medium

Red Team

OPERATIVE	PRIMARY	SECONDARY	SLOT 1	SLOT 2	UNIFORM
Price	MP5-S10SD	.45 Mark 23-SD	Flashbang	Flashbang	Street 2 Medium
Murad	MP5-S10SD	.45 Mark 23-SD	Heartbeat Sensor	Flashbang	Street 2 Medium

Green Team

OPERATIVE	PRIMARY	SECONDARY	SLOT 1	SLOT 2	UNIFORM
Noronha	MP5-S10SD	.45 Mark 23-SD	Flashbang	Flashbang	Street 2 Medium
Rakuzanka	MP5-S10SD	.45 Mark 23-SD	Heartbeat Sensor	Flashbang	Street 2 Medium

Gold Team

OPERATIVE	PRIMARY	SECONDARY	SLOT 1	SLOT 2	UNIFORM
Bogart	MP5-S10SD	.45 Mark 23-SD	Flashbang	Flashbang	Street 2 Medium
Raymond	MP5-S10SD	.45 Mark 23-SD	Heartbeat Sensor	Flashbang	Street 2 Medium

Note
In this mission, there are 14 innocent bystanders. After the shooting begins, they usually run to the walls and crouch down. Although the tangos don't target them directly, if you're standing near one when a tango opens fire, the bystander could be hit. If any are killed, the mission is a failure.

Map 9-1. The Turkish Bazaar

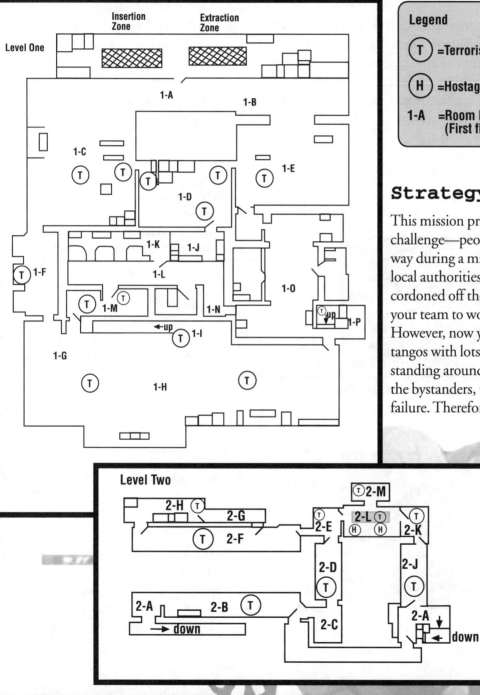

Legend

(T) = Terrorist

(H) = Hostage

1-A = Room Designation (First floor, first room)

Strategy

This mission presents a new challenge—people getting in your way during a mission. In the past, local authorities have always cordoned off the area to allow your team to work uninterrupted. However, now you must take out tangos with lots of innocents standing around. If you kill any of the bystanders, the mission is a failure. Therefore, aim carefully.

Before you shoot, make sure the target is carrying a gun. That is the only way to tell the difference between the tangos and the innocents.

The strategy is to use two of your teams for infiltrating the bazaar and securing the hostages while the other two provide cover to prevent tangos from sneaking up behind the first two teams. Your teams must enter the bazaar through one of two market areas. Beware. The tangos have positioned snipers on the upper levels at 2-H and 2-M overlooking these areas.

The hostages are both located in room 2-L with four tangos nearby. Blue and Red Teams must fight their way to the hostages and then clear a path to the extraction zone.

Blue Team

Blue Team is the main team to enter the bazaar, locate the hostages, secure them, and escort them to safety. You should take control of this team.

Wait until the tango patrolling 1-C moves back into the alley.

Begin by moving carefully toward market area 1-C. There's usually one tango patrolling this area and one near the wall common with 1-D. Also watch out for the sniper above in 2-H. He'll look out of a window and can cause a lot of problems.

You must take out the sniper in 2-H before he hurts your Operatives or innocent bystanders.

The key to this section is timing. Wait until the patrolling tango in 1-C heads back to 1-F. Then move and take out the sniper and the other tango in 1-C before moving toward 1-F. Continue down this alley to engage another tango and the one from 1-C. Hold up near the entrance to 1-G and watch for tangos in 1-G and 1-H. There can be two or three

patrolling around. Take them out and then move to 1-I. A tango is guarding the stairs going up. Drop him and climb the stairs.

Clear out the southern marketplace before moving toward the stairs.

A tango patrols between rooms 2-A and 2-B. Clear these rooms and room 2-F across the way. Move into 2-C and neutralize the tango patrolling between there and 2-D, then another tango at 2-J if he's still active. When this area is clear, enter and clear 2-E, then burst into 2-L and drop the tango guarding the hostages. Don't forget the sniper at 2-M.

You must quickly take out the tango in 2-L before he can kill the hostages.

When you've neutralized all the tangos in the immediate area, escort the hostages to safety.

By now, the bazaar should be clear of most tangos, and it's time to get the hostages out. Escort them through 2-K to 2-I and down the stairs. Continue through 1-O, to 1-E, and on to the extraction zone.

Red Team

Red Team's job is to help Blue Team get through the bazaar and assist in securing the hostages. Move to 1-A and hold for Alpha. When the shooting begins and Alpha is given, rush through 1-C and into 1-D, clearing it of all tangos. Take up a position covering the doors to 1-E and 1-J. Cover here until code Bravo.

Red Team advances through the middle of the bazaar, through a restaurant and some small shops.

At Bravo, move through 1-J into 1-K. There are a couple of tangos in this small shop area, usually in or near 1-M. Be careful when you open the door from 1-K into 1-L. It has a bell that rings. Advance through 1-L and 1-N, cross 1-O to the stairs at 1-P. Climb carefully because a tango is usually patrolling them.

Watch out for the tango patrolling the stairs. He will usually not appear on the heartbeat sensor, so keep your weapon always aimed up the stairway while ascending.

At the top, go through the door and take out the tango at 2-J. Hold here and cover facing the door to 2-K for code Charlie. Once the code is given, rush through and clear 2-K and then go on into 2-L. Defend the hostages while holding for code Delta.

At Delta, clear the way for Blue Team and the hostages by leading them through 2-K to 2-I and down the stairs. Move through 1-O and 1-E to the extraction zone.

Green Team

Green Team's job is very simple. They must cover the main entrance to market area 1-E and prevent tangos from sneaking around and hitting the other teams from behind.

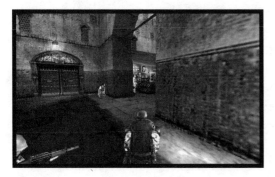

Green Team covers the northeast entrance to the marketplace.

At the beginning of the mission, move to 1-B and hold while taking up a Cover position facing the entrance to 1-E. Make sure your team isn't visible to the sniper at 2-M.

At code Delta, Green Team can move to the extraction zone.

Gold Team

Gold Team is another covering team. At the start of the mission, Gold Team should move to area 1-A and hold for Alpha. When the code is given, Gold Team moves through area 1-C and into 1-D, taking up a Cover position near and facing the entrance to 1-E from 1-D.

Gold Team usually takes out a couple of tangos as they move around in the northeastern marketplace, trying to sneak up on Red and Blue Teams.

Remain here until code Delta, then advance through 1-E to the extraction zone.

Notes

For this mission, you should control Blue Team. They set the timing for the mission. As they're ready to begin clearing area 1-C, give code Alpha to bring Red and Gold Teams in to help.

While the other three teams take up covering positions, Blue Team makes its way up to the second level. After clearing the western part of this level, give code Bravo to bring Red Team in to help. You should clear 2-B and 2-F first because the tangos here can fire down on Red Team if they're not neutralized. Watch the map and as soon as you

see Red Team climbing the stairs to 2-I, move out to 2-C and clear the upper area on the west while Red Team takes the east. Once both teams are ready, give code Charlie to send them in to secure the hostages.

With the hostages secured and the sniper at 2-M eliminated, give code Delta and follow Red Team back down the stairs and out to the extraction zone. However, by this time in most missions, you'll have neutralized all tangos and the mission will end without you having to escort the hostages at all.

Mission 2—Operation: Virgin Moon

04.03.03 1230
London

Mission Orders

Radical Irish Loyalists, fleeing after a bomb blast in central London, have barricaded themselves in an underground railway station. Your mission is to retake the station and rescue the commuters who are held hostage.

Normally, the SAS handles incidents like this on British soil. Unfortunately, their London HRT team is already engaged with a hostage situation in Whitehall, and they've asked for our help.

The explosion was in a flat in Smithfield. When the police showed up, the suspects traded shots with them, then made a run for it. They only got as far as the underground station before they were surrounded. They're panicked and extremely well armed—a very dangerous combination.

Objective

1. Rescue All Hostages

The tangos are holding hostages on levels 3 and 4. You must rescue them all.

Team Assignments

Blue Team

OPERATIVE	PRIMARY	SECONDARY	SLOT 1	SLOT 2	UNIFORM
Chavez	MP5-S10SD	.45 Mark 23-SD	Lockpick Kit	Flashbang	Black Medium
Woo	MP5-S10SD	.45 Mark 23-SD	Heartbeat Sensor	Flashbang	Black Medium

Red Team

OPERATIVE	PRIMARY	SECONDARY	SLOT 1	SLOT 2	UNIFORM
Walther	MP5-S10SD	.45 Mark 23-SD	Lockpick Kit	Primary Mag	Black Medium
Loiselle	MP5-S10SD	.45 Mark 23-SD	Heartbeat Sensor	Flashbang	Black Medium

Green Team

OPERATIVE	PRIMARY	SECONDARY	SLOT 1	SLOT 2	UNIFORM
Petersen	AW Covert	.45 Mark 23-SD	Lockpick Kit	Primary Mag	Black Medium
Pak	MP5-S10SD	.45 Mark 23-SD	Heartbeat Sensor	Primary Mag	Black Medium

Gold Team

OPERATIVE	PRIMARY	SECONDARY	SLOT 1	SLOT 2	UNIFORM
Hanley	MP5-S10SD	.45 Mark 23-SD	Primary Mag	Flashbang	Black Medium
Haider	MP5-S10SD	.45 Mark 23-SD	Heartbeat Sensor	Flashbang	Black Medium

Map 9-2. The London Underground

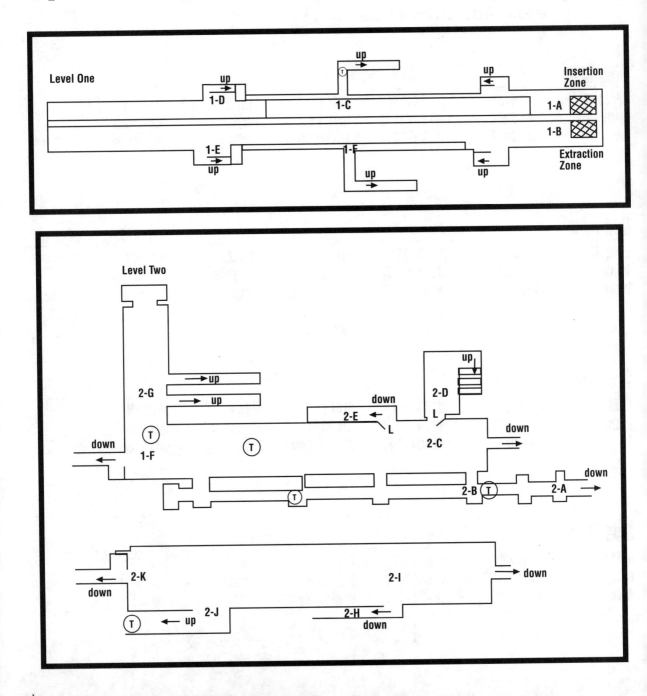

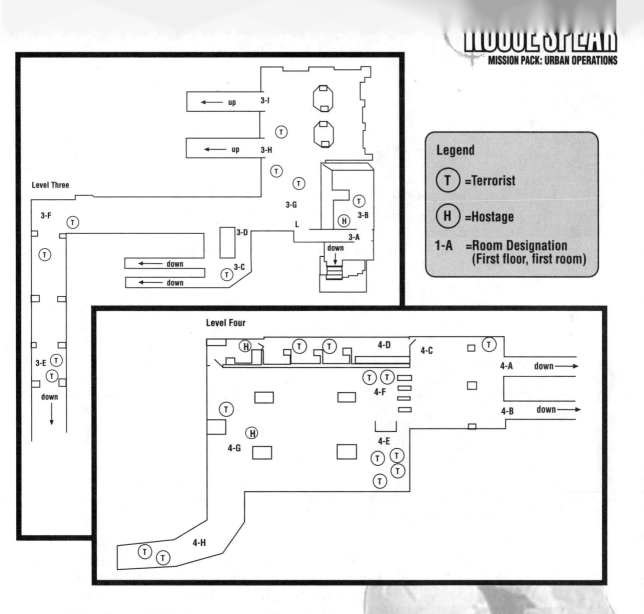

Legend

(T) =Terrorist

(H) =Hostage

1-A =Room Designation
(First floor, first room)

Level Three

3-I up
3-H up
3-F
3-G
3-D
3-C down
down
3-E
down
3-A
3-B
L
down

Level Four

4-D
4-C
4-A down
4-F
4-B down
4-E
4-G
4-H

Strategy

Tangos are crawling all over in this mission. To get to the hostages, you'll have to use four teams working closely together. The good thing is that there are no innocent bystanders here—just the tangos and their hostages. If a person isn't on his knees with his hands behind his head, shoot. Your teams are inserted along the subway tracks and must work their way up to levels 3 and 4 to find the hostages.

Blue Team

Blue Team is one of your assault teams. Its job is to help clear the way to the hostages, along with the other two assault teams. Move to 1-A and hold for code Alpha.

Blue Team rushes through the subway train to get to the station platform.

At Alpha, climb up into the subway train to 2-A and then through 2-B, and 2-C to 2-D. The door is locked, so use the lockpick kit to speed up the job. Ascend the stairs to 3-A and hold for code Bravo.

When you receive Bravo, rush into room 3-B and take out the tango guarding the hostage. Defend this area until code Charlie. At Charlie, move out of this office to 3-I and hold for code Delta.

One hostage is located in a ticket office on level 3. He is guarded by a single tango. The windows of this office are bulletproof.

At Delta, rush up the escalator to 4-A and then take up a Cover position at 4-F facing 4-G. Cover here until code Alpha, then return to the extraction zone.

Red Team

Red Team is the second assault team. At the start of the mission, move to 1-B and hold while covering toward 1-E until code Alpha. At Alpha, move into the subway train to 2-A, then through 2-B and 2-C to the locked door to 2-E, Open it and descend through

the tunnel, checking for hiding tangos before advancing alongside the rails to 1-D. Climb up the ramp to 2-F and on then onto 2-G.

Watch out for the tango waiting to ambush you as you ascend the first flight of escalators.

Climb the escalator carefully. There's a tango crouched at 3-C. Take him out, then set up a cover position at 3-D facing 3-G. Hold here for code Charlie. Then move to 3-I and hold for code Delta.

Red Team covers the lobby of level 3 while using the escalators for cover.

When you receive Delta, blitz up the escalator, and neutralize the tango at the top behind the corner near 4-A. Move to 4-C and open the door to the office. Take out both tangos inside and defend the hostages until code Alpha. Then escort them down to level 3 and through 3-A, down the stairs, and out to the extraction zone.

Green Team

Green Team is your sniper team. You should take control of them initially. At the beginning, move to 3-A and assume a Sniper position, aiming at the enemy snipers through the window at 3-E. These tangos can fire down on your operatives as they move around the subway tracks and, therefore, must be taken out early in the mission.

Green Team takes out the snipers overlooking the subway platform area. You don't need to see their heads to get a shot. In fact, it's better not to so they won't shoot at you.

Once you've eliminated the snipers behind the window, aim down at the other end of the tracks, near 1-D and take out several tangos as they appear. When you're using the AW Covert sniper rifle, the tangos will have a difficult time spotting you, and you can pretty much pick them off at your leisure. Stay here until code Bravo.

Take out all tangos that appear at the far end of the area.

Green Team covers the other teams as they begin their assault across the lower levels.

At Bravo, move through the subway train to ascend the stairs at 2-D up to 3-A. Stay by the door into 3-G and provide cover for the other teams until code Charlie.

At Charlie, move to 3-G and assume a Sniper position aimed at the window at 4-E to make sure no tangos try to snipe at your other operatives. Hold here until code Alpha. Then enter 3-B and escort the hostage down the stairs and on to the extraction zone.

Gold Team

Gold Team is the third assault team. At the beginning of the mission, move to 1-B and hold while covering down toward 1-D. At code Alpha, advance along the southern side of the tracks under the overhang to 1-E. Ascend the ramp and head to the stairs at 2-J. Take out the tango guarding these stairs and then ascend to 3-E. Clear out any remaining tangos here before moving to 3-F and holding for code Charlie while covering toward 3-G.

Watch out for the tango guarding the stairway at 2-J.

Before code Charlie, take control of Gold Team and slowly walk backward toward 3-G while facing 3-F and looking up. Above you is a window overlooking the hallway. Take out the tango sniper here. Red Team will cover your back. Once the window is clear and code Charlie is given, move to 3-H and hold for Delta.

NEW BRIDGE

To take out the sniper on level 4, you must walk backward while aiming at the window until you have a shot at the tango.

At Delta, rush up the escalator to 4-B and then advance normally on to 4-E. Clear out any tangos, here as well as one guarding a hostage near 4-G. Continue past the hostage to take out two more tangos at 4-H, then return to defend the hostage at 4-G until code Alpha. At Alpha, escort the hostage and follow the other teams down the escalators. Then descend the stairs to 2-D and out to the extraction zone.

Notes

For this mission, you must take control of two different teams at various stages of the mission. Begin with Green Team and move carefully to the first position. Here, crouch so you can see the two snipers and take them out. Take out several more tangos as they appear in the distance. When it seems all of the tangos in this area have been neutralized, give code Alpha to send the other three teams on their way.

Remain in control of Green Team to cover their advance in case any tangos appear at the far end of this lower level. Once Blue Team is holding for code Bravo and the other two are waiting for Charlie, give code Bravo and switch to Gold Team. At Bravo, Blue Team will rush the office to secure the first hostage while Green Team ascends to level 3. As Gold Team, take out the tango above at 4-E. Then give code Charlie. Watch the window above until Green Team is holding for Alpha, then move to the escalators at 3-H.

When Blue, Red, and Gold Teams are all holding for Delta, give the code and rush up the escalators. As Gold Team clears the southern part of the fourth level, watch out for the tangos in the office near 4-D. They'll fire through the windows at you. Once the level is secure and all teams are holding for code Alpha, give it to send them all down to the extraction zone with hostages in tow. However, if you eliminated all of the tangos in this mission by this time, the mission will end and you need not escort the hostages at all.

Mission 3—Operation: Aztec Palace

06.20.03 1400
Venice

Mission Orders

Members of an apocalyptic cult have seized control of a Venetian library housing a collection of rare medieval manuscripts. They've planted a bomb in the building that we believe are set to detonate within the hour. Your mission is to regain control of the library and prevent the bomb from detonating.

The group holding the library calls itself Universal Harmony. They're mostly American—a fringe New Age cult out of New Mexico. Apparently, they believe that one of the books in the Alberti collection has some sort of mystical significance. They haven't issued any demands, but our surveillance indicates that they've set explosives in the building. Intel thinks we may have a mass suicide in the making. Your job is to retake the place before they can blow it up.

Objectives

1. Disarm the Bomb
2. Neutralize All Terrorists

You must advance to the library and disarm the bomb. To get through this mission will require your teams to work together and provide cover fire for one another.

Team Assignments

Blue Team

OPERATIVE	PRIMARY	SECONDARY	SLOT 1	SLOT 2	UNIFORM
Chavez	UMP 45SD	.45 Mark 23-SD	Frag Grenades	Frag Grenades	Gray Medium
Yacoby	UMP 45SD	.45 Mark 23-SD	Heartbeat Sensor	Frag Grenades	Gray Medium

Red Team

OPERATIVE	PRIMARY	SECONDARY	SLOT 1	SLOT 2	UNIFORM
Price	HK G3A3	.45 Mark 23-SD	Frag Grenades	Primary Mag	Gray Medium
Murad	HK G3A3	.45 Mark 23-SD	Frag Grenades	Heartbeat Sensor	Gray Medium

Green Team

OPERATIVE	PRIMARY	SECONDARY	SLOT 1	SLOT 2	UNIFORM
Novikov	HK G3A3	.45 Mark 23-SD	Frag Grenades	Primary Mag	Gray Medium
McAllen	HK G3A3	.45 Mark 23-SD	Demolitions Kit	Heartbeat Sensor	Gray Medium

Gold Team

OPERATIVE	PRIMARY	SECONDARY	SLOT 1	SLOT 2	UNIFORM
Narino	PSG-1	.45 Mark 23-SD	Primary Mag	Frag Grenades	Gray Medium
Rakuzanka	UMP 45SD	.45 Mark 23-SD	Heartbeat Sensor	Frag Grenades	Gray Medium

Map 9-3. The Canals of Venice

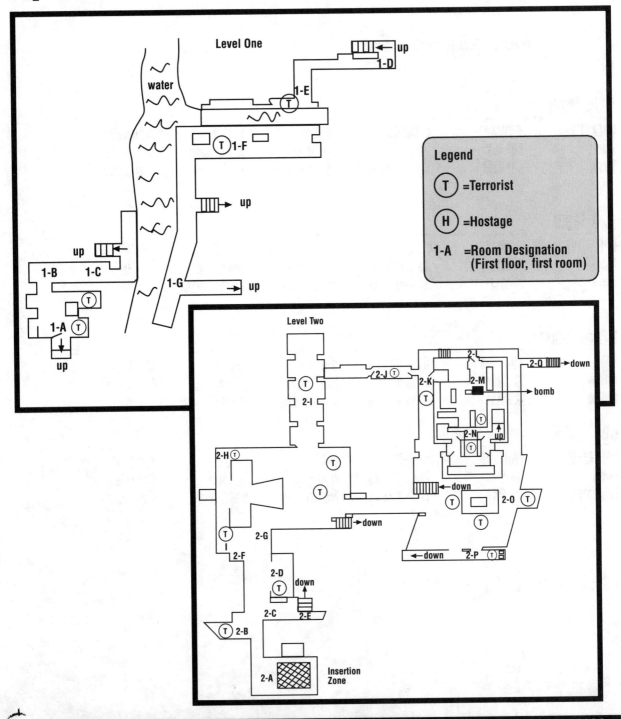

MISSION PACK: URBAN OPERATIONS

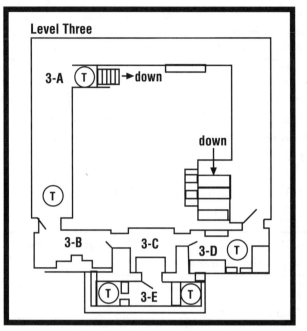

Level Three

3-A T →down

down

3-B   3-C   3-D T

T 3-E T

Strategy

For this mission, you must get your team into the library and disarm the bomb. However, there are tangos patrolling everywhere and two positions from where they can snipe at your Operatives. Because you must neutralize all the tangos to complete this mission, you might as well clear as you advance on the library.

Use two main assault teams, a sniper team, and a recon-covering team. The key to getting to the library is to limit the exposure to the enemy as your Operatives move across open areas. Also try to clear out these open areas as much as possible from cover before moving across them.

Blue Team

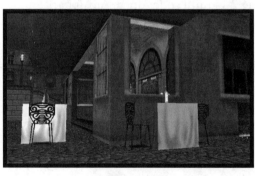

Take out the tango hiding in the cafe.

Blue Team is your recon-cover team. You should take control of Blue Team for the first part of the mission. Their main job is to clear the lower level near the insertion zone. At the start of the mission, crouch and advance to 2-C and take out the tango in 2-D. Then move toward 2-E and on to the stairs down to 1-A. Try to take out the tango by the door first if possible. Then throw a couple of frag grenades through the door with as much power as possible so they'll travel farther across the room.

Move carefully toward the stairs and take out the tango by the door as soon as you can see him.

Immediately after the grenades go off, rush down the stairs and clear 1-A. If you set the ROE to Recon, the second team member will pull out a heartbeat sensor so you can see if any tangos are hiding behind crates or in 1-C. When this whole area is clear, move to 1-C, open the door and Cover facing 1-G until code Delta and the remainder of the mission.

Blue Team holds and covers the canal to prevent tangos from sneaking in behind your other teams.

Red Team

Red Team is your main assault team. From the start, move quickly to 2-B, watching for a tango positioned there, and Cover facing 2-G until code Alpha. At Alpha, advance to 2-F and hold there for code Bravo while covering toward 2-H.

Run quickly to 2-H, staying low to avoid getting hit by enemy fire.

At Bravo, blitz while crouching to 2-H, using the platform for some cover. At 2-H, hold for code Charlie and cover facing the balcony at 3-E. Try to take out the snipers if possible or at least keep their heads down until the sniper team is in position to target them. When code Charlie is given, stay crouched and blitz to 2-I, and then move on to 2-J to take out another sniper covering the canal and the bridge. Hold at 2-K and defend until code Delta.

Aim just like this from the balcony and throw a frag grenade as hard as you can to take out the tango hiding below behind the archway.

At Delta, open the door and take out the tango on the stairs. Then ascend to 3-A. Move through 3-B and 3-C to 3-D to take out a tango before moving out onto the balcony at 3-E. From the balcony, you can take out the tango below at 2-O. You can also take out the tango hiding at 2-P. Aim at the archway nearest him and while looking level, throw a frag grenade. If the range is correct, it will go through the archway and explode, killing the hiding tango. You may have to throw a second or third to get the range right. Red Team can hold here and defend until the end of the mission.

Tip

When moving to 2-H, it is important for Red, Gold, and Green Teams to run or blitz to make it harder for the tangos on the other side of the canal to hit them.

Green Team

Green Team is the secondary assault team. Its job is to help Red Team, disarm the bomb, and clear out the lower level on the opposite side of the canal. At the start move to 2-C and hold for code Alpha. Cover facing 2-G while waiting.

At Alpha, move to 2-G and hold for code Charlie while covering toward 2-I. Green Team must help clear the large open area on this side of the canal while Red and Gold Teams advance. At Charlie, move around to the west of the platform and then through 2-H, 2-I, and 2-J to 2-L. Hold here for code Delta while assuming a Defend posture.

Green Team completes one of the mission objectives by disarming the bomb.

At Delta, open the door to the library and enter just enough to take out the tango inside. Hold again for code Alpha while defending. When you receive this Go code, move to the bomb at 2-M and disarm it. Then advance to take out the tangos at 2-N before heading down the stairs

at 2-Q. Use caution while descending. A tango can be patrolling down there near 1-D. When you get to 1-E, ease left past the corner to take out the tango at 1-F and the other one just to the right and around the corner.

Green Team finishes mopping up the tangos by clearing out the first level near the canal under the library.

Gold Team

Gold Team covers the alley and helps clear out the open area during the first part of the mission.

Gold Team is your sniper team. It has a limited, yet important task for this mission. At the start, move to 2-A and hold for code Bravo while sniping toward 2-G. At code Bravo, blitz past 2-F to 2-H and assume a sniping position aimed at the balcony at 3-H. Take out all tangos that poke up their heads. Remain at this position for the remainder of the mission.

Gold Team must cover the balcony while Green and Gold Teams advance to the library.

Notes

For this mission, you should take control of different teams at various stages. Start in control of Blue Team. Before you do anything else, activate the sniper control so Gold Team automatically fires when there's a tango in

their sights. While you take Blue Team down to the first level and clear out the tangos hiding there, the other three teams will be taking out tangos as they appear near 2-G. Once Blue Team is holding at 1-C, switch to Red Team and give code Alpha. When you get to 2-F and Green Team is holding at 2-G, give code Bravo and race to 2-H. Cover the balcony area until Gold Team is in position next to you and can take over covering.

Give code Charlie to bring Green Team in behind you as you head down 2-I toward the library. Once Green team is in position and holding, give code Delta and rush into the library and up the stairs to clear out the third level. Once it's clear and you have taken out the two tangos in the courtyard below from the balcony, switch to Green Team. Move forward into the library, disarm the bomb, and work your way around to clear out the rest of the library and then the first level below.

Mission 4—Operation: Infinite Seven

08.18.03 0545
Mexico City

Mission Orders

Marxist revolutionaries have raided an international economic summit in Mexico City. After being driven back by police, the terrorists have retreated to their headquarters in a warehouse district near downtown. Your mission is to flush the terrorists out and neutralize them.

The group calls itself the Popular National Liberation Army. They've been making trouble in the countryside for years, but the local authorities didn't think they had the resources to mount an urban attack. "Force F"—Mexico's own CT squad—is handling mop-up operations at the summit, so we've been tapped to run the assault. Watch your sixes in there; it's a real hamster run.

Objective

1. Kill All Terrorists

These slums in Mexico City are crawling with tangos.

Team Assignments

Blue Team

OPERATIVE	PRIMARY	SECONDARY	SLOT 1	SLOT 2	UNIFORM
Bogart	HK21E3	.50 Desert Eagle	Primary Mag	Frag Grenade	Street 2 Heavy
Burke	M249 SAW	.50 Desert Eagle	Primary Mag	Frag Grenade	Street 2 Heavy

Red Team

OPERATIVE	PRIMARY	SECONDARY	SLOT 1	SLOT 2	UNIFORM
Chavez	HK G3A3	.50 Desert Eagle	Primary Mag	Frag Grenade	Street 2 Medium
Haider	HK G3A3	.50 Desert Eagle	Heartbeat Sensor	Frag Grenade	Street 2 Medium

Green Team

OPERATIVE	PRIMARY	SECONDARY	SLOT 1	SLOT 2	UNIFORM
Price	HK G3A3	.50 Desert Eagle	Primary Mag	Frag Grenade	Street 2 Medium
Loiselle	HK G3A3	.50 Desert Eagle	Heartbeat Sensor	Frag Grenade	Street 2 Medium

Gold Team

OPERATIVE	PRIMARY	SECONDARY	SLOT 1	SLOT 2	UNIFORM
Noronha	HK G3A3	.50 Desert Eagle	Primary Mag	Frag Grenade	Street 2 Medium
Murad	HK G3A3	.50 Desert Eagle	Heartbeat Sensor	Frag Grenade	Street 2 Medium

Map 9-4. The Slums of Mexico City

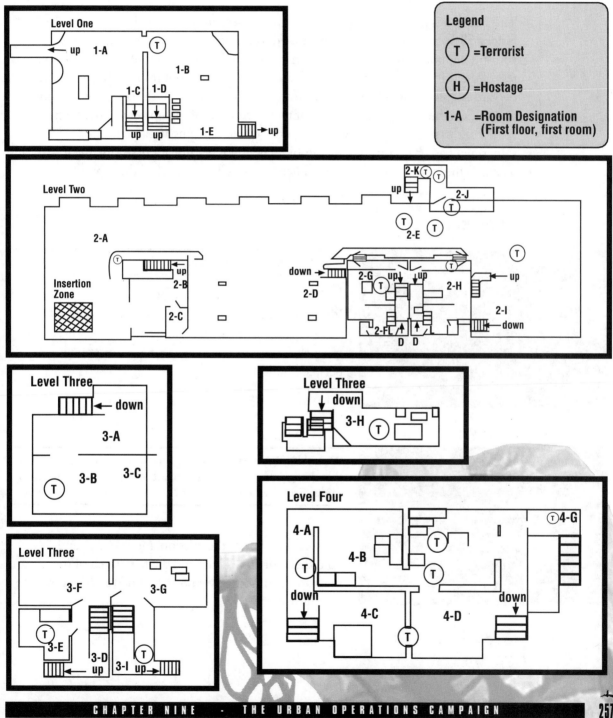

Legend

(T) =Terrorist

(H) =Hostage

1-A =Room Designation
(First floor, first room)

Level One

up   1-A

1-B

1-C 1-D

up   up   1-E up

Level Two

2-K
up
2-J
2-E
2-A
Insertion Zone
down   up   up   up
2-G   2-H
2-D
2-B
2-C
2-I
2-F down
D D

Level Three

down
3-A
3-B 3-C

Level Three

down
3-H

Level Three

3-F   3-G
3-E
3-D   3-I
up   up

Level Four

4-A   4-G
4-B
down   down
4-C   4-D

Strategy

This mission is purely close-quarters combat. There are a lot of tangos and they're hidden all over, waiting to ambush you. For this mission, you'll have four teams. One is your fire support and carries light machine guns to lay down a lot of fire to help cover the rest of the teams. The second team will also provide cover, but from up high. The other two are assault teams. Their job is to clear the main building in the center. While one team clears, the other covers to prevent tangos from sneaking up behind the first team.

For this mission, you'll want to control different teams at different stages. The AI sometimes has a hard time taking out hidden tangos because it doesn't use the heartbeat sensor to find them around corners. Therefore, you'll have to clear the rooms.

Blue Team

Blue Team takes up position.

Blue Team's job is to provide fire support for the other three teams. Armed with light machine guns, this team must clear the streets and keep tangos from moving between buildings.

With their light machine guns, Blue can take out any tangos that dare venture out into the street. Also, Blue can't be hit by sniper fire when positioned at 2-A.

At the start of the mission, move to 2-A and hold there for code Delta and the remainder of the mission. Assume a Cover posture aimed at 2-E. That's it for this team.

Red Team

Red Team is your high cover team. Its job is to clear the first building and then use the upper-level windows for covering the assault teams. Take control of Red Team at the start.

> **Tip** *Remember to use the heartbeat sensors. The second operative in Red, Green, and Gold Teams each carry one. To order them to pull it out and use it, change the ROE to Recon.*

Red Team clears out level 3 of the first building.

At the start, move to 2-B and head up the stairs. There may be a tango on the stairway. If not, there will probably be two on level 3. Take them both out, and then carefully move over to the window at 3-C. Fire at the tango sniping from 3-E and the one at 3-H, and hold there until code Delta or for the rest of the mission.

Carefully look out the window at 3-C and take out the tango at 3-E.

Green Team

Green Team is your main assault team. From the start, move to 2-C and hold for code Alpha. Then go out the door and on to 2-D. You need to take control of Green Team for what follows. From 2-D, throw a grenade up into the window to 3-E, and take out any tangos remaining inside. Then move down the steps to 1-A and clear out the tangos inside. Hold near 1-A for code Bravo.

When throwing a grenade into 3-E, aim slightly above the window. Be ready to run away if the grenade misses the window, bounces off the wall, and comes back at you.

Take out the tangos guarding the flooded basement.

At Bravo proceed up the stairs at 1-C to 2-F. Move through 2-G and then up the stairs to 3-D. Use the heartbeat sensor carried by the second operative to check the level for tangos. There's usually one on the stairway up to the fourth level, between 3-D and 3-E. Once level 3 is clear, go up the stairs to level 4. Clear it of all tangos. Watch out—they're are all over this level. If you locate a group, try throwing a grenade into the room to take some out and scatter the rest. There's also a tango on the fire escape at 4-G. If you can't see him by looking out the window, don't climb out. You'll get him later.

There are several tangos on level 4 of the central building.

Now head back down to level 3 using the stairs by 4-F. Continue down the stairs at 3-I to level 2 and clear out 2-H before descending to level 1. Hold near 1-A for code Charlie. Then rush up the stairs near 2-D and move to 2-E, then hold for code Delta while covering facing 2-J.

Gold Team

Gold Team is your second assault team. It works with Green Team to clear the tangos out of two of the buildings. From the start, move to 2-C and hold for code Alpha. Then rush down the stairs, clearing out the flooded basement before moving to 1-B and holding for code Charlie. Assume a Cover posture facing the stairs at 1-D and also watching the stairs at 1-E. Gold's job is to make sure no tangos use the basement to sneak up behind Green Team.

Watch out for the tango on the fire escape at 4-G.

Gold Team prepares to enter the final building and clear it.

At code Charlie, move up the stairs at 1-E and take out the tango on the fire escape at 4-G. Then advance through 2-I toward 2-J. Before you get there, stop in front of this last building and throw a couple frag grenades through the window into 3-H to help clear this room. Then enter 2-J and climb the stairs to 3-H. There's usually a tango in the stairway who'll survive the grenade attack. Clear 3-H and stay there until the mission is complete.

Notes

For this mission, you take control of three different teams at various stages of the mission. Blue Team is fine on its own. Start off in command of Red Team. Lead them up to level 3 of the first building and fire at the tango snipers. Once they're down or at least hiding, switch to Green Team and give code Alpha. Take your new team out the door

and toward the second building. Throw a grenade through the window and then descend into the basement. Once both Green and Gold Teams are holding, give code Bravo and advance up the stairs to clear out the center building.

When Green finishes and arrives back at 1-A, switch to Gold Team and give code Charlie. Take Gold up to level 2 and then clear out the third and final building. This mission is straightforward, and the hiding tangos are the only tricks the enemy will throw at you.

Mission 5—Operation: Jade Key

10.06.03 2300
Hong Kong

Mission Orders

Chinese gangsters have attacked the hotel where Hong Kong's Chief Executive was dining with a delegation of prominent foreign business leaders. Your mission is to rescue the kidnapped dignitaries with minimum loss of life.

Given the extremely high profile of the hostages, Beijing has asked you to work with HKPD to resolve the situation. Their Special Duties Unit has established a basic perimeter, but you'll be making the hit. You'll have to move quickly. The intel we're getting suggests that the gunmen are prepped to move the hostages out of the building. You need to take them out *now*.

Objective

1. Rescue All Hostages

Two of the hostages are located in the restaurant on the third level. If the tangos guarding them hear gunfire, they'll take the hostages to two separate locations and may even shoot them.

Team Assignments

Blue Team

OPERATIVE	PRIMARY	SECONDARY	SLOT 1	SLOT 2	UNIFORM
Chavez	UMP 45SD	.45 Mark 23-SD	Primary Mag	Flashbang	Street 1 Medium
Maldini	UMP 45SD	.45 Mark 23-SD	Primary Mag	Flashbang	Street 1 Medium
Yacoby	UMP 45SD	.45 Mark 23-SD	Primary Mag	Heartbeat Sensor	Street 1 Medium

Red Team

OPERATIVE	PRIMARY	SECONDARY	SLOT 1	SLOT 2	UNIFORM
Price	UMP 45SD	.45 Mark 23-SD	Primary Mag	Flashbang	Street 1 Medium
Loiselle	UMP 45SD	.45 Mark 23-SD	Primary Mag	Flashbang	Street 1 Medium
Filatov	UMP 45SD	.45 Mark 23-SD	Primary Mag	Heartbeat Sensor	Street 1 Medium

Green Team

OPERATIVE	PRIMARY	SECONDARY	SLOT 1	SLOT 2	UNIFORM
Johnston	AW Covert	.45 Mark 23-SD	Primary Mag	Primary Mag	Street 1 Medium

Gold Team

OPERATIVE	PRIMARY	SECONDARY	SLOT 1	SLOT 2	UNIFORM
Petersen	AW Covert	.45 Mark 23-SD	Primary Mag	Primary Mag	Street 1 Medium

Map 9-5. Hong Kong Hotel

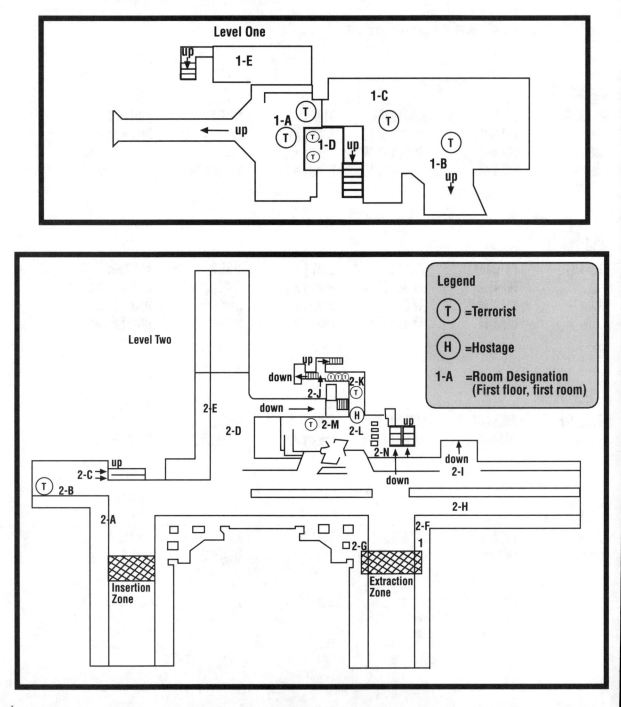

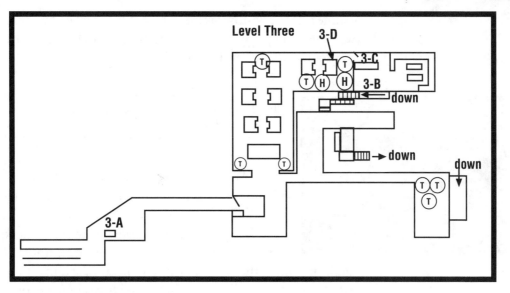

Strategy

This mission can be tough. In addition to a couple of snipers positioned to cover the street out in front, there are also tangos hiding in ambush and two three-man patrols that move all over the hotel. To succeed, you need to coordinate the actions of all your teams.

Two of the hostages are on the third level in the restaurant. However, if the tangos guarding them hear any noise, they'll escort these hostages down to level 1 to two separate areas—1-D and 1-E. If they run into dead tangos along the way, they may kill the hostages, so it's imperative you get to them before they leave the restaurant.

You'll need two assault teams and two sniper teams for this mission. All must use silenced weapons. The snipers actually will have a more active role in this mission because their long-range firepower will help clear out several of the tangos.

There are two insertion zones for this mission. Red Team should begin at Insertion Zone 2 while the other three teams begin at 1.

Blue Team

Blue Team is one of the assault teams. At the start, hold at the insertion zone for code Alpha while covering toward the hotel. When Alpha is given, move while crouched to 2-H, using the concrete divider for cover. Go around the right side and on to 2-I. Carefully take out the two tangos in area 1-B before they can sound an alarm. Then move to 1-C and hold there for code Bravo. A tango will patrol the area around 1-A,

so take him out. Assume a Cover posture aimed at 1-D. Actions taken by the other teams should bring the two three-man patrols down to the first level. To help the other teams, take out the patrols as soon as they come into sight.

Blue Team rushes down to the first level, taking out two tangos guarding this ramp.

At Bravo, move through 1-D and 1-A to 1-E. Climb the stairs to the third level and on into the kitchen at 3-B. Hold there for code Charlie. At Charlie, move into 3-C, face 3-D, and slowly sidestep to the corner of the wall. Then peek right around the corner until you can see the tango in green at the far end of the restaurant area. Quickly take him out, then get the tango in blue right by the door. A third tango starts taking the hostages out of the restaurant, right toward you. Take out the tango and not the hostages. The tango is wearing blue. With these three tangos down, escort the hostages through the kitchen and down the stairs to level 1. Go through 1-E and 1-A, then up to 2-D and all the way back to the extraction zone.

Peek around the corner and quickly take out the two tangos in sight, starting with the one looking right at you.

With the hostages secure, escort them through the kitchen and then down to level 1.

Red Team

Red Team is the second assault team. You should take control of Red at the start of the mission. Immediately, move out to take care of the two snipers. Move to 2-A, and then sidestep around the corner to take out the tango at 2-B. With the first down, head up the walkway at 2-C to level 3 and take out the tango at 3-A who is looking toward 2-H. Hold here until code Alpha.

You have to fire quickly to take out the first sniper because he's looking right in your direction.

At Alpha, rush back down the walkway to level 2 and advance to 2-D. Hold here for code Bravo, assuming a Cover posture facing down the ramp to 1-A. Red Team must help take out the three-man teams as they come down to level 1.

Red Team takes out the two tangos guarding the third hostage in quick succession.

When code Bravo is given, rush down into 1-A then to 1-E and hold there for code Charlie. At this Go code, rush up the stairs to level 2 to 2-K. Take out the tango between you and the hostage at 2-L, then quickly rush around the corner to the right and take out a second tango at 2-M who could fire at the hostage if you aren't quick enough. With both tangos down,

escort the hostage to the door at 2-N. Go through and descend the stairs to level 1 and exit via the ramp at 1-B. Continue all the way to the extraction zone with the hostages in tow.

Green Team

Green Team is one of the sniper teams. Their job is to cover the entrance to the hotel during the first phase, then cover the entrance to the restaurant.

Green Team keeps an eye on the front entrance.

At the start of the mission, move to 2-F and hold for Alpha. Assume a sniping position aimed at the bus crashed through the front door of the hotel.

As the assault teams prepare to enter the hotel, Green Team covers the entrance to the restaurant to make sure no tangos try to move out of this door and get in behind the other teams.

When code Alpha is given, rush to 2-C, and up the walkway to a position near 3-A so you have a good shot at the entrance to the restaurant. Snipe at the doors until code Delta. When you receive this last Go code, go back down the walkway and to the extraction zone.

Gold Team

Gold Team is also a sniper team and will actually do a lot of the shooting for this mission. At the start, move to 2-G and hold for code Alpha. From here, snipe at the entrance to the parking garage at 2-I.

Gold Team covers the parking ramp while Red Team deals with the snipers.

At Alpha, move to 2-E. You need to take control of Gold Team at this point. While aiming the sniper rifle down the ramp to 1-A, slowly sidestep to the left until you see the first tango. If Blue Team has not taken out the one by the van, do so. Then continue moving left until you can just see the tango crouched behind a window. Take him out before he can fire, then position yourself so you can crouch and see the door through the window. The three-man teams will come down the stairs and enter 2-D through this door. Take out each team as it comes into your sights.

When the three-man teams come down to level 1, you have to shoot quickly.

Hold at this spot, covering the first level until code Delta. Then move back to the extraction zone.

Notes

For this mission, you need to carefully coordinate the actions of all your teams. You also need to take control of three of the teams at critical points in the mission.

Start off with Red Team. While the other teams are holding near the first insertion zone, take out the two tango snipers in the west. Once the second one is down, give code Alpha and switch to Gold Team. Lead Gold to 2-E and follow the instructions above to take out several tangos. When no more tangos appear below, give code Bravo and switch to Blue Team. Move through 1-D, taking out any remaining tangos in this room before heading up the stairs to level 3. Just before peeking around the corner to take out the tangos guarding the hostages, give code Charlie to send Red Team rushing up to level 2 to get the third hostage. Once both assault teams are out of the hotel and headed to the extraction zone, give code Delta to bring the two sniper teams home.

This mission is quite tough, so it may take a few tries. You'll have to adjust the planning to get each team in just the right covering position. However, once it's all together, it goes very smoothly.

For those of you who played the original *RAINBOW Six*, the five missions that make up the Classic Campaign will seem very familiar. Although the maps are nearly the same, additions have been made to a few. Now you can play these original missions with the new *Rogue Spear* game engine and the improved AI with all the new weapons and equipment. If you never had the opportunity to play these missions in *RAINBOW Six*, then they're all new to you. Enjoy.

Mission 1—Operation: Sun Devil

08.03.00 0630
Brazil

Mission Orders

American and Brazilian workers have been kidnapped from the site of a new research station under construction in the Amazon rain forest. Ramon Calderon,

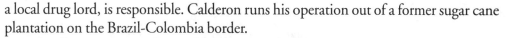

a local drug lord, is responsible. Calderon runs his operation out of a former sugar cane plantation on the Brazil-Colombia border.

Intelligence reports that Calderon's stronghold is well guarded. Guards armed with automatic weapons patrol inside and outside the house. The workers are being held in the basement, and Calderon's bedroom lies on the second floor.

You'll be inserted on the road to Calderon's house, a short distance from his front gate. Return with the hostages to this location to be airlifted out.

Objectives

1. Rescue All Hostages
2. Kill Ramon Calderon

Calderon must be eliminated and the hostages rescued to complete this mission.

Team Assignments

Blue Team

OPERATIVE	PRIMARY	SECONDARY	SLOT 1	SLOT 2	UNIFORM
Walther	UMP 45SD	.45 Mark 23-SD	Flashbang	Frag Grenade	Wood Heavy
Arnavisca	UMP 45SD	.45 Mark 23-SD	Heartbeat Sensor	Frag Grenade	Wood Heavy

Red Team

OPERATIVE	PRIMARY	SECONDARY	SLOT 1	SLOT 2	UNIFORM
Chavez	UMP 45SD	.45 Mark 23-SD	Flashbang	Frag Grenade	Wood Heavy
Raymond	UMP 45SD	.45 Mark 23-SD	Heartbeat Sensor	Frag Grenade	Wood Heavy

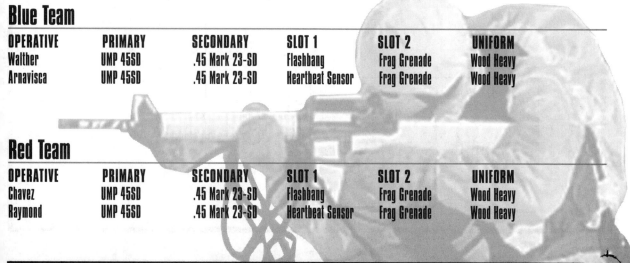

Green Team

OPERATIVE	PRIMARY	SECONDARY	SLOT 1	SLOT 2	UNIFORM
Bogart	G3A3	.45 Mark 23-SD	Primary Mag	Frag Grenade	Wood Heavy
Yacoby	G3A3	.45 Mark 23-SD	Primary Mag	Frag Grenade	Wood Heavy

Map 10-1. The Plantation House

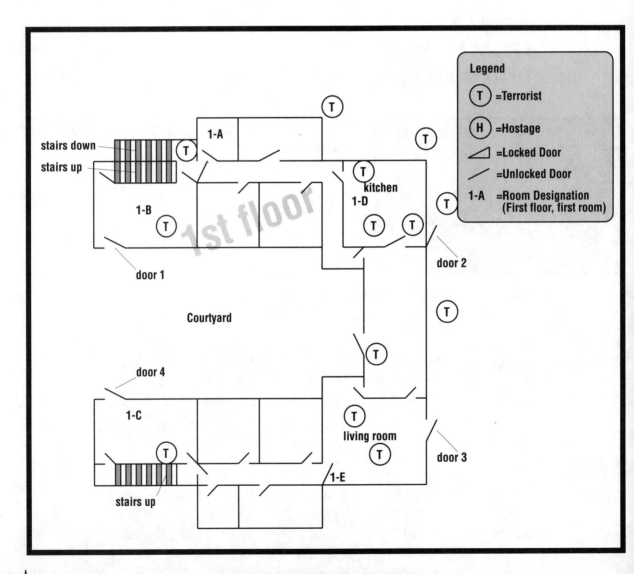

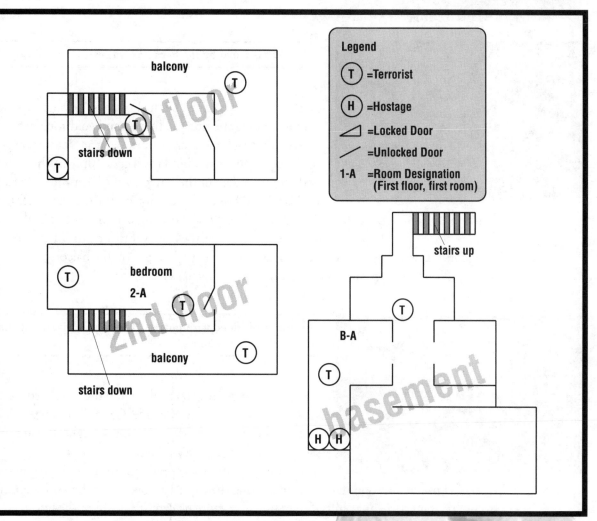

Strategy

This mission is straightforward, but difficult to execute. One of your teams will be the outside fire support and will clear the exterior of the house from a distance. The other teams will enter the building. As one rescues the hostages, the other will find the drug lord and execute him. As in the previous mission, you should control each team during its most difficult task to prevent unnecessary casualties. All the tangos have automatic weapons and are very dangerous. Heartbeat sensors allow infiltrating teams to detect tangos hiding in ambush around corners.

Blue Team

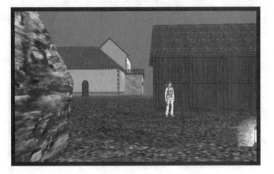

Take out the tango by the barn near the exit from the cave.

Blue Team's job is to rescue the hostages. Advance up the walkway along the ridge to the left and go through the cave to approach the manor from the rear. Before you get to the end of the cave, hold until code Alpha. When the code comes, take out the tango by the barn and then run to door 2 and hold for code Bravo. At the code, enter the kitchen, and then move on to the hallway. There may be a tango at the far end of the hall. If not, he's probably in room 1-A. Use the heartbeat sensor to locate him and the tango in 1-B. Be careful not to enter 1-B—there are two tangos on the balcony overlooking this room. Next, head downstairs to the basement.

The kitchen is filled with tangos. Be sure you have a full clip before opening the door.

Hold at the basement door and use the heartbeat sensor to locate the tangos inside. Carefully open the door and take out the terrorist in your line of sight. If you can't see him, wait until he comes out into the open. Then move carefully into the basement. Another tango guards the two hostages in room B-A. Advance along the right-hand wall and then sidestep left to put the tango in your sights. Shoot quickly before he can fire at you or the hostages.

Take out the tango guarding the hostages before he has a chance to execute them.

With the basement clear, escort the hostages to the kitchen and await code Delta. Then head to the extraction zone.

Red Team

Red Team's task is to execute the drug lord, Ramon Calderon. First, advance through the cave with Blue Team and hold for code Alpha. Then run to door 3 and hold for code Bravo. Hold in room 1-E with a Defend posture until code Charlie. Then move to room 1-C and take out the tango there. Use the heartbeat sensor to find him. Then make your way to the stairs.

Red Team approaches the manor through the cave.

Take out the tango in room 1-C before heading to the stairs.

Calderon is in the room at the top of the stairs, around the corner. Throw a frag grenade up the stairs to take out a tango guarding him. Then cautiously climb the stairs. Use the heartbeat sensor to locate Calderon. If he's around the corner, throw another frag grenade to take him out. After the grenade goes off, rush in to make sure he's dead and finish him off if he's only stunned. Also take out the tango outside on the balcony if he's still alive.

Go down the stairs and hold in room 1-C for code Delta. Then make your way to the extraction zone.

Green Team

Green Team provides fire support and clears the outside of the plantation house of all tangos. Because all their shots will be from long range, members are assigned assault rifles for more firepower.

Green team clears the balcony ...

... then deals with the patrols.

Begin by moving to the wall around the plantation house. Using an edge for cover, take out the guard on the balcony. There are two two-man patrols moving around outside the house. Take out both patrols and then hold for code Delta while covering toward the house.

At Delta, return to the extraction zone.

Notes

Begin in control of Green Team, because its job is the first you must do. After all the patrolling tangos are down on this side of the house, give code Alpha. Blue and Red Teams will run to their positions outside the house at doors 2 and 3, respectively.

Switch to Blue Team and give code Bravo. Lead Blue Team in through the kitchen to free the hostages. The tangos waiting in ambush along the way make this difficult, and you can probably do better than the computer. When the hostages are free, lead them back to the kitchen to await Delta.

Switch to Red Team. Give code Charlie, and then advance to room 1-C. After Calderon is dead, return downstairs. Finally, give code Delta to order all teams to return to the extraction zone.

Mission 2—Operation: Fire Walk

09.10.00 0700
Idaho

Mission Orders

The Phoenix Group is operating a secret biological warfare installation in southern Idaho. The team must secure the compound with minimal casualties. Lethal biological agents may be present in the main laboratory building. Breach of biosuit integrity in this environment may result in death.

You'll be inserted over the wall in the rear of the compound. If they detect your presence, Phoenix members carrying virus samples will try to escape through the front gate, so secure this area first.

If you allow anyone to leave the compound, your mission fails..

Intelligence indicates the compound's occupants won't expect an attack. They'll be unarmed, offering little resistance.

Objectives

1. Kill All Terrorists
2. Prevent Both Leaders from Leaving

The leaders try to make a break for the Escape Vehicle. Kill them before they escape with the biological agents.

Team Assignments

Blue Team

OPERATIVE	PRIMARY	SECONDARY	SLOT 1	SLOT 2	UNIFORM
Hanley	Steyr Aug	.45 Mark 23-SD	Frag Grenades	Frag Grenades	Biosuit
Raymond	Steyr Aug	.45 Mark 23-SD	Frag Grenades	Heartbeat Sensor	Biosuit

Red Team

OPERATIVE	PRIMARY	SECONDARY	SLOT 1	SLOT 2	UNIFORM
Burke	Steyr Aug	.45 Mark 23-SD	Frag Grenades	Frag Grenades	Biosuit
Sweeney	Steyr Aug	.45 Mark 23-SD	Frag Grenades	Heartbeat Sensor	Biosuit

Green Team

OPERATIVE	PRIMARY	SECONDARY	SLOT 1	SLOT 2	UNIFORM
Arnavisca	HK G36K	.45 Mark 23-SD	Frag Grenades	Frag Grenades	Wood Heavy
Maldini	HK G36K	.45 Mark 23-SD	Frag Grenades	Heartbeat Sensor	Wood Heavy

Gold Team

OPERATIVE	PRIMARY	SECONDARY	SLOT 1	SLOT 2	UNIFORM
Woo	M-14	.45 Mark 23-SD	Frag Grenades	Frag Grenades	Wood Heavy
Yacoby	M-14	.45 Mark 23-SD	Frag Grenades	Heartbeat Sensor	Wood Heavy

Map 10-2. Phoenix Group Laboratory

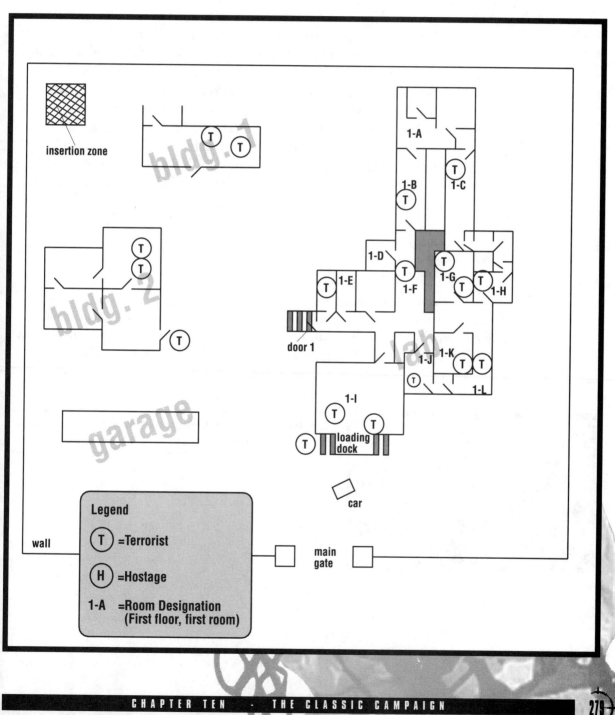

insertion zone

bldg. 1

bldg. 2

lab

garage

1-A

1-B 1-C

1-D 1-E

1-F 1-G 1-H

door 1

1-J 1-K

1-L

1-I

loading dock

car

Legend

wall

(T) =Terrorist

(H) =Hostage

1-A =Room Designation
(First floor, first room)

main gate

Strategy

This mission is tough. The briefing states that you're unexpected and can take the camp without firing a shot. That intelligence is extremely faulty. The tangos fight back, and they all wear body armor, too. You must pull out the heavy artillery. All your operatives should carry assault rifles. These give you a bit more punch than the submachine guns. Silenced weapons would be nice, but the surprise would be short-lived.

This mission requires four teams. One of the four teams covers the main gate to prevent escapes. The second team clears the two smaller buildings. The remaining two teams enter the lab and kill everyone inside. Because the lab contains dangerous biological agents, all operatives who enter it must wear biosuits. These suits aren't very protective against bullets, and a puncture can mean death. Therefore, you must exercise great caution inside the lab. Use heartbeat sensors to locate hiding tangos. Throw frag grenades as much as possible to kill tangos around corners.

Blue Team

Blue Team is your main lab infiltrator. Advance to building 1 and hold for Alpha code. Then move up to door 1 of the lab and wait for a second Alpha—then enter the lab. There's a tango in room 1-E or one of the other nearby offices. Throw a frag grenade around the corner to take him out. Then wait for other tangos to come and investigate. The heartbeat sensor enables you to see them before they come into visual range. Mow them down with your rifles as you await a third Alpha.

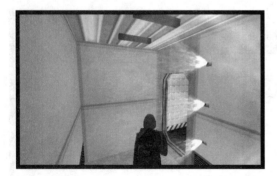

Blue Team must move through decontaminating rooms with disinfecting spray to find and kill all the terrorists.

Throw a grenade to clear out 1-J.

Throw a frag grenade into 1-J to take out the tango hiding behind the locker; then advance toward 1-B. A tango is stationed in 1-B. (He may be there or you may have killed him already.) Continue around to 1-A, and then through the disinfecting spray to 1-C. Here you'll find one or two tangos. Dispatch them quickly with a frag grenade or full-automatic bursts. Advance to room 1-H and hold for Alpha. There are two tangos in 1-G. Sidestep out of 1-H, shoot out the glass window of 1-G, and throw in a frag grenade. Carefully approach room 1-K and do the same to the tango inside. A final tango waits in hall 1-L. Kill him and exit the lab.

Red Team

Red Team is the other team to enter the lab and so needs protective biosuits. Initially, head to the compound's northeast corner, and then advance down the other side of the lab until you have a view of the loading dock from the side. Wait there for code Bravo. Shoot any tangos that come out of the loading dock before they can escape in the car.

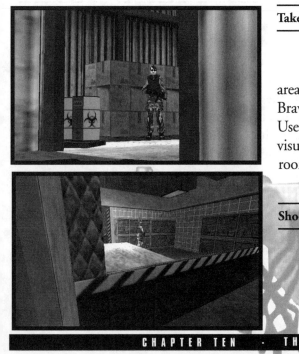

Take out the tangos in the loading area.

When you receive code Bravo, enter the loading area (1-I) and hold in the doorway to hall 1-F for another Bravo code. Shoot any tangos who come into your sights. Use the heartbeat sensor to monitor tangos out of your visual range. When you get the next code, advance to room 1-J, careful to take out any tangos hiding in there.

Shoot through the window to get the tango in 1-K.

Watch out for the tango in 1-H.

Pause there until you get yet another Bravo. Enter room 1-L through the spray room. You can take out the tango in 1-K through the window. Use caution when rounding the corner: the tango in room 1-H will have a shot at you. Take him out and kill the one in 1-G, then wait for Blue Team to meet up with you.

Green Team

Green Team's task is to clear the other two buildings in the compound. Advance down the west wall past building 2. Turn east to take out a tango next to the lab loading dock. Hold for code Charlie. Another tango patrols the center of the compound. Drop him as he comes into view. Using the heartbeat sensor, locate the two tangos in building 2 before entering. If they're not in the first room when you enter, then throw frag grenades through the doorways to kill them where they hide.

Green Team clears the smaller buildings.

When the building is clear, head to building 1. One of the tangos may have come out the door to investigate the gunshots. Drop him. Otherwise, use caution as you approach the door and when you open it. Throw a frag grenade into the corner of the room where the tangos are, and then rush in to finish the job. You also can try throwing a grenade through the window. Hold outside building 1 and cover door 1 of the lab in case any tangos try to escape.

Gold Team

Gold Team covers the main gate to prevent tango leaders from escaping with biological agents. Advance down the west wall to the south corner; then move east to the edge of the garage, where you have a good view of the loading dock, the Escape Vehicle, and the area between. This is your killing ground. Shoot any tangos in this area to prevent their escape. That's all you have to do in this mission.

Notes

Begin in control of Green Team. The two small buildings must be cleared before Blue Team approaches the lab, because the tangos in these buildings can fire through the windows at your operatives. Give Charlie codes so Green can clear building 2, and then building 1. Gold Team will automatically go to its post and take out any tangos attempting to leave. Red Team also has a good field of fire into this area from the other side of the lab. When Green Team finishes its job, give code Alpha for Blue Team to approach door 1 of the lab.

Now take control of Blue. You can do a better job than the computer can for this next difficult task. Give code Alpha again to enter the lab. Code Bravo tells Red Team to enter the lab through the loading dock. Together, you should be able to catch several tangos in a crossfire. Once Blue Team clears 1-F and 1-J, give Red another Bravo code and have them wait in 1-J while you take Blue Team through the rest of the lab.

Inside the lab, you'll find humans being used as test subjects for deadly biological weapons.

Mission 3—Operation: Yellow Knife

**09.23.00 0800
Alexandria**

Mission Orders

Information provided by Dr. Winston links Presidential Science Advisor Anne Lang to the Phoenix Group. By bugging Lang's home phone, RAINBOW may gain valuable information about Phoenix's plans.

Lang lives in a walled estate outside Alexandria, Virginia. Armed guards patrol the grounds. The team must enter and leave the compound undetected to gather useful intelligence.

You'll be inserted over the wall at the back of Lang's property and extracted from the same location.

Your team has two new operatives for this mission.

Use of deadly force is not sanctioned on this mission.

Objectives

1. Deactivate Security
2. Bug Upstairs Phone
3. Bug Downstairs Phone
4. Get to Extraction Zone

Several security guards protect Anne Lang's home. If they spot you, the mission fails.

Team Assignments

Blue Team

OPERATIVE	PRIMARY	SECONDARY	SLOT 1	SLOT 2	UNIFORM
Lofquist	Empty	.45 Mark 23-SD	Heartbeat Sensor	Electronics Kit	Black Light

Red Team

OPERATIVE	PRIMARY	SECONDARY	SLOT 1	SLOT 2	UNIFORM
DuBarry	Empty	.45 Mark 23-SD	Heartbeat Sensor	Electronics Kit	Black Light

Map 10-3. Anne Lang's Home

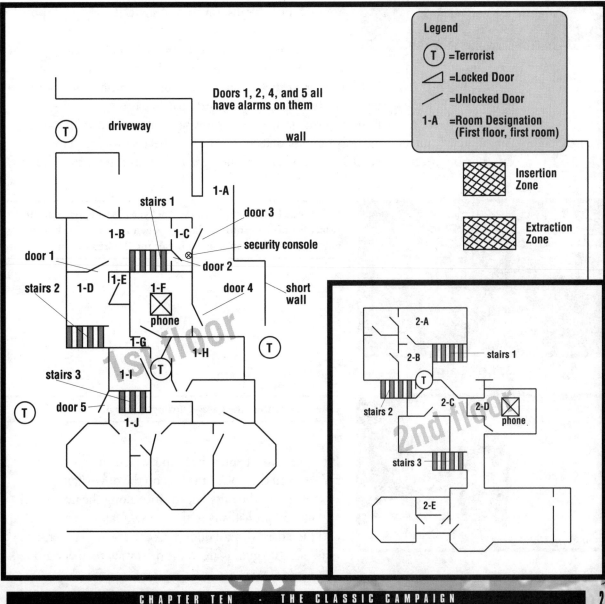

Strategy

A security system in room 1-C of the garage protects the home. You must deactivate it before you can enter.

Because you don't have to kill anybody, this mission may seem easy. But, this requirement actually makes it tougher. Your operatives must stay out of sight. If any guard spots them, the mission fails.

Also, you can't kill any guards. You're taking weapons only because an empty slot for them isn't an option. The key to this mission is timing. You may have to play it several times to get it right—not because your strategy is flawed, but because of the difficulty of timing the guards' patrol paths.

You need two teams for this mission, each comprising a single electronics specialist. Any more will increase the possibility of detection. The heartbeat sensors are a must for this mission, because you must know where the enemy is without being spotted yourself.

Blue Team

Watch out for the guard in the backyard. As he heads south, insert Blue Team into the house. When he walks back to the north, Red Team can make a break for the front door.

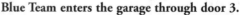

Blue Team enters the garage through door 3.

Blue Team must enter the home, deactivate the security system, and then plant the bug on the downstairs phone. At the start of the mission, advance along the north wall and halt about halfway to the house. Wait for code Alpha, and then dash toward door 3. Use the heartbeat sensor to make sure no guards are in the driveway; then enter the

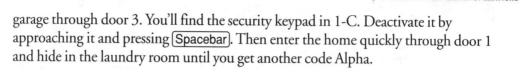

garage through door 3. You'll find the security keypad in 1-C. Deactivate it by approaching it and pressing Spacebar. Then enter the home quickly through door 1 and hide in the laundry room until you get another code Alpha.

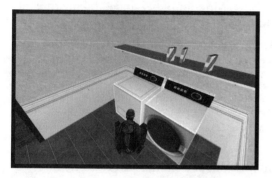

The laundry room is a good place to hide: the downstairs guard doesn't patrol this part of the house.

At the next code Alpha, advance down hall 1-D and through 1-G to room 1-F. Quickly plant the bug on the telephone (press Spacebar), and then run back to the laundry room. Hold for code Delta; then run out through door 3 and follow the north wall back to the extraction zone.

Office 1-F is a difficult room to plant a bug in. The downstairs security guard enters it regularly, and the upstairs guard checks it routinely through the opening above.

Red Team

Red Team must plant the bug on the upstairs phone and monitor the guard on this level so Blue Team will know when it's safe to plant the bug on the other phone. Advance along the south wall and hold about halfway to the house for code Bravo. Then advance quickly around the south side of the house. When the guards on the front lawn are walking away, move to door 5 at the front of the house. Make sure the downstairs guard isn't around before entering the front door. Immediately climb stairway 3.

Red Team plants the bug on the upstairs phone. Afterward, wait in the alcove and monitor the upstairs guard for Blue Team.

Pause at the top of the stairs to make sure the upstairs guard isn't looking before you run into closet 2-E.

Wait until the upstairs guard begins walking away from you, past room 2-D. Then rush in, plant the bug on the phone, and return to 2-E. Monitor the upstairs guard for Blue Team and await a second code Bravo.

Next, run to stairway 2 when the upstairs guard is walking away from you and the downstairs guard is in the south part of the house. Move into the garage. Taking care the backyard guard can't see you in the garage, hide behind a wall. Use the heartbeat sensor to make sure there are no guards in the driveway to the north and that the backyard guard is headed south. At code Delta, which comes when the coast is clear, run along the north wall to the extraction zone.

Notes

Again, timing and stealth are the keys to this mission. You should lead Red Team, because its main job is to monitor guards and make sure the way is clear for Blue Team. At the first Bravo code waypoint (about halfway to the house), watch the backyard guard through the Sniper view of your submachine gun. Make sure the safety is on so you don't accidentally shoot. When the guard heads south past the large window, give code Alpha. Blue Team will dash to the garage, enter, and disarm the security system.

When the guard heads back north, give code Bravo and run to the south side of the house. When the front yard is clear, go through the front door to the upstairs closet. When it's clear, bug the upstairs phone and return to the closet. With Red Team in 2-E and Blue in the laundry room, it's time to use those heartbeat sensors. Switch to Map view. Switching teams enables you to monitor both upstairs and downstairs guards. When the latter is in the south part of the house and the former moves south toward room 2-D, give code Alpha. Blue Team will dash into the office, plant the bug, and return to the laundry room.

The final step is getting your teams to safety. Continue monitoring the guards. When the path is clear, get Red Team downstairs and into the garage. Monitor the outside guards and give code Delta when it's safe to leave the home and head to the extraction zone.

Mission 4—Operation: Deep Magic

09.26.00 0400
San Francisco

Mission Orders

Horizon Corporation has been linked to the Phoenix Group. Horizon's central computer system is believed to contain information about Phoenix's plans to release the *Ebola brahma* virus.

The computer system is at Horizon's headquarters in downtown San Francisco. Access is through a terminal in John Brightling's office on the top floor. To escape detection, the team first must disable the security cameras in the control room on the floor below. Armed guards patrol both areas.

A helicopter will insert you on the roof and extract you the same way. The team must enter and leave the building completely undetected if it is to gather useful intelligence.

Use of deadly force is not sanctioned on this mission.

Objectives

1. Deactivate Security
2. Download Files
3. Get to Extraction Zone

Your teams must infiltrate the Horizon Corporation office building and download files from the computer database.

Team Assignments

Blue Team

OPERATIVE	PRIMARY	SECONDARY	SLOT 1	SLOT 2	UNIFORM
Lofquist	Empty	.45 Mark 23-SD	Heartbeat Sensor	Electronics Kit	Blue

Red Team

OPERATIVE	PRIMARY	SECONDARY	SLOT 1	SLOT 2	UNIFORM
DuBarry	Empty	.45 Mark 23-SD	Heartbeat Sensor	Electronics Kit	Gray Light

Map 10-4. The Horizon Office Building

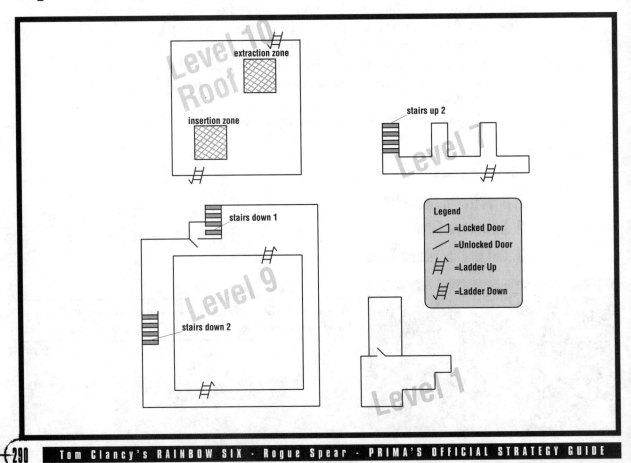

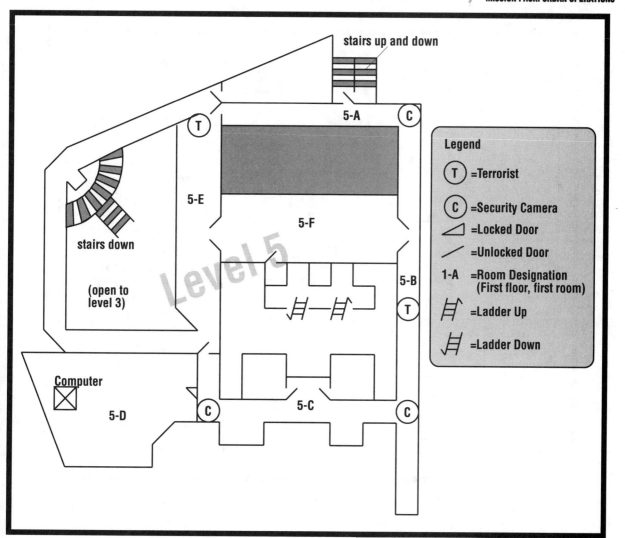

Strategy

This mission is similar to the last. In fact, you can use the same teams in different uniforms.

Your objective is to download files from the computer database. To do this, you must get into John Brightling's office on level 5. However, security cameras cover the corridors to the office and his office door has an alarm. Therefore, you must deactivate the security system first. One team must get to the security system on level 3 and shut it down while the other gets the computer files. Then get both your teams back to the extraction zone on the roof.

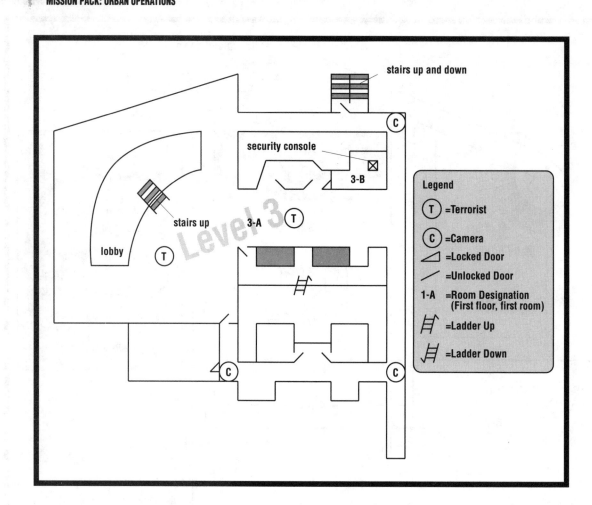

stairs up and down

security console

3-B

stairs up

Level 3

3-A

T

lobby

T

Legend

T = Terrorist

C = Camera

◿ = Locked Door

╱ = Unlocked Door

1-A = Room Designation
(First floor, first room)

▤ = Ladder Up

▤ = Ladder Down

C

The mission will end if you move in front of these cameras before they're deactivated.

Again, stealth and timing are vital to mission success. All told, only three guards patrol levels 3 and 5. Avoid them: if they spot you, the mission fails. You may not shoot them.

Blue Team

Download the files from the database in Brightling's office on level 5.

Blue Team's task is to get the files from the computer database. From where the helicopter drops you on the roof, descend stairway 1 to level 3. Hold in the stairwell until you get code Alpha, signifying the security system has been deactivated.

Use the heartbeat sensor to locate this level's two guards. Wait until they're both out near the lobby walkways in area 5-E. Exit the stairway into hall 5-A and run down halls 5-B and 5-C until you reach 5-D's door. If the doors to the right of 5-D are open, close them so the guards can't observe your actions. Pick the lock and enter the office. Walk to the computer and press ⓪ on the numeric keypad to download the files.

You have what you came for, so exit the level the way you entered, careful to avoid the guards. If you have to, you can duck into 5-F as an intermediate hiding place on your way to the stairwell. Or, if the area is clear, descend the stairs near 5-E to the lobby below and run either to the stairway or to the elevator shaft Red Team used. Return to the roof and a helicopter will pick you up and take you to safety.

Both teams wait on the roof for their ride out of here.

Red Team

Don't make too much noise in the elevator shaft. It may attract a guard. If one goes in to look around while you're deactivating the security system, then you'll have to get out via the stairs.

Red Team must deactivate the security system so Blue Team can complete its task. From the roof, descend stairway 2 to level 7. Then, in the elevator shaft, climb down two ladders to level 3. Walk to the door, but be careful: it has a window. Use the heartbeat sensor to locate this level's single guard. When he heads away from hall 3-A, give code Bravo, exit the elevator shaft access, and run to room 3-B. Pick the lock and enter.

Go to the security system and press [0] on the numeric keypad to deactivate it. Now all monitors will show a loop of prerecorded feed, and the door to Brightling's office is off the alarm circuit. Your job is done. Return to the roof, either the way you came or up stairway 1.

Red Team must deactivate the security system before Blue Team can get the computer files.

Notes

Control Red Team during the first part of this mission. Get the team down to level 3, deactivate the security system, and then send it back to the roof for extraction. Meanwhile, Blue Team will hold for code Alpha in stairway 1 on level 5. Take control of this team. Lead it into the office to download the files and then get it back to the roof. The heartbeat sensor again proves invaluable.

Note *This level makes for a great multiplayer game. There are lots of little offices and the elevator shaft provides a way to sneak up behind the enemy undetected.*

Mission 5—Operation: Black Star

09.30.00 0700
Brazil

Mission Orders

The Phoenix Group has raided a research station in Brazil and taken a group of Rainforest 2000 VIPs hostage. Intelligence indicates this raid is meant to cover Anne Lang's disappearance. Surveillance reveals Lang waits with her "captors" in the main building; the other VIPs are held in a nearby prefab. The terrorists await reinforcements before killing their hostages and moving Lang out to a safe location.

Your team will be inserted by inflatable boat upriver from the station.

Objective

1. Rescue All Hostages

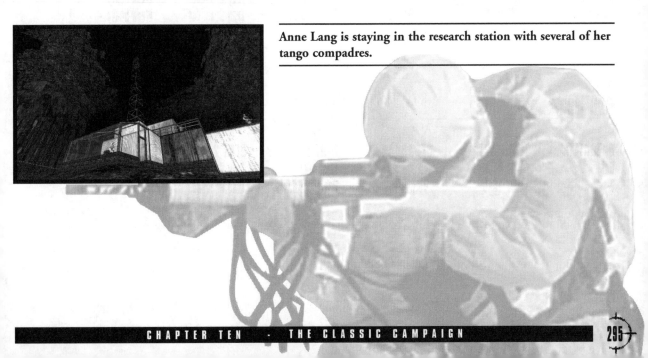

Anne Lang is staying in the research station with several of her tango compadres.

Team Assignments

Blue Team

OPERATIVE	PRIMARY	SECONDARY	SLOT 1	SLOT 2	UNIFORM
Chavez	MP5/10SD	.45 Mark 23-SD	Flashbang	Frag Grenades	Wood Heavy
Yacoby	MP5/10SD	.45 Mark 23-SD	Heartbeat Sensor	Frag Grenades	Wood Heavy

Red Team

OPERATIVE	PRIMARY	SECONDARY	SLOT 1	SLOT 2	UNIFORM
Walther	UMP 45SD	.45 Mark 23-SD	Flashbang	Frag Grenades	Wood Heavy
Raymond	UMP 45SD	.45 Mark 23-SD	Heartbeat Sensor	Frag Grenades	Wood Heavy

Green Team

Operative	Primary	Secondary	Slot 1	Slot 2	Uniform
Arnavisca	UMP 45SD	.45 Mark 23-SD	Flashbang	Frag Grenades	Wood Heavy
Maldini	UMP 45SD	.45 Mark 23-SD	Heartbeat Sensor	Frag Grenades	Wood Heavy

Gold Team

OPERATIVE	PRIMARY	SECONDARY	SLOT 1	SLOT 2	UNIFORM
Haider	UMP 45SD	.45 Mark 23-SD	Flashbang	Frag Grenades	Wood Heavy
Woo	UMP 45SD	.45 Mark 23-SD	Heartbeat Sensor	Frag Grenades	Wood Heavy

Map 10-5. Research Station

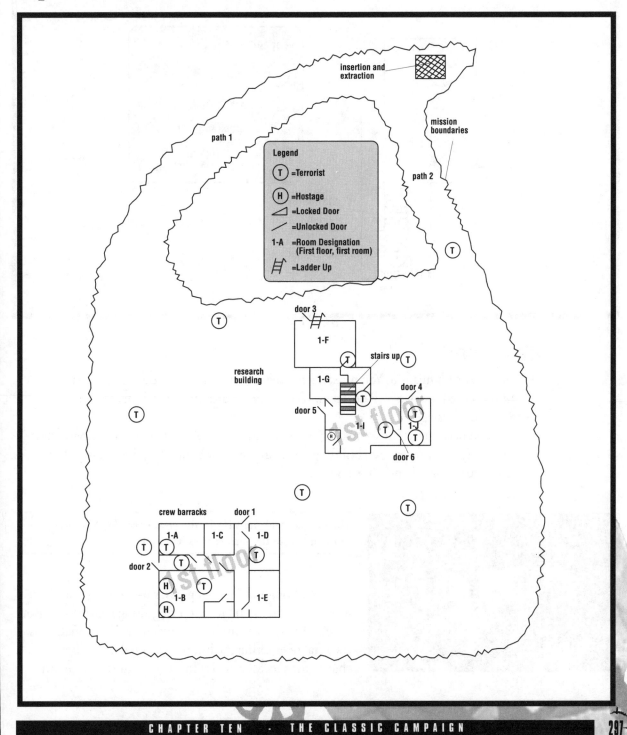

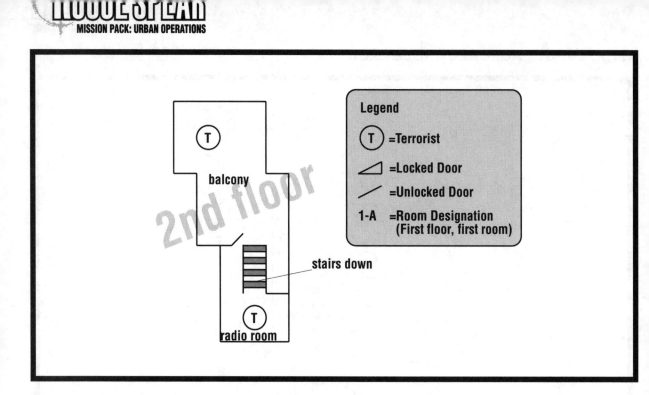

Strategy

This is a stealth mission. You must keep quiet and use silenced weapons, at least until you've secured the two VIP hostages. If the tango guards hear gunshots, they may execute the hostages.

You need four teams—two for each building. The VIPs are in the crew barracks; Anne Lang is in the research building. Securing the first building is the priority. The tangos won't harm Lang: she's one of them.

The tangos hold the VIPs in the crew barracks. You must get to them before the terrorists execute them.

Although the buildings are small and contain few rooms, it's still a good idea to bring along heartbeat sensors to see what's in a room before you enter. Coordination is essential in entering the buildings. You'll have a better chance for success if two teams rush in at the same time

from different entrances. (Be careful of blue-on-blue, or friendly fire.) After you rescue the hostages, get them back to the extraction zone.

Blue Team

Blue Team is the advance group for the other teams. Climb the rope ladder and take path 1 toward the station. Hold for code Alpha at the clearing entrance. However, while you're here, switch to Sniper view and take out the three tangos near the crew quarters. You must kill all three quickly. Survivors will run inside and kill the hostages. If you move into the clearing a bit, you also can take out the tango on the balcony of the research building. Scan the rest of the area for other tangos on patrol.

Blue Team can open up most of the clearing with long-range fire using Sniper view from the end of the jungle path.

At code Alpha, run to the crew quarters and wait by door 2 for code Charlie. Then rush in with Green Team and clear out the building. The hostages are in room 1-B. A tango may be with them. There's another tango in 1-A and possibly one in 1-E.

When the hostages are secure, exit the quarters and make a quick patrol around the building. Then lead Green Team and the hostages to safety at code Delta, following the route you took into the station clearing.

Red Team

Red Team must clear the research building. Follow path 2 to the clearing. You may find a tango along the way. Take him down before he can sound an alarm. Hold just short of the clearing and wait for Alpha. Then make your way to the ladder outside room 1-F. Climb it to the balcony and enter the door to the radio room. A tango may be hiding in the corner. Sidestep around the corner and drop him with a burst of gunfire.

Carefully descend the stairs to room 1-G. There may be a tango in room 1-H. Take him out if he's there. Hold in room 1-G for code Bravo. When the code comes, rush into 1-I, along with Gold Team, and take out the two tangos there. Take care not to shoot Anne Lang. Wait for code Delta, and then lead Gold Team and Lang back to the extraction zone.

Tangos are prowling all over the grounds around the two buildings. Keep an eye out for them.

Green Team

Green Team provides support to Blue Team. Take path 1 to the clearing and hold for Alpha. At the code, run to door 1 of the crew barracks and wait for code Charlie. This is the go for rushing into the building along with Blue Team. Take out tangos in 1-E and 1-B to secure the hostages. When you're ready to escort them, wait for code Delta to begin leading them back down path 1 to the extraction zone.

Green Team must rescue the two hostages and escort them to safety.

Gold Team

Gold Team provides support for Red Team. Follow path 2 to the clearing and hold for Alpha. Then rush toward the green house, room 1-J, attached to the research building and take out the two tangos there, as well as any others you see outside the buildings. Wait at door 6 for code Bravo; then rush into room 1-I to clear it and capture Anne Lang. Prepare to escort her down path 2 to the extraction zone at code Delta.

Notes

Controlling Blue Team lets you take care of things from long range at the edge of the clearing using Sniper view. After you eliminate the tangos outside the two buildings, the rest of the mission isn't that difficult, but beware of a couple tangos who seem to appear out of nowhere. Just when you think everything is safe and you let your guard down, they show up to blow away a team or two.

Anne Lang is posing as a hostage. However, while you're supposedly coming to her rescue, you're really arresting her.

It's important to coordinate your actions. Code Alpha sends all teams to their positions outside the buildings; Bravo sends Red and Gold into room 1-I; Charlie orders Blue and Green to rush the crew barracks. Try giving both Alpha and Charlie together. Red and Gold can handle their tasks under computer control. When all hostages are secure, give code Delta to send the four teams back down the jungle paths to the extraction zone.

CHAPTER ELEVEN
THE NEW MULTIPLAYER MAPS

Rogue Spear: Urban Operations includes eight new maps that aren't used for any of the campaigns. They're only for multiplayer games or custom missions. This chapter provides tips and hints for each of the maps. Although they're intended for multiplayer games, most of the tactics also can be used during custom missions on each of these maps. At the end of this chapter are some general hints and tips for playing multiplayer games against human opponents.

Note *I would like to thank the members of Clan Warbones for their assistance in playing through the multiplayer maps and devising strategies for each. Clan Warbones consists of Ryan Lynch (Orion Blade), Danny Rentschler (Snowlord), Jason Wyatt (Darkpup), Brian Sliman (Leviathan), Brandon Sliman (Saleen) and Lance Gardner (Gomer Pyle). Watch for them online.*

Bunkers

01.22.03 2050
Osajek

Map 11-1. The Bunkers

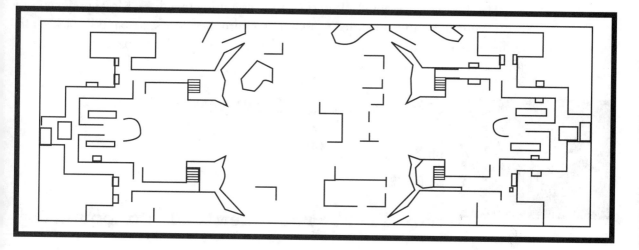

The key to bunkers is patience. There are several tactics that seem to consistently work—such as setting up sniper positions on the small ramps and waiting for someone's head to pop up. Although these tactics have their advantages, they're often easily compromised.

By setting up two people behind structures, you can catch advancing enemies in a crossfire.

Our favorite attack is to have two people provide constant cover fire with heavy machine guns. Under the cover of fire, the rest of the team assaults the front of the enemy's bunkers, throwing grenades into key hiding locations (behind the bunkers, inside the bunkers, or into the trenches). As the second team reaches the enemy's realm, the machine gunners move out to provide additional support.

An unsuspecting enemy walks right into an ambush.

Guns 4 Hire (=G4H=) taught us a valuable strategy, using us as unsuspecting fodder. As soon as the players spawned in, the =G4H= crew setup a defensive position behind each bunker, which allowed them to view the map from behind a covered position. By simply waiting behind the bunkers and covering the entry points into their base, =G4H= effectively prevented all attackers from assaulting their base. Most opponents became impatient and attempted to assault, in return they were systematically picked off as they entered. About two minutes before the mission's time limit ran out, the entire team assaulted the enemy's base.

Chemical Compound

06.20.03 1250
Smolensk

Map 11-2. The Chemical Compound

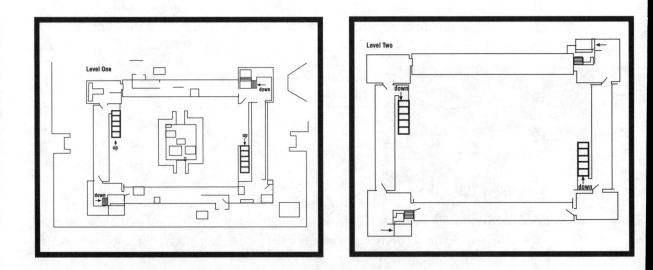

This map is one of the most intricate in the multiplayer lineup. What will grab your attention right away is the inclusion of the automatic doors. You'll quickly grow accustomed to the sound of a door opening in the distance and, after a while, the sound will make the hairs on the back of your neck stand on end.

With teams starting at opposite corners of the map, there are a few options for attack, depending upon your tastes. The first option is a spiral pattern assault. Sweep along the outside of the compound, staying alert to the corners and windows above. Complete a circle around the compound, move inside and continue the sweep, clearing each room and hallway as you go. Once the inside sweep is complete, move your team upstairs to the catwalk, paying special attention to the inside courtyard and the outer perimeter. This map is a good place to master "Bound and Over Watch."

Another option is to create a choke point. There are several places in the compound for an effective ambush. Be sure to use each map's subtle nuances to your advantage, like the doors on the stairways leading to the catwalk. By covering and listening for the automatic doors on the catwalk level, a two- or three-man assault team can conceivably cover each point of entry.

At the start of the game, throwing Hail Mary grenades toward the corners of the maps doesn't hurt. You may catch the enemy off guard.

Graveyard

10.02.03 0145
Pennsylvania

Map 11-3. The Graveyard

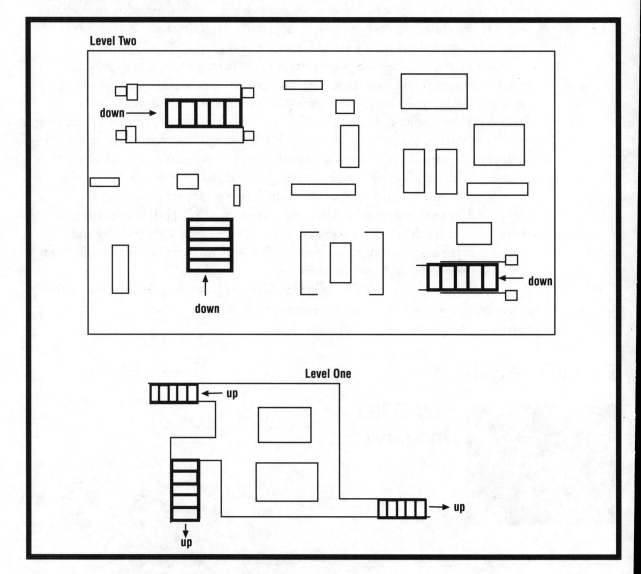

This map lends itself well to night vision. Although night vision evens out the contrast of your surroundings, it's very difficult to distinguish between friend and foe. It also doesn't improve your depth of view. Your map will be your best friend here, but it will cost you valuable time in the heat of battle. We don't like to condone it, but camping with a SAW, or any other machine gun, works well on this map. Each team member takes a corner, crouches down, and lights up any movement.

This map, due to its short depth of view, creates several challenges for everyone playing. Strategy can be developed, but often falls short due to Murphy's Law. Try moving slowly as a unit, clearing the map in a diamond formation that covers all points of the compass. Rear security should use the map to keep track of your team's movement, so increase the size of your map to make it easy on yourself if you're in that position. Because your enemy seems to materialize out of thin air, it's important to cover a 360-degree field of fire.

Old Train Tracks

03.15.03 1300
Nevada

Map 11-4. The Old Train Tracks

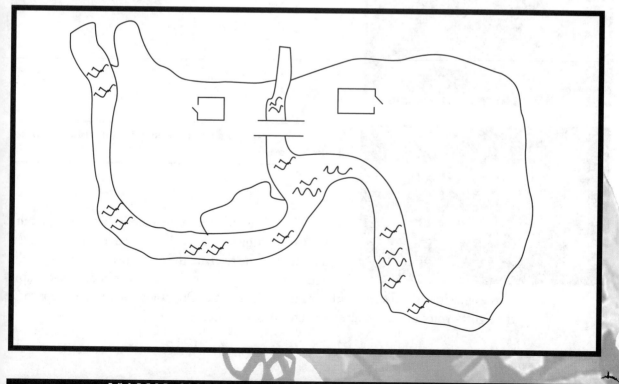

This is a great map for snipers and assaulters alike. In a minimum team of two, a sniper covers the bridge while the other teammates assault along the river. With the sniper laying down cover fire, the assaulting river rats can make a sneaky, effective attack. Also, grenades can be the river rat's most effective weapons, especially from the middle fork of the river under the bridge.

Teaming up a sniper and a spotter works well for this map, as well as for several others.

Watch out for enemies sneaking up along the river.

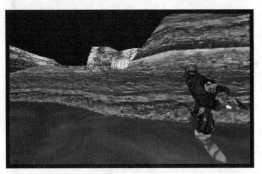

Try throwing frag grenades at the enemy while using the river-banks for cover.

The "Coal car" side of the map is the more difficult of the two starting locations. An immediate rush for cover or a jump into the river are the only options against a well-versed sniper crew from the "Engine car" side of the map. However, with a good sniper rifle like the PSG-1 or the Dragunov—and a few steps to the right—you can catch some unaware tangos out in the open.

When starting on the "Engine car" side of the map, hug the cliff wall and take immediate cover behind the shack. You can then choose from which side of the shack to attack. Switching from one corner of the shack to another can often confuse the other side, allowing you an advantage. As soon as your enemy spawns in, your sniper can take aim across the map and catch the opponent while they're sprinting for cover. Do watch your own cover; while taking the enemy by surprise, you leave yourself wide open.

Snow Base

06.25.03 2400
Minsk

Map 11-5. The Snow Base

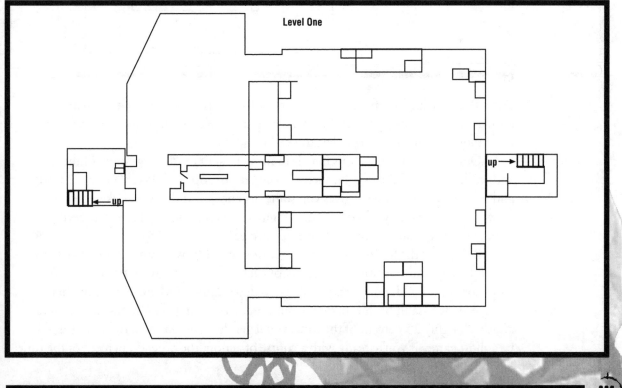

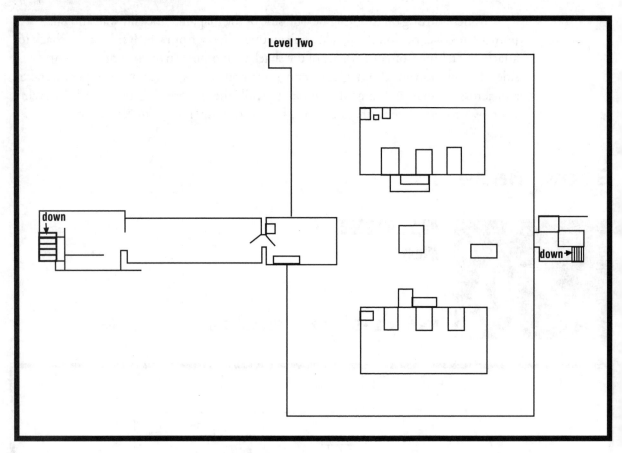

Snow Base is a fast-and-furious chess game where you're one step away from a checkmate. The starting points for this map place you close to your enemies, so you must move out quickly or risk defeat.

One way to dominate this map is to move upstairs at the beginning of the match and work to control the two entrances leading to the top level. Place C4 on the bridge and near the rear stairs. This gives you some distance from the two choke points upstairs, allowing you to catch your opponents off guard. There's nothing finer than seeing an opponent open a door to reveal your explosive package behind it.

Because of the limited number of options available, we found that it's better to develop a standard operating procedure for each. We pick an attack route so, at first, we're not caught with our pants down. Then depending on where our opponents move, we're ready to assault or shift to one of our predetermined defenses against a particular attack. Roughly 25 percent of the time, you'll get the drop on them right away and it'll be a short game. If you're ready with a course of action, the other 75 percent of the time,

you'll be able to shift quickly and move into a position to counter their attack. Preparation is your best defense.

This map is also a camper's paradise, with its numerous boxes to hide on or behind and balcony viewpoints to cap the occasional unsuspecting victim. In the end, the way to win this map is to learn from your opponent's attacks or plan aggressive attacks that throw them off balance.

Storage Depot

02.15.03 1210
North Carolina

Map 11-6. The Storage Depot

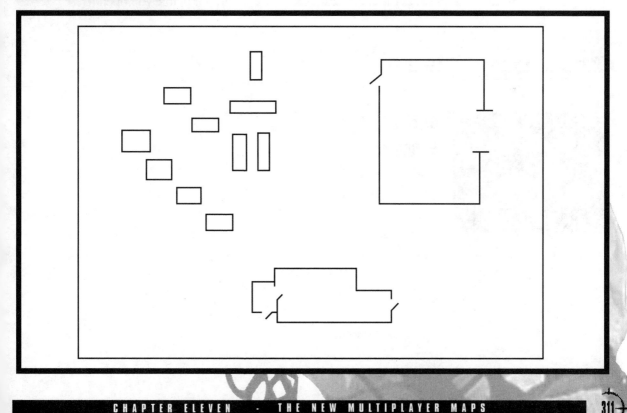

The warehouse is by far the most difficult of the two starting locations, especially with a small team. The door should never be considered a viable exit, as the shack has a clear shot from the window. The garage door should be used to move your team to the rear of the warehouse or flank the left side of the shack. Smoke grenades work well to distract your assault from either the rear of the warehouse or the side shack's door. Don't hold up in the tubes of the obstacle course; a good sniper can keep you pinned down indefinitely while his teammate flushes you out.

Sniping at the enemy through a window.

When beginning in the shack, a good strategy is to cover the door and the corner of the warehouse from the window. You can easily cut off any sort of flanking from the obstacles or ditch. To exit the shack, use the rear door, then follow the ditch along the far wall and flank either side of the warehouse. Try not to exit the side door closest to the warehouse, as the enemy can easily cover that door before you open it.

Training Maze

07.19.03 2150
Hereford

Map 11-7. The Training Maze

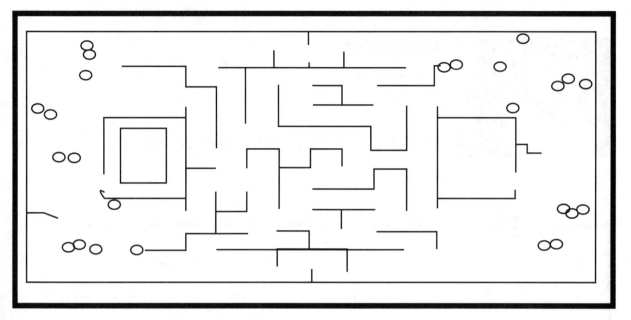

This is by far one of our favorite maps, and it's perfect for shotguns and machine guns. The close-quarter battle and disorientation associated with the maze makes it a fast-paced adrenaline rush. Assaulting is the best line of defense. Attack, attack, attack, and never stop moving.

The speed at which this map forces you to move creates very comical scenarios. You'll find yourself bumping into the enemy, scaring yourself to death, and forgetting that you were suppose to shoot them. Try not to shoot your teammates on accident; it's difficult to distinguish your uniform from the enemy's at such high speeds of game play.

One of the starting attacks we like to use is to charge and throw a grenade over the dividing wall on the left or right side of the map. Then charge through and hope you don't die.

We've stumbled on a tactic that works beautifully in this map. We like to call it "dropping the bomb." Since the action is so fast paced, you find yourself often running right past an enemy. Instead of turning around and attempting to go head-to-head, try switching to a frag and charge it for about one to two seconds, then, just before you round the next corner, drop it at your feet. If you do this correctly, the enemy you just passed, whom you hope turned to follow you, will be staring at a live frag, and you'll be safely protected around the corner.

Underwater Habitat

12.30.03 2300
Pacific Ocean

Map 11-8. The Underwater Habitat

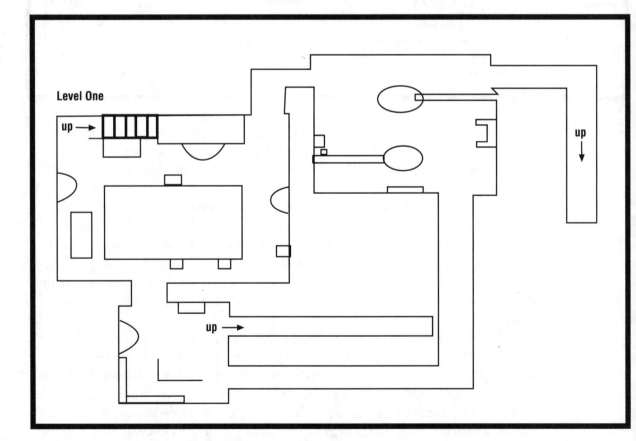

Level One

up →

up →

up ↓

up →

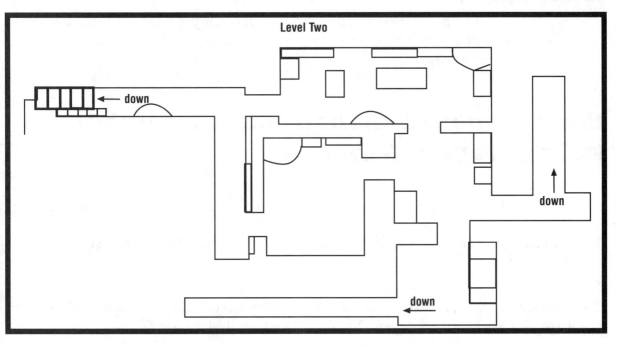

Level Two

← down

down ↑

down ←

This can be a very disorienting map because of the number of distractions present. The layout, steam, noise, and echoes of battle create all new levels of paranoia, where you'll find yourself losing control and looking over your shoulder for phantom tangos.

The steam (caused by damaging the pipes in the ceiling) was a stroke of genius by the developers of this game. We like to run down stairs emptying a magazine into the pipes overhead, which creates a room full of white streams of concealment. Then just pick a corner and wait for the prey to come to Daddy. You can use C4 and grenades to open up the steam as well.

Force the enemy to come at you through the steam. See how difficult a crouched operative is to see through the steam?

The diverse color patterns of this map, combined with different levels of lighting, give the player several hiding positions that are in plain sight. For example, the entrances seem to blend into the walls, making a room with four entrances appear to have only two. Keep your eyes peeled and your ears open.

Use the catwalks above the sub bay to gain the high ground on your enemy, remember to keep one teammate available to watch your back so the enemy doesn't sneak up on you.

More General Hints and Tips for Multiplayer Games

Here are some tried-and-tested tips and hints straight from Clan Warbones.

1. Peek around corners! It'll save your life many times. It's harder to hit half a head than it is to hit a half a body.

2. In real life, if you saw a pile of your teammates' bodies lying next to a window or door, would you really go there to see what killed them? Why do it in the game then? Choose life.

3. Along the same lines, if you peek around a corner and someone nearly shoots your head off, don't stick your head back around. You may or may not get them in a shoot out, but isn't it better to leave them thinking you're there and then go flank them or get some teammates and set up an ambush?

4. Remember the golden rule: when in doubt, *frag out*!

5. Teamwork is essential. Find each team member's special skill or ability and work on those strengths. For example, if you have someone who's a quick shot and very accurate, use him as a sniper and develop tactics around him to utilize that skill. He can always move to a high spot or provide cover fire for your assaulters.

6. When you have to move across an area that you're sure the enemy is covering, throw smoke and lay down scattered rounds where you think they're hiding—while part of your team moves. You may not know where they are, but if dirt clouds are hitting near them, they're less likely to poke their guns around the corner and see what the commotion is about.

7. Don't discount stealth. More often than not, it's the sneak commando who gets the kill. A good mix of playing styles and plans that capitalize on your team's talents will go a long way to making you victorious!

8. Develop standard operating procedures and break contact drills. This way, everyone knows what to do when the bullets start flying. Often, the best tactic is to get out of there (break contact) and set up an ambush somewhere else on your terms.

9. Learn to use formations and overlapping fields of fire. The map is helpful. With the diamond formation, your rear-guard is walking backward 90 percent of the time, covering your six. He can watch the map to stay in position with the rest of the team and still do his job (he's no good if he's looking toward the front to see where his team is).

10. When patrolling, stay in formation. Only move as fast as your slowest man, which is usually your rear guard. Although it should be your point man if he wants to live a long time.

11. Not all maps provide for planned, slow movements. Many of these new multiplayer maps are small, with fast action—and you need to move decisively and quickly. You must develop plans for each one, as you won't have time to once the game starts. Again, each team member should know his job and be able to count on his teammates doing theirs!

Name	Specialty	Assault	Demolitions	Electronics
Arnavisca, Santiago	Assault	100	24	34
Beckenbauer, Lars	Demolitions	76	100	91
Bogart, Daniel	Assault	98	20	20
Burke, Andrew	Assault	93	75	53
Chavez, Ding	Assault	100	71	67
DuBarry, Alain	Electronics	84	76	100
Filatov, Genedy	Assault	91	62	36
Galanos, Kure	Sniper	50	45	22
Haider, Karl	Assault	89	42	55
Hanley, Timothy	Assault	91	75	65
Johnston, Homer	Sniper	42	55	50
Lofquist, Annika	Electronics	85	61	97
Loiselle, Louis	Assault	94	49	70
Maldini, Antonio	Recon	90	65	65
McAllen, Roger	Demolitions	96	97	71
Morris, Gerald	Demolitions	80	99	54
Murad, Jamal	Assault	87	16	50
Narino, Emilio	Sniper	39	60	56
Noronha, Alejandro	Assault	94	50	32
Novikov, Arkadi	Assault	94	32	85
Pak Suo-Won	Recon	89	25	67
Petersen, Einar	Sniper	36	24	49
Price, Eddie	Assault	96	71	63
Rakuzanka, Kazimiera	Assault	96	50	52
Raymond, Renee	Assault	97	30	23
Sweeney, Kevin	Recon	90	30	96
Walther, Jorg	Assault	96	71	89
Weber, Dieter	Assault	45	53	61
Woo, Tracy	Recon	80	30	85
Yacoby, Ayana	Recon	97	30	86

Grenades	Sniper	Stealth	Aggression	Leadership	Self-Control	Stamina
65	49	82	72	81	94	83
80	31	72	55	78	77	81
50	51	73	89	96	93	97
67	36	78	91	85	75	94
74	63	100	95	100	92	97
81	66	73	72	81	76	91
85	59	70	82	82	87	83
83	96	99	100	88	90	90
71	61	74	100	75	71	96
84	43	85	93	86	84	100
70	100	100	89	83	87	98
69	58	69	80	92	77	82
70	50	78	90	85	100	85
50	38	100	50	60	80	95
100	65	70	70	70	70	98
97	63	71	40	72	80	79
78	42	88	99	86	99	65
67	97	90	95	80	54	84
75	56	73	91	91	91	82
60	75	70	74	99	80	83
65	51	99	60	70	88	100
75	99	89	88	75	100	98
77	52	89	80	95	90	87
70	73	80	85	85	60	96
85	68	96	75	79	90	91
50	59	99	45	65	95	85
83	71	97	76	97	90	96
72	95	96	93	73	84	100
50	61	98	50	75	85	96
60	54	97	95	65	70	95